The Memoirs Of François René

François-René Chateaubriand (vicomte de)

THE
MEMOIRS OF CHATEAUBRIAND

VOL. I

THE MEMOIRS OF FRANÇOIS RENÉ VICOMTE DE CHATEAUBRIAND SOMETIME AMBASSADOR TO ENGLAND

BEING A TRANSLATION BY ALEXANDER TEIXEIRA DE MATTOS OF THE MÉMOIRES D'OUTRE-TOMBE WITH ILLUSTRATIONS FROM CONTEMPORARY SOURCES. IN 6 VOLUMES. VOL. I

" NOTRE SANG A TEINT
LA BANNIÈRE DE FRANCE"

LONDON: PUBLISHED BY FREEMANTLE AND CO. AT 217 PICCADILLY   MDCCCCII

CONTENTS

PART THE FIRST

1768–1800

BOOK I

BOOK II

BOOK III

BOOK IV

BOOK V

BOOK VI

LIST OF ILLUSTRATIONS

VOL. I

THE TRANSLATOR'S NOTE

THE TRANSLATOR'S NOTE

MANY years ago, M. Pierre Louÿs, who had not then achieved his astonishing successes, and I sat talking literature in a Paris café. The future author of *Aphrodite* had praise for none save the moderns, of whom he has now become a recognized type and leader. I turned to him suddenly and asked :

"Is there any nineteenth-century French writer at all whom you others read nowadays and approve of?"

"Yes," said Louÿs, "Chateaubriand."

"How do you mean?" said I. "The novels? *Atala?* The essays?"

"Ah no," he answered: "but the *Mémoires d'outre-tombe*, yes. That—that is monumental; that will live for ever."

Our talk drifted to other things; I remembered what Louÿs had said—for two days: had I come across these Memoirs in the course of my rambles along the quays, I should have bought them; I did not, and bought other books instead.

In the winter of 1898, I spent two months at the house of my kinsman, David Teixeira de Mattos, in Amsterdam. It stands on one of the oldest of the canals. It is a quaint, spacious seventeenth-century house, and the habits of the house are of the same date as the architecture: there are few books in it. Knowing this, I had brought books with me, but not enough to last out my stay; and, before very long, I was driven to rummage in the one small, old-fashioned book-case which contained David Teixeira's library. I found it to consist in the main of volumes bearing upon the history of the reigning House of Orange, in whose restoration my kinsman's near pre-decessors had been concerned; of family records; of the Dutch poets of the early nineteenth century: until, suddenly, I came across a poor little pirated edition of Chateaubriand's masterpiece, printed in Brussels in twenty small parts, and bound up into five small volumes. I carried them to my room, spent three weeks in their perusal, started to read them a second time, and came back to London de-termined to find a publisher who would undertake the risk of an English translation.

I found one at almost the first asking, and it will ever remain a mystery to me why no complete trans-lation of this admirable work has seen the light in England during the more than fifty years that have elapsed since the *Mémoires d'outre-tombe* were first published.

The British Museum Library contains two at-tempts at a translation. One, published in the "Parlour Library of Instruction," is entitled, "*An Auto-biography*. By François René, Viscount de Chateaubriand. London and Belfast: Simms & M'Intyre, 1849." It consists of four slim volumes containing in all less than half of the work. The other appeared, under the title of "*Memoirs of Chateaubriand. Written by Himself.* London: Henry Colburn, 1848–49. To be completed in ten parts," in "Colburn's Standard Library." Only three parts were published, embracing not more than a quarter of the *Mémoires d'Outre-tombe.*

In both cases the translator is anonymous; in both cases the translation seems careless and hastily made; in both cases the English version, as I have said, is far from complete.

The present translation, by arrangement with the publishers, is complete in so far that no attempt whatever has been made at compression or condensation; nor has a single passage been omitted without the insertion of a footnote pointing out exactly where the omission occurs. The omissions are very few, and consist of the following:

1. All that portion of Chateaubriand's account of the career of Napoleon Bonaparte which touches the period during which the author was not himself residing in France and which is of historical rather than autobiographical interest. This portion Messrs. Freemantle hope to publish later, as a supplemental volume to the Memoirs. Left where it stood, it hampered the action of the work, and its omission is in no way noticeable.

2. Part of the account of the journey to Jerusalem

which Chateaubriand quotes from the Itinerary of his body-servant Julien, side by side with his own; also some discursive correspondence and quotations following upon the Itinerary.

3. A selection from the writings of Chateaubriand's sister Lucile (Madame de Caud). This selection is a short one; but it is of interest to none save the author and her brother, and nothing is lost by the omission.

4. Some of the longer quotations from the French or Italian poets, besides a few poems by Chateaubriand himself.

5. One passage, or at most two, which, without being in any sense immoral, seemed to me to contain a little too much of the *esprit gaulois* to prove acceptable to English taste. I was anxious that not a line should appear which would prevent the universal reading of so fine a work.

For the rest, I have striven to perform my task of translation, which has taken me over two years to accomplish, conscientiously, correctly, and above all respectfully. If here and there I have seemed to follow the original a little too closely, my excuse must be that I had too great a respect for this great man to take liberties with his writing. To reproduce his style in another language has been no easy matter: I have done my best.

The volumes will be found to be fully annotated. The author's own notes are so marked; those signed "B." are by M. Edmond Biré, the accomplished editor of the latest edition of the Memoirs, from which edition my version has, in the main, been made; those signed "T" are mine. I claim no merit of erudition for these notes: my aim has been merely to give the essential details concerning each new person, belonging to whatever period, mentioned in the work, and, whenever possible, to add the date of his birth and death. More particularly in the case of Chateaubriand's contemporaries, I thought it not without value to furnish a clue to the age and to the stage of their career which they had attained at the time when they were brought into contact with the writer. A full index of all persons mentioned in the *Mémoires d'outre-tombe* will be found at the end of the last volume.

My thanks are due to M. Louis Cahen, of Paris, who has read and collated most of the proofs and suggested a happy solution of many a difficulty, and to Mr. Frederic J. Simmons for the care with which he has selected the illustrations to the several volumes.

A. T. DE M.

CHELSEA, *December* 1901.

THE AUTHOR'S PREFACE

THE AUTHOR'S PREFACE[1]

Sicut nubes . . . quasi naves . . . velut umbra.—Job.[2]

As it is not possible for me to foresee the moment of my
end ; as at my age the days accorded to man are but days of
grace, or rather of reprieve, I propose, lest I be taken by
surprise, to make an explanation touching a work with which
I intend to cheat the tedium of those last forlorn hours which
we neither desire, nor know how to employ.

The Memoirs prefaced by these lines embrace and will
embrace the whole course of my life : they were commenced in
the year 1811 and continued to the present day. I tell in that
portion which is already completed, and shall tell in that which
as yet is but roughly sketched, the story of my childhood, my
education, my youth, my entrance into the service, my arrival
in Paris, my presentation to Louis XVI., the early scenes
of the Revolution, my travels in America, my return to Europe,
my emigration to Germany and England, my return to France
under the Consulate, my employment and work under the
Empire, my journey to Jerusalem, my employment and work
under the Restoration, and finally the complete history of the
Restoration and of its fall.

I have met nearly all the men who in my time have played
a part, great or small, in my own country or abroad : from
Washington to Napoleon, from Louis XVIII. to Alexander,
from Pius VII. to Gregory XVI., from Fox, Burke, Pitt,
Sheridan, Londonderry, Capo d'Istrias to Malesherbes, Mirabeau and the rest ; from Nelson, Bolivar, Mehemet Pasha of
Egypt to Suffren, Bougainville, La Pérouse, Moreau and so
forth. I have been one of an unprecedented triumvirate :

---

[1] This preface is first printed in the edition of 1899, from which the present
version is made.—T.

[2] " I am brought to nothing : as a wind thou hast taken away my desire : and
my prosperity hath passed away *like a cloud.*"—Job, xxx. 15.
" My days have passed by *as ships* carrying fruits, as an eagle flying to the
prey."—Job, ix. 26.
" Man cometh forth like a flower and is destroyed, and fleeth *as a shadow,* and
never continueth in the same state."—Job, xiv. 2.—T.

three poets of different interests and nationality, who filled, within the same decade, the post of minister of Foreign Affairs—myself in France, Mr. Canning in England, Señor Martinez de la Rosa in Spain. I have lived successively through the empty years of my youth and the years filled with the Republican Era, the annals of Bonaparte and the reign of the Legitimacy.

I have explored the seas of the Old World and the New, and trod the soil of the four quarters of the globe. After camping in Iroquois shelters and Arab tents, in the wigwams of the Hurons, amid the remains of Athens, Jerusalem, Memphis, Carthage, Grenada, among Greeks, Turks and Moors, in forests and among ruins; after wearing the bearskin of the savage and the silken caftan of the mameluke; after enduring poverty, hunger, thirst and exile, I have sat, as minister and ambassador, in a gold-laced coat, my breast motley with stars and ribbons, at the tables of kings, at the feasts of princes and princesses, only to relapse into indigence and to receive a taste of prison.

I have been connected with a host of personages famous in the career of arms, the Church, politics, law, science and art. I have endless materials in my possession: more than four thousand private letters, the diplomatic correspondence of my several embassies, that of my term at the Foreign Office, including documents of an unique character, known to none save myself. I have carried the soldier's musket, the traveller's cudgel, the pilgrim's staff: I have been a sea-farer, and my destinies have been as fickle as my sails; a halcyon, and made my nest upon the billows.

I have meddled with peace and war; I have signed treaties and protocols, and published numerous works the while. I have been initiated into secrets of parties, of Court and of State: I have been a close observer of the rarest miseries, the highest fortunes, the greatest renowns. I have taken part in sieges, congresses, conclaves, in the restoration and over-turning of thrones. I have made history, and I could write it. And my life, solitary, dreamy, poetic, has gone on through this world of realities, catastrophes, tumult, uproar, in the company of the sons of my dreams, Chactas, René, Eudore, Aben-Hamet, of the daughters of my imagination, Atala, Amélie, Blança, Velléda, Cymodocée. Of my age and not of it, I perhaps exercised upon it, without either wishing or seeking to do so, a three-fold influence, religious, political and literary.

There are left to me but four or five contemporaries of established fame. Alfieri, Canova and Monti have disappeared; Italy has only Pindemonte and Manzoni left over from her brilliant days. Pellico has wasted his best days in the cells of the Spielberg: the talents of the land that gave Dante birth are condemned to silence or driven to languish on foreign soil; Lord Byron and Mr. Canning have died young; Walter Scott is no longer with us; Goethe has left us, full of years and glory. France has scarce anything remaining from her abundant past; she is commencing a new era, while I linger behind to bury my period, like the old priest who, in the sack of Béziers, was to toll the bell before falling himself when the last citizen had expired.

When death lowers the curtain between me and the world, it shall be found that my drama was divided into three acts.

From my early youth until 1800, I was a soldier and a traveller; from 1800 to 1811, under the Consulate and the Empire, my life was given to literature; from the Restoration to the present day, it has been devoted to politics.

During each of my three successive careers, I have always placed some great task before myself: as a traveller, I aimed at discovering the polar world; as a man of letters, I have striven to reconstruct religion from its ruins; as a statesman, I have endeavoured to give to the people the true system of representative monarchy, accompanied with its various liberties: I have at least assisted in winning that liberty which is worth all the others, which replaces them and serves in stead of any constitution, the liberty of the press. When, frequently, I have failed in my enterprises, there has been in my case a failure of destiny. The foreigners who have succeeded in their designs were aided by fortune; they had powerful friends behind them and a peaceful country. I have been less lucky.

Of the modern French authors of my own period, I may be said to be the only one whose life resembles his works: a traveller, soldier, poet, publicist, it is amid forests that I have sung the forest, aboard ship that I have depicted the sea, in camp that I have spoken of arms, in exile that I have learnt to know exile, in Courts, in affairs of State, in Parliament that I have studied princes, politics, law and history. The orators of Greece and Rome played their part in the republic and shared its fate. In Italy and Spain, at the end of the Middle Ages and at the Renascence, the leading intellects in letters and the arts took part in the social movement. How stormy and how fine were the lives of Dante, of Tasso, of Camoëns, of Ercilla, of Cervantes!

In France our ancient poets and historians sang and wrote in the midst of pilgrimages and battles: Thibaut Count of Champagne, Villehardouin, Joinville borrow the felicity of their style from their adventurous careers; Froissart travels the highways in search of history, and learns it from the mouths of the knights and abbots whom he meets, by whose side he rides along the roads. But, commencing from the reign of Francis I., our writers have been men leading detached lives, and their talents have perchance expressed the spirit but not the deeds of their age. If I were destined to live, I should represent in my person, as represented in my Memoirs, the principles, the ideas, the events, the catastrophes, the idylls of my time, the more in that I have seen a world end and a world commence, and that the conflicting characters of that ending and that commencement lie intermingled in my opinions. I have found myself caught between two ages as in the conflux of two rivers, and I have plunged into their waters, turning regretfully from the old bank upon which I was born, yet swimming hopefully towards the unknown shore at which the new generations are to land.

These Memoirs, divided into books and parts, have been written at different times and in different places: each section naturally entails a kind of prologue which recalls the occurrences that have arisen since the last date and describes the place in which I resume the thread of my narrative. In this way the various events and the changeful circumstances of my life enter one into the other; it happens that, in moments of prosperity, I have to tell of times of penury, and that, in days of tribulation, I retrace my days of happiness. The diverse opinions formed in diverse periods of my life, my youth penetrating into my old age, the gravity of my years of experience casting a shadow over my lighter years, the rays of my sun, from its rise to its setting, intercrossing and commingling like the scattered reflections of my existence, all these give a sort of indefinable unity to my work; my cradle bears the mark of my tomb, my tomb of my cradle; my hardships become pleasures, my pleasures sorrows, and one no longer knows whether these Memoirs proceed from a dark or a hoary head.

I do not say this in self-praise, for I do not know that it is good; I say what is the fact, what happened without reflection on my part, through the very fickleness of the tempests loosed against my bark, which often have left me but the rock that caused my shipwreck upon which to write this or that fragment of my life.

I have applied to the writing of these Memoirs a really paternal predilection; I would wish to be able to rise at the ghostly hour to correct the proofs: the dead go fast.

The notes accompanying the text are of three kinds: the first, printed at the end of each volume, consist of explanatory documents, proofs and illustrations; the second, printed at the foot of the pages, are contemporary with the text; the third, also printed as foot-notes, have been added after the text was written, and bear the date of the time and place at which they were written. A year or two of solitude spent in some corner of the earth would suffice to enable me to complete my Memoirs; but the only period of rest that I have known was the nine months during which I slept in my mother's womb: it is probable that I shall not recover this antenatal rest until I lie in the entrails of our common mother after death.

Several of my friends have urged me to publish a portion of my story now: I could not bring myself to accede to their wish. In the first place, I should be less candid and less veracious, in spite of myself; and then, I have always imagined myself to be writing seated in my grave. From this my work has assumed a certain religious character, which I could not remove without impairing its merit; it would be painful to me to stifle the distant voice which issues from the tomb, and which makes itself heard throughout the course of this narrative. None will be surprised that I should preserve certain weaknesses, that I should be concerned for the fate of the poor orphan destined to survive me upon earth. Should Minos judge that I had suffered enough in this world to become at least a happy Shade in the next, a little light thrown from the Elysian Fields to illumine my last picture would serve to make the defects of the painter less prominent. Life does not suit me; perhaps death will become me better.

PARIS, 1 *December*, 1833.

THE AUTHOR'S PREFACE

TO THE FIRST EDITION

THE AUTHOR'S PREFACE

TO THE FIRST EDITION [1]

Sicut nubes . . . quasi naves . . . velut umbra.—JOB.

As it is not possible for me to foresee the moment of my end; as at my age the days accorded to man are but days of grace, or rather of reprieve, I propose to make an explanation.

On the 4th of September next I shall have completed my seventy-eighth year: it is high time that I should quit a world which is quitting me and which I do not regret.

The Memoirs prefaced by these lines follow, in their divisions, the natural divisions of my several careers.

The sad necessity which has always held me by the throat has obliged me to sell my Memoirs. None can know what I have suffered by being compelled thus to hypothecate my tomb; but I owed this last sacrifice to my vows and to the consistency of my conduct. With an almost pusillanimous attachment, I looked upon these Memoirs as confidants from whom I would not care to part; my intention was to leave them to Madame de Chateaubriand; she would have published them at will, or suppressed them, as I would have desired more than ever to-day.

Ah, if, before quitting the earth, I could have found some one rich enough, confiding enough, to buy up the shares of the "Syndicate," and one who would not, like the Syndicate, be under the necessity of sending the work to press so soon as my knell had sounded! Some of the shareholders are my friends; several of them are obliging persons who have sought to assist me; nevertheless the shares have perhaps been sold, they will have been transferred to third parties with whom I am not acquainted, and with whom family interests must take the first place; to the latter it is natural that the prolongation of my days should mean to them, if not an annoyance, at least

---

[1] 1848–1850.—T.

an actual loss. Lastly, if I were still the owner of these Memoirs, I would either keep them in manuscript or delay their appearance for fifty years.

These Memoirs have been put together at different dates and in different countries. Hence the necessary prologues, which depict the environments upon which I cast my eyes, the thoughts which occupied me at the time when I resume the thread of my narrative. The changeful circumstances of my life have in this way entered one into the other: it has happened that, in moments of prosperity, I have had to tell of times of penury; in days of tribulation, to retrace my days of happiness. My youth penetrating into my old age, the gravity of my years of experience casting a shadow over my lighter years, the rays of my sun, from its rise to its setting, intercrossing and commingling: all these have produced in my recital a sort of confusion, or, if you will, a sort of indefinable unity; my cradle bears the mark of my tomb, my tomb of my cradle; my hardships become pleasures, my pleasures sorrows, and I no longer know, as I finish reading these Memoirs, whether they proceed from a dark or a hoary head.

I cannot tell if this medley, to which I can apply no remedy, will please or displease; it is the fruit of the inconstancy of my fate; often the tempests have left me no writing-table save the rock that has caused my shipwreck.

I have been urged to publish portions of these Memoirs during my life; I prefer to speak from the depths of my grave: my narrative will then be accompanied by those voices which are in a measure consecrated, because they issue from the tomb. If I have suffered enough in this world to become a happy Shade in the next, a ray escaping from the Elysian Fields will cast a protecting light over my last pictures. Life does not suit me; perhaps death will become me better.

These Memoirs have been the object of my predilection. St. Bonaventure obtained from Heaven permission to continue his after death; I hope for no such favour, but I would wish to rise at the ghostly hour at least to correct the proofs. However, when Eternity shall with its two hands have stopped my ears, in the dusty family of the deaf, I shall hear nobody.

If any part of this work has interested me more than another, it is that which relates to my youth, the least-known side of my life. There I have had to reveal to the world what was known to myself alone; in wandering among that vanished company I have met only remembrances and silence: of all the persons I have known, how many are alive to-day?

The inhabitants of Saint-Malo applied to me, on the 28th of August 1828, through the medium of their mayor, on the subject of a floating dock they wished to build. I hastened to reply, begging, in exchange for my good will, a concession of a few feet of ground, for my tomb, on the Grand-Bé.[1] This encountered some difficulty, owing to the opposition of the military engineering authorities. At last, on the 27th of October 1831, I received a letter from the mayor, M. Hovius. He said:

"The resting-place which you desire by the side of the sea, at a few steps from your birthplace, will be prepared by the filial piety of the Malouins. A sad thought is mingled with this task. Ah, may the monument remain long unoccupied! But honour and glory survive all that dies upon earth."

I quote these beautiful words of M. Hovius with gratitude; there is but one word too much: "glory."

I shall therefore rest on the shore of the sea which I have loved so well. If I die out of France, I hope that my body will not be brought back to the land of my birth until fifty years shall have been completed since my first burial. Let my remains be spared a sacrilegious autopsy; let not my chilled brain and my dead heart be searched for the mystery of my being. Death does not reveal the secrets of life. A corpse riding post fills me with horror; bones, bleached and light, are easily moved: they will be less fatigued by this last journey than when I dragged them hither and thither, laden with the burden of my cares.

PARIS, 14 *April*, 1846.
    Revised 28 *July*, 1846.

---

[1] A small island situated in the roadstead of Saint-Malo.—*Author's Note.*

PART THE FIRST
1768–1800

THE

MEMOIRS OF CHATEAUBRIAND

PART THE FIRST

1768–1800

BOOK I[1]

Birth of my brothers and sisters—My own birth—Plancoët—I am vowed—
Combourg—My father's scheme of education for me—Villeneuve—Lucile—
Mesdemoiselles Couppart—I am a bad pupil—The life led by my maternal
grandmother and her sister at Plancoët—My uncle, the Comte de Bedée,
at Monchoix—I am relieved from my nurse's vow—Holidays—Saint-Malo
—Gesril—Hervine Magon—Fight with two ship's lads.

FOUR years ago, on my return from the Holy Land, I purchased near the little village of Aulnay, in the neighbourhood
of Sceaux[2] and Châtenay, a small country-house, lying hidden
among wooded hills. The sandy and uneven ground attached
to this house consisted of a sort of wild orchard, at the end
of which was a ravine and a coppice of chesnut-trees. This
narrow space seemed to me fitted to contain my long hopes:
spatio brevi spem longam reseces.[3] The trees which I have
planted here are thriving. They are still so small that I
can shade them by placing myself between them and the sun.
One day they will give me shade and protect my old age as I
have protected their youth. I have selected them, in so far as
I could, from the different climes in which I have wandered;
they recall my travels and foster other illusions in my heart.

If ever the Bourbons reascend the throne, I will ask from

---

[1] This book was written at the Vallée-aux-Loups between October 1811
and June 1812.—T.

[2] Seven miles south of Paris, in the Department of Seine.—T.

[3] HORACE, *Od.* I. xi.—T.

them no greater reward for my loyalty than that they should make me rich enough to add to my fee-simple the skirts of the surrounding woods: I have grown ambitious, and would wish to expand my walks by a few roods. Knight-errant though I be, I have the sedentary tastes of a monk: I doubt whether, since taking up my abode in this retreat, I have thrice set foot without my boundary. If my pines, my fir-trees, my larches, my cedars ever keep their promise, the Vallée-aux-Loups will become a veritable hermitage. When, on the 20th of February 1694,[1] Voltaire saw the light at Châtenay, what was then the appearance of the hill to which the author of the *Génie du Christianisme* was to retire in 1807?

This spot pleases me; it has taken the place of my paternal acres; I have bought it with the price of my dreams and my vigils; I owe the little wilderness of Aulnay to the vast wilderness of Atala; and I have not, in order to acquire this refuge, imitated the American planter and despoiled the Indian of the Two Floridas.[2] I am attached to my trees; I have addressed elegies to them, sonnets, odes. There is not one of them which I have not tended with my own hands, which I have not rid of the worm attached to its roots, the caterpillar clinging to its leaves; I know them all by their names, as though they were my children: they are my family, I have no other, and I hope to die in their midst.

Here, I have written the *Martyrs*, the *Abencerages*, the *Itinéraire* and *Moïse*; what shall I do now during these autumn evenings? This 4th day of October 1811, the anniversary of my saint's-day[3] and of my entrance into Jerusalem,[4] tempts me to commence the history of my life. The man who to-day is endowing France with the empire of the world only so that he may trample her under foot, the man whose genius I admire and whose despotism I abhor, that man surrounds me with his tyranny as it were with a new solitude; but though he may crush the present, the past defies him, and I remain free in all that precedes his glory.

[1] Voltaire was not born on the 20th of February 1694, and he was not born at Châtenay. In 1864, M. A. Jal (*Dictionnaire critique de biographie et d'histoire*, pp. 1283, *et seq.*), after searching the register of the Parish of Saint-André-des-Arcs, established the fact that Voltaire was born in Paris on Sunday, 21 November 1694.—B.

[2] The district now known as Florida was formerly divided into Eastern and Western Florida, with St. Augustine and Pensacola for their respective capitals.—T.

[3] The 4th of October is the feast of St. Francis of Assisi.—T.

[4] Chateaubriand made his entrance into Jerusalem on the 4th of October 1806.—B.

The greater part of my feelings have remained buried in the recesses of my soul, or are displayed in my works only as applied to imaginary beings. To-day, while I still regret, without pursuing, my illusions, I will reascend the acclivity of my happier years: these Memoirs shall be a shrine erected to the clearness of my remembrances.

Let us commence, then, and speak first of my family. This is essential, because the character of my father depended in a great measure upon his position and, in its turn, exercised a great influence upon the nature of my ideas, by determining the manner of my education.[1]

I am of noble birth. In my opinion I have improved the hazard of my cradle and retained that firmer love of liberty which belongs principally to the aristocracy whose last hour has struck. Aristocracy has three ages: the age of superiority, the age of privilege, the age of vanity; issuing from the first, it degenerates in the second to become extinguished in the third.

He who is curious for information concerning my family may consult Moréri's[2] Dictionary, the different Histories of Brittany by d'Argentré,[3] Dom Lobineau,[4] Dom Morice, Père Du Paz' *Histoire généalogique de plusieurs maisons illustres de Bretagne*, Toussaint de Saint-Luc, Le Borgne, and lastly Père Anselme's *Histoire des grands officiers de la Couronne*.[5]

[1] Following M. Edmond Biré in his edition of 1899, I have borrowed this paragraph from the manuscript known as the *Manuscrit de 1826*, which was in the handwriting, for the most part, of Madame Récamier, and which was published by Madame Charles Lenormant in 1874. It is certainly preferable to the paragraph in all other editions of the *Mémoires d'Outre-Tombe*, which runs as follows:

"My father's birth and the trials of his first position caused his character to become one of the gloomiest ever known. Now this character influenced my ideas because it terrified me in childhood, saddened me in youth, and determined the manner of my education."

The Comte de Marcellus (*Chateaubriand et son temps*, p. 6) remarks that this paragraph interrupts the narrative and in no way assists it.—T.

[2] Louis Moréri (1643–1680) took orders at Lyons, and in 1673 published in that town his *Dictionnaire historique et géographique*, which forms the basis of Bayle's *Dictionnaire critique* (1697–1702).—T.

[3] Bertrand d'Argentré (1519–1590), Seneschal of Rennes, and author of an *Histoire de Bretagne* and *Commentaires sur la coutume de Bretagne.*—T.

[4] Père Lobineau of the Benedictines (1666–1727), author of the *Histoire de Bretagne* (1707), *Histoire des Saints de la Bretagne*, and other historical works.—T.

[5] This genealogy is summarised in the *Histoire généalogique et héraldique des Pairs de France*, by M. le Chevalier de Courcelles.—*Author's Note.*

The full title of the work by Pierre de Gibours, known as Père Anselme, is *Histoire généalogique et chronologique de la maison de France et des grands officiers de la Couronne* (1674). Its importance is mainly due to the labours of the compilers who continued it, Du Fourni and Père Ange de Sainte-Rosalie (1726–1733).—T.

My proofs of descent were made out by Chérin,[1] for the admission of my sister Lucile as a canoness of the Chapter of the Argentière, whence she was to be transferred to that of Remiremont. They were reproduced for my presentation to Louis XVI., again for my affiliation to the Order of Malta, and lastly, when my brother was presented to the same unfortunate Louis XVI.

My name was first written "Brien," and then "Briant" and "Briand," following the invasion of French spelling. Guillaume le Breton says "Castrum-Briani." There is not a French name that does not present these literal variations. What is the spelling of Du Guesclin?

About the commencement of the eleventh century, the Briens gave their name to an important Breton castle, and this castle became the burgh of the Barony of Chateaubriand. The Chateaubriand arms at first consisted of fir-cones with the motto, *Je sème l'or*. Geoffrey Baron of Chateaubriand accompanied St. Louis to Palestine. He was taken prisoner at the battle of the Mansourah,[2] but returned, and his wife Sybil died of joy and surprise at seeing him. St. Louis, in reward for his services, granted to him and his heirs, in lieu of his old arms, an escutcheon gules, strewn with fleur-de-lis or: "*Cui et ejus hæredibus*," a cartulary of the Priory of Bérée bears witness, "*sanctus Ludovicus tum Francorum rex, propter ejus probitatem in armis, flores lilii auri, loco pomorum pini auri, contulit.*"

The Chateaubriands were divided, soon after their origin, into three branches: the first, that of the Barons of Chateaubriand, was the stock of the two others, and commenced in the year 1000 in the person of Thiern, son of Brien, grandson of Alan III., Count or Chief of Brittany; the second was called the Lords[3] of the Roches Baritaut, or of the Lion d'Angers; the third bore the title of Lords[4] of Beaufort.

When the line of the Lords of Beaufort became extinct in the person of Dame Renée, one Christopher II., of a collateral branch of that line, came into possession of the estate of the Guerrande in Morbihan.[5] At this period, the middle of the

---

[1] Bernard Chérin (1718–1785), genealogist and historiographer of the Orders of St. Lazarus, St. Michael, and the Holy Ghost.—B.

[2] 1250, when St. Louis defeated the Saracens, but was subsequently taken prisoner, with a number of his knights.—T.

[3] *Seigneurs.*—T.   [4] *Sires.*—T.

[5] The estate of the Guerrande is situated not in Morbihan, but in the parish of Hénan-Bihen, now one of the communes of the Canton of Matignon, Arrondissement of Dinan (Côtes-du-Nord).—B.

seventeenth century, great confusion prevailed in the order of the nobility. Names and titles had been usurped. Louis XIV. ordered a visitation, so that each might be reinstated in his rights. Christopher, upon giving proofs of his ancient nobility, was confirmed in his title and in the ownership of his arms, by judgment of the Chamber instituted at Rennes for the reforming of the nobility of Brittany. This judgment was issued on the 16th of September 1669, and ran as follows:

"Judgment of the Chamber instituted by the King for the reforming of the nobility in the.Province of Brittany, delivered the 16th of September 1669: between the King's Attorney-General and M. Christophe de Chateaubriand, Sieur de La Guerrande; which declares the said Christophe to issue from an ancient noble house, permits him to take the quality of knight, and confirms his right to bear arms gules strewn with fleur-de-lys or without number, and this after production by him of his authentic titles, from which it appears, &c., &c. The said judgment signed Malescot."

This judgment declares that Christophe de Chateaubriand de La Guerrande was descended in the direct line from the Chateaubriands, Lords of Beaufort; the Lords of Beaufort were connected through historical evidences with the first Barons of Chateaubriand. The Chateaubriands de Villeneuve, du Plessis and de Combourg were younger branches of the Chateaubriands de La Guerrande, as is proved by the descent of Amaury, brother of Michel, the said Michel being the son of the Christophe de La Guerrande whose descent was confirmed by the above-quoted decree of the reforming of the nobility of 16 September 1669.

After my presentation to Louis XVI., my brother proposed to increase my portion as a younger son by endowing me with some of those benefices known as *bénéfices simples*. There was but one practical means of doing this, since I was a layman and a soldier, and that was to have me received into the Order of Malta. My brother sent my proofs to Malta, and soon after, he presented a petition, in my name, to the Chapter of the Grand Priory of Aquitaine, held at Poitiers, with a view to the appointing of a commission to declare urgency. M. Pontois was at the time archivist, vice-chancellor and genealogist of the Order of Malta at the Priory.

The president of the Chapter was Louis Joseph des Escotais, *bailli*, Grand Prior of Aquitaine, having with him the Bailli de

Freslon, the Chevalier de La Laurencie, the Chevalier de Murat, the Chevalier de Lanjamet, the Chevalier de La Bourdonnaye-Montluc and the Chevalier du Bouëtiez. The petition was allowed at the sittings of the 9th, 10th, and 11th of September 1789. It is stated, in the terms of admission of the "Memorial," that I deserved the favour which I solicited "by more than one title," and that "considerations of the greatest weight" made me worthy of the satisfaction which I claimed.

And all this took place after the fall of the Bastille,[1] on the eve of the scenes of the 6th of October 1789,[2] and of the removal of the Royal Family to Paris. And at its sitting of the 7th of August in this same year 1789, the National Assembly had abolished titles of nobility! How could the knights, the examiners of my proofs, find that I deserved "by more than one title the favour which I solicited" and so forth, I, who was nothing more than a petty sub-lieutenant of Foot, unknown, without credit, interest or fortune?

My brother's eldest son (I add this in 1831 to my original text, written in 1811), the Comte Louis de Chateaubriand, married Mademoiselle d'Orglandes, by whom he had five daughters and one son, the latter called Geoffroy. Christian, Louis' younger brother, the great-grandson and godson of M. de Malesherbes, to whom he bore a striking resemblance, served with distinction in Spain in 1823 as a captain of the Dragoons of the Guard. He became a Jesuit in Rome. The Jesuits supply the place of solitude in proportion as the latter vanishes from the earth. Christian died recently at Chieri, near Turin: old and ailing as I am, I should have preceded him; but his virtues summoned him to Heaven before me, who have yet many faults to deplore.

In the division of the family patrimony, Christian had received as his share the property of Malesherbes, and Louis the estate of Combourg. Christian did not look upon an equal division as just, and on retiring from the world, determined to disburden himself of a property which did not belong to him and restore it to his elder brother.

To judge from my parchments, it would but rest with myself if I inherited the infatuation of my father and brother, and believed myself to represent a younger branch of the Dukes of Brittany, descending from Thiern, grandson of Alan III.

These Chateaubriands aforesaid had twice mixed their blood with the Blood Royal of England, Geoffrey IV. of Chateaubriand

[1] 14 July 1789.—T.
[2] The massacre of the *gardes-du-corps* at Versailles.—T.

having married as his second wife Agnes of Laval, granddaughter of the Count of Anjou and of Maud, daughter of Henry I., while Margaret of Lusignan, widow of the King of England and grand-daughter of Louis the Fat,[1] married Geoffrey V., twelfth Baron of Chateaubriand. With respect to the Royal House of Spain, we find Brien, a younger brother of the ninth Baron of Chateaubriand, who would seem to have married Joan, daughter of Alphonsus, King of Aragon. It is stated, moreover, in so far as the great families of France are concerned, that Edward of Rohan took Margaret of Chateaubriand to wife; and again that a Croï married Charlotte of Chateaubriand. Tinténiac, the victor of the Battle of the Thirty,[2] and Du Guesclin, the Constable, allied themselves with our three branches. Tiphaine Du Guesclin, grand-daughter of Bertrand's brother, made over the property of the Plessis-Bertrand to Brien of Chateaubriand, her cousin and heir. In treaties, Chateaubriands are given as sureties for the peace to the Kings of France, to Clisson,[3] to the Baron of Vitré. The Dukes of Brittany send records of their assizes to the Chateaubriands. The Chateaubriands become grand officers of the Crown and *illustres* in the Court of Nantes; they receive commissions to defend the safety of their province against the English. Brien I. is present at the Battle of Hastings: he was the son of Eudon, Count of Penthièvre. Guy of Chateaubriand is one of the lords whom Arthur of Brittany appoints to accompany his son upon his embassy to the Pope in 1309.

I should never come to an end if I finished stating all that of which I intended to give only a brief summary: the note[4] which I have at last determined to write, from consideration for my two nephews, who doubtless do not hold these bygone trifles as cheaply as I do, will supply the place of my omissions in the text. Still, nowadays we go too

---

[1] The second wife of Edward I. was Margaret, daughter of Philip the Bold, and grand-daughter of St. Louis, not of Louis the Fat. The reference is perhaps to Isabella of Angoulême, the affianced bride of Hugh of Lusignan, Count of the Marche, who was carried off and married by King John of England.—T.

[2] The Lord of Beaumanoir in 1351 sent his famous challenge to the English Lord of Ploërmel. Thirty Bretons and thirty Englishmen met in mortal combat at the foot of the oak midway between Ploërmel and Josselin. Eight of the English were killed, and the remainder surrendered. In the heat of the fight, Beaumanoir, parched with heat and fatigue, drank the blood flowing from his own wounds.—T.

[3] Olivier de Clisson, Constable of France, surnamed the Butcher. He succeeded Du Guesclin as Constable in 1380 and held the office until 1392. He died in his castle of Josselin, in Brittany, in 1407.—T.

[4] See this note at the end of these Memoirs.—*Author's Note.*

much to the other extreme; it has become the custom to declare that one comes of a stock liable to villain service, that one has the honour to be the son of a man bound to the soil. Are these declarations as proud as they are philosophical? Is it not taking the side of the strongest? Are the marquises, the counts, the barons of the present day, who have neither privileges nor furrows, three-fourths of whom are starving, blackening one another, refusing to recognize each other, mutually contesting each other's birth : are these nobles, whose very names are denied them or only allowed with reserve, able to inspire any fear?

For the rest, I ask pardon for being obliged to stoop to this puerile recital, in order to account for my father's dominant passion, which forms the key to the drama of my youth. As for myself, I neither boast nor complain of the old or the new society. If in the first I was the Chevalier or the Vicomte de Chateaubriand, in the second I am François de Chateaubriand: I prefer my name to my title. Monsieur my father would readily, like a certain mighty land-owner of the Middle Ages, have called God "the gentleman on high" and surnamed Nicodemus (the Nicodemus of the Gospels) "a holy gentleman." And now, passing over my immediate progenitor, let us come from Christopher, feudal lord of the Guerrande, descending in the direct line from the Barons of Chateaubriand, to me, François, lord without vassals or money of the Vallée-aux-Loups.

To trace backwards the line of the Chateaubriands, consisting, as it did, of three branches : after the two first had failed, the third, that of the Lords of Beaufort, represented by a branch, the Chateaubriands of the Guerrande, grew poor, as the inevitable result of the law of the land; the eldest sons of the nobility received two-thirds of the property, by virtue of the custom of Brittany, while the younger sons divided among all of them one-third only of the paternal inheritance. The degeneration of the frail stock of the latter worked with a rapidity which became the greater as they married; and as the same distribution into two-thirds and one-third existed in the case of their children, these younger sons of younger sons soon came to dividing a pigeon, a rabbit, a duck or two, and a hound, although they did not cease to be "high knights and mighty lords" of a dove-cote, a toad-pool and a rabbit-warren. In the old noble families we see a number of younger sons; we follow them during two or three generations, and then they disappear, descending gradually to the plough or absorbed by the labouring classes, no man knowing what has become of them.

The head in name and blazon of my family at the commencement of the eighteenth century was Alexis de Chateaubriand, Seigneur de La Guerrande, son of Michel, the said Michel having a brother named Amaury. Michel was the son of the Christophe confirmed in his descent from the Lords of Beaufort and the Barons of Chateaubriand in the judgment above-quoted. Alexis de La Guerrande was a widower and a confirmed drunkard, spent his days in rioting with his maid-servants, and used his most precious family documents as covers for his butter-jars.

Contemporary with this head in name and blazon lived his cousin François, son of Amaury, Michel's younger brother. François, born 19 February 1683, owned the small lordships of the Touches and the Villeneuve. He married, on the 27th of August 1713, Pétronille Claude Lamour, Dame de Lanjégu, by whom he had four sons: François Henri, René (my father), Pierre Seigneur du Plessis and Joseph Seigneur du Parc. My grandfather, François, died 28 March 1729; in my grandmother, whom I knew in my childhood, lingered a beautiful expression of the eyes, which seemed to smile in the shade of her many years. At the time of her husband's death, she was living in the manor of the Villeneuve, in the neighbourhood of Dinan. My grandmother's whole fortune did not exceed 5,000 livres a year, of which her eldest son took 3,333 livres, leaving 1,666 livres a year to be divided among the three younger sons, of which sum the eldest again first took the largest share.

To crown the misfortune, my grandmother's plans were thwarted by the characters of her sons: the eldest, François Henri, to whom the magnificent heritage of the lordship of the Villeneuve had fallen, refused to marry and became a priest; but instead of seeking the benefices which his name would have procured for him, and with which he could have supported his brothers, prompted by pride and indifference, he asked for nothing. He buried himself in a country vicarage, and was successively Rector of Saint-Launeuc and of Madrignac in the Diocese of Saint-Malo. He had a passion for poetry; I have seen a goodly number of his verses. The jovial character of this sort of high-born Rabelais, the cult of the Muses practised by this Christian priest in his presbytery, aroused no little interest. He gave away all he possessed and died insolvent.

My father's fourth brother, Joseph, went to Paris and shut

himself up in a library: every year his younger son's portion of 416 livres was sent to him. He lived unknown amidst his books, occupying himself with historical research. During his life, which was a short one, he wrote to his mother on each first of January: the only sign of existence he ever gave. Strange destiny! There you have my two uncles, one a man of erudition, the other a poet; my elder brother wrote agreeable verse; one of my sisters, Madame de Farcy, had a real talent for poetry; another of my sisters, the Comtesse Lucile, a canoness, might have become known through a few admirable pages; I myself have blackened no little paper. My brother died on the scaffold, my two sisters quitted a life of pain after languishing in the prisons; my two uncles did not leave enough to pay for the four boards of their coffin; literature has caused my joys and my sorrows, and I do not despair, God willing, of ending my days in the alms-house.

My grandmother, having exhausted her means in doing something for her eldest and her youngest sons, was unable to do anything for the two others, René, my father, and Pierre, my uncle. This family, which had "strewn gold," according to its motto, looked out from its small manor upon the rich abbeys which it had founded and in which its ancestors lay entombed. It had presided over the States of Brittany, by virtue of possessing one of the nine baronies; it had witnessed with its signature the treaties of sovereigns, had served as surety to Clisson, and would not have had sufficient credit to obtain an ensigncy for the heir of its name.

One resource was left to the poor Breton nobles, the Royal Navy. An endeavour was made to use this on behalf of my father; but he must first go to Brest, live there, pay masters, buy his uniform, arms, books, mathematical instruments: how were all these expenses to be met? The brevet applied for to the Minister of Marine was not sent, for want of a protector to solicit its despatch: the Lady of Villeneuve sickened with grief.

It was then that my father gave the first sign of that decision of character for which I have known him. He was about fifteen years of age; observing his mother's distress, he approached the bed on which she lay, and said:

"I will no longer be a burden to you."

Thereupon my grandmother began to weep: I have heard my father describe the scene a score of times.

"René," said she, "what do you wish to do? Till your fields."

"They will not keep us; let me go away."

"Well, then," said the mother, "go where God wills that you should go."

She embraced the child with sobs. That same evening my father left the maternal farm and arrived at Dinan, where one of our kinswomen gave him a letter of recommendation to an inhabitant of Saint-Malo. The orphan adventurer was taken as a volunteer on board an armed schooner, which set sail a few days later.

At that time, the little commonwealth of Saint-Malo alone maintained the honour of the French ensign at sea. The schooner joined the fleet which the Cardinal de Fleury was despatching to the assistance of Stanislaus, who was besieged at Dantzic by the Russians. There my father landed, and was present at the memorable combat which 1,500 Frenchmen, commanded by the Breton de Bréhan, Comte de Plélo,[1] delivered, on the 29th of May 1734, against 40,000 Muscovites under Munich.[2] De Bréhan, diplomatist, warrior and poet, was killed; my father was twice wounded. He returned to France, and embarked once more. Wrecked upon the Spanish coast, he was attacked and stripped by robbers in Galicia, took a passage on board ship to Bayonne, and landed once again beneath the paternal roof. His courage and his orderly conduct had brought him into notice. He went to the West Indies, made money in the colonies, and laid the foundations of a new fortune for his family.

My grandmother entrusted to her son René the care of her son Pierre, M. de Chateaubriand du Plessis,[3] whose son, Armand de Chateaubriand, was shot, by order of Bonaparte, on Good Friday[4] 1809. He was one of the last of the French nobles to die for the cause of the monarchy. My father took charge of his brother's fate, although the habit of suffering had endowed him with a sternness of character that

[1] Louis Robert Hyppolite de Bréhan, Comte de Plélo (1699–1734). French Ambassador at Copenhagen, a grand-nephew of Madame de Sévigné, and author of some light poems.—T.

[2] Christopher Burchard, Count Munich (1683–1767), a native of Oldenburg and a favourite field-marshal, privy-councillor and eventually prime-minister of the Empress Anne of Russia. He was exiled on the accession of Elizabeth, and recalled by Peter III. after enduring twenty years of banishment.—T.

[3] Pierre Marie Anne de Chateaubriand, Seigneur du Plessis et du Val-Guildo (1727–1794), commanded several of his brother's merchant-ships. On the 12th of February 1760 he married Marie Jeanne Thérèse Brignon, daughter of Nicolas Jean Brignon, Seigneur de Laher, merchant, and of Marie Anne Le Tendu. He was imprisoned during the Terror and died in Saint-Malo jail, 3 Fructidor Year II. (20 August 1794).—B.

[4] 31 March.—T.

lasted through his life. *Non ignara mali* is not always a true saying: unhappiness has its harsh as well as its gentle side.

M. de Chateaubriand was tall and spare; he had an aquiline nose and thin, pale lips; his eyes were deep-set, small, and of a bluish or sea-green colour, like the eyes of lions or of the barbarians of olden time. I have never seen an expression like theirs: when inflamed with anger, each flashing pupil seemed to shoot out and strike you like a bullet.

My father was governed by one sole passion, that of his name. His general condition was one of deep sadness, which increased with age, and of a silence from which he issued only in fits of anger. Avaricious in the hope of restoring to his family its pristine splendour, haughty of demeanour with the nobles at the States of Brittany, harsh with his dependants at Combourg, taciturn, despotic and threatening at home, the feeling which the sight of him inspired was one of fear. Had he lived until the Revolution, and had he been younger, he would have played a great part, or got himself massacred in his castle. He was certainly possessed of genius: I have no doubt that, at the head of an administration or an army, he would have been a man out of the ordinary.

He first thought of marriage on returning from America. Born on the 23rd of September 1718, he was thirty-five years of age when, on the 3rd of July 1753, he married Apolline Jeanne Suzanne de Bedée, born 7 April 1726, and daughter of Messire Ange Annibal Comte de Bedée, Seigneur de La Bouëtardais. He took up his residence with her at Saint-Malo, within seven or eight leagues of which both of them had been born, so that their house commanded the horizon under which they had first seen the light. My maternal grandmother, Marie Anne de Ravenel de Boisteilleul, Dame de Bedée, born at Rennes on the 16th of October 1698, had been brought up at Saint-Cyr during the last years of Madame de Maintenon: her education had left its mark upon her daughters.

My mother was endowed with great wit and intelligence, and with a prodigious imagination; her mind had been formed by the works of Fénelon, Racine, Madame de Sévigné, and stored with anecdotes of the Court of Louis XIV.; she knew the whole of *Cyrus*[1] by heart. Apolline de Bedée was dark, short and ill-favoured, with large features; the elegance of

---

[1] MADELEINE DE SCUDÉRI, *Le Grand Cyrus*, one of the longest of the old French romances, published 1650, in ten volumes 8vo.—T.

her manners, the vivacity of her temperament, formed a contrast with my father's stiffness and calm. Loving society as much as he loved solitude, as humoursome and animated as he was cold and unimpassioned, she had no tastes but what were opposed to her husband's. The antagonism which she encountered saddened her naturally gay and light-hearted disposition. Obliged to hold her tongue when she would have wished to speak, she made amends to herself by a kind of clamorous melancholy broken with sighs which alone interrupted my father's silent gloom. For piety my mother was an angel.

My mother was brought to bed at Saint-Malo of an eldest son, who died in the cradle and was christened Geoffroy, like almost all the first-born of my family. This son was followed by another and by two daughters, none of whom lived more than a few months.

These four children died of an extravasation of blood on the brain. At last my mother bore a third son, who was named Jean-Baptiste: it was he who later married M. de Malesherbes' grand-daughter. After Jean-Baptiste came four daughters: Marie-Anne, Bénigne, Julie and Lucile, all four endowed with rare beauty; the two eldest alone survived the storms of the Revolution. Beauty, that serious trifle, remains when all the rest has passed away. I was the last of the ten children. Probably my four sisters owed their existence to my father's desire to assure the perpetuation of his name through the arrival of a second boy; I resisted, I had an aversion to life.

Here is my baptismal certificate:[1]

"Extract from the civil register of the Commune of Saint-Malo for the year 1768.

"François René de Chateaubriand, son of René de Chateaubriand and of Pauline Jeanne Suzanne de Bedée, his

[1] The full text runs as follows:—
"François René de Chateaubriand, son of the high and mighty René de Chateaubriand, Knight, Comte de Combourg, and of the high and mighty dame, Apolline Jeanne Suzanne de Bedée, Dame de Chateaubriand, his wife, born 4 September 1768, baptized on the following day by us, Messire Pierre Henri Nouail, grand-chanter and canon of the cathedral church, official and grand-vicar of Monseigneur the Bishop of Saint-Malo. Godfather, the high and mighty Jean-Baptiste de Chateaubriand his brother, and godmother, the high and mighty dame, Françoise Marie Gertrude de Contades, Dame and Comtesse de Plouër, who sign with the father. Signed: Jean-Baptiste de Chateaubriand, Brignon de Chateaubriand, Contades de Plouër, de Chateaubriand, Nouail, vicar-general."—B.

wife, born 4 September 1768, baptized on the following day by us Pierre Henri Nouail, grand-vicar of the Bishop of Saint-Malo. Godfather, Jean-Baptiste de Chateaubriand, his brother, and godmother, Françoise-Gertrude de Contades, who sign with the father. Thus signed on the register: Contades de Plouër, Jean-Baptiste de Chateaubriand, Brignon de Chateaubriand, de Chateaubriand, and Nouail, vicar-general." [1]

It will be observed that I have made a mistake in my Works: I say that I was born on the 4th of October [2] and not on the 4th of September; my Christian names are François René and not François Auguste. [3]

The house in which my parents were then living at Saint-Malo stands in a dark and narrow street called the Rue des Juifs: [4] it has now been turned into an inn. [5] The room in which my mother was confined overlooks a bare portion of the city wall, and from the windows one can contemplate an endless expanse of sea, which breaks upon the rocks. My godfather, as appears from my baptismal certificate, was my brother, and my godmother the Comtesse de Plouër, daughter of the Maréchal de Contades. [6] I was almost dead when I first saw the light. The roaring of the waves, upheaved by a squall which heralded the autumnal equinox, deadened my cries: I have often been told these details; their sadness has never been erased from my memory. A day seldom passes on which, reflecting on what I have been, I do not see again in thought the rock upon which I was born, the room in which my mother inflicted life upon me, the tempest whose sound first lulled me to sleep, the unfortunate brother who gave me a name which I have nearly always dragged through misfortune. Heaven seemed to unite these several circumstances in order to lay within my cradle a symbol of my destiny.

[1] Twenty days before my birth, on the 15th of August 1768, was born, in another island, at the other extremity of France, the man who abolished the old society, Bonaparte.—*Author's Note.*

[2] In the *Itinéraire de Paris à Jérusalem.*—T.

[3] *Atala*, the *Génie du Christianisme*, the *Martyrs* and the *Itinéraire* are all signed François Auguste de Chateaubriand. The author's object in suppressing the name of René on the title-pages of his early works was to avoid a false interpretation on the part of those who might have been tempted to identify him with the immortal episode in his works which has *René* for its title.—B.

[4] Now Rue de Chateaubriand.—T.

[5] The Hôtel de France et de Chateaubriand.—T.

[6] Louis George Érasme Marquis de Contades (1704-1795), for some time Commander-in-Chief of the French Army, a marshal of France, and Governor of Alsace from 1763 to 1788.—T.

Chateaubriands birth place at St. Malo.

On leaving my mother's breast I underwent my first exile: I was banished to Plancoët, a pretty village situated between Dinan, Saint-Malo and Lamballe. My mother's only brother, the Comte de Bedée, had built a house near the village, to which he gave the name of Monchoix. My maternal grandmother's property stretched from this neighbourhood to the market-town of Courseul, the Curiosolites of Cæsar's Commentaries. My grandmother, since many years a widow, lived with her sister, Mademoiselle de Boisteilleul, in a hamlet divided from Plancoët by a bridge, and known as the Abbaye, from a Benedictine abbey dedicated to Our Lady of Nazareth.

My nurse was sterile; another poor Christian took me to her breast. She vowed me to the patron of the hamlet, Our Lady of Nazareth, and promised that I should wear blue and white in her honour for seven years. I had lived but a few hours, and already the weight of years was marked upon my brow. Why did they not let me die? God in His wisdom granted to the prayer of humbleness and innocence the preservation of a life for which a vain renown was lying in wait.

This vow of the Breton peasant woman is no longer in the spirit of the age: yet nothing can be more touching than the intervention of a Divine Mother coming between Heaven and the child and sharing the terrestrial mother's solicitude.

After three years I was brought back to Saint-Malo. Already seven years had elapsed since my father had recovered the domain of Combourg. He wished to gain possession of the estates where his ancestors had lived and died; and unable to treat for the purchase of the manor of Beaufort, which had passed to the Goyon family, or for the barony of Chateaubriand, which had fallen into the hands of the House of Condé, he turned his attention to Combourg, which is spelt "Combour"[1] in Froissart, and which has been held by various branches of my family through their intermarriages with the Coëtquens. Combourg served as a defence to Brittany in the Norman and English marches: it was built in 1016 by Junken, Bishop of Dol; the great tower dates to 1100. The Maréchal de Duras,[2] who held Combourg by right of his wife, Maclovie de Coëtquen, whose mother was a Chateaubriand, came to terms with my father. The Marquis

---

[1] It was so spelt long after Froissart's time, following the ancient form, "Comburnium." The final "g" was first added between 1660 and 1680.—B.

[2] Emmanuel Félicité de Durfort, Duc de Duras (1715–1789), a peer and marshal of France, First Lord of the Bedchamber, and a member of the French Academy. He married in 1736 Louise Françoise Maclovie Céleste de Coëtloquen, who died 7 January 1802.—B.

du Hallay,[1] an officer in the Mounted Grenadiers of the Royal
Guards, perhaps too well known for his valour, is the last of
the Coëtquen Chateaubriands: M. du Hallay has a brother.
The same Maréchal de Duras, in his quality as our ally, subsequently presented my brother and myself to Louis XVI.

I was intended for the Royal Navy: a distaste for Court
life was natural to any Breton, and particularly to my father.
This feeling was strengthened in him by the aristocratic
character of our States.

When I was brought home to Saint-Malo, my father was
at Combourg, my brother at Saint-Brieuc College; my four
sisters were living with my mother. All the latter's affections
were centred upon her eldest son: not that she did not love
her other children, but she showed a blind preference for
the young Comte de Combourg. True, I had, as a boy,
as the youngest-born, as the "chevalier," as I was called,
certain privileges not shared by my sisters; but, upon the
upshot, I was left to the care of the servants. Moreover, my
mother, full of intelligence and virtue, was largely taken up
with social claims and religious duties. The Comtesse de
Plouër, my godmother, was her intimate friend; she also saw
Maupertuis'[2] family and the Abbé Trublet's.[3] She loved
politics, excitement, society: for people talked politics at
Saint-Malo like the monks in the Cedron hollow;[4] and she
threw herself with ardour into the La Chalotais[5] affair. She
would bring home with her a cross humour, an absent-minded-

---

[1] Jean Georges Charles Frédéric Emmanuel Marquis du Hallay-Coëtquen
(1799–1867). He was a captain in the 1st Mounted Grenadiers of the Royal
Guard under the Restoration, and a Lord of the Bedchamber. The reference to
his valour applies to his reputation as a judge in points of honour and a referee
in matters of the duel. His brother, the Comte du Hallay-Coëtquen, served as
a page to Louis XVIII. in 1814, and was subsequently a guard to Monsieur and a
lieutenant in the 4th Mounted Chasseurs.—B.

[2] Pierre Louis Moreau de Maupertuis (1698–1759), the distinguished geometrician and French Academician, and President of the Berlin Academy.
Maupertuis was a native of Saint-Malo.—T.

[3] Nicholas Charles Joseph Trublet (1697–1770), Archdeacon and Canon of
Saint-Malo, his native city. He was a writer of little merit, although elected
a member of the French Academy in 1761, and was the hero of Voltaire's satire,
Le Pauvre Diable.—T.

[4] See the *Itinéraire* for this anecdote.—T.

[5] Louis René de Caradeuc de La Chalotais (1701–1785) was Attorney-
General to the Parliament of Brittany. He was accused of instigating the
opposition of the States and Parliament of Brittany to certain financial edicts
affecting the Breton liberties. After a long confinement in the Citadel of Saint-
Malo (1765), he was exiled to Saintes and was not permitted to return to Rennes
until ten years later, on the accession of Louis XVI., when he resumed his
functions. The affair created a great and prolonged local commotion.—T.

ness, a spirit of parsimony, which at first prevented one from recognising her admirable qualities. She was methodical, and showed no method in the management of her children; generous, and appeared avaricious; gentle, yet ever scolding: my father was the terror of the servants, my mother their scourge.

Such were the dispositions of my parents, whence sprang the earliest feelings of my life. I attached myself to the woman who took care of me, an excellent creature called Villeneuve, whose name I write with a movement of gratitude and with tears in my eyes. Villeneuve was a sort of superintendent of the household; she carried me in her arms, gave me, by stealth, anything she could come across, wiped away my tears, kissed me, pushed me into a corner, took me out, and constantly muttering: "There's one who won't grow up proud, who has a good heart, who does not snub poor people! Here, little fellow," she would stuff me with sugar and wine.

Soon my childish affection for Villeneuve was controlled by a worthier friendship. Lucile, my fourth sister, was two years older than I.[1] Neglected as the youngest, she was given none save her sisters' left-off clothes to wear. Imagine a little thin girl, too tall for her age, with loose-jointed arms, shy, speaking with difficulty, and unable to learn a thing; dress her in a frock taken from a child of a different size and shape; confine her chest in a quilted corset the gores of which cut wounds into her ribs; hold up her neck with an iron collar cased in brown velvet; dress her hair back upon the top of her head, fasten it with a cap of black stuff, and you see before you the wretched object that struck my eyes on returning to the paternal roof. No one would have suspected in the puny Lucile the talent and beauty with which she was one day to shine.

She was given me as a plaything; I did not abuse my power; instead of submitting her to my will, I became her defender. She and I were taken every morning to the sisters Couppart, two hunch-backed old women dressed in black, who taught children to read. Lucile read very badly; I still worse. She was scolded; I scratched the sisters' faces; great complaints were carried to my mother. I began to pass for a ne'er-do-weel, a rebel, an idler, in short, an ass. These ideas sank into my parents' heads: my father said that all the Chevaliers de Chateaubriand had been hare-hunters, drunkards, and brawlers. My mother sighed and grumbled when she saw the disordered condition of my jacket. Child

---

[1] Lucile was four, not two years, older than her brother. She was born on the 7th of August 1764.—B.

though I was, my father's remark revolted me; when my mother crowned her remonstrances with a panegyric on my brother, whom she called a Cato, a hero, I felt inclined to do all the ill that they seemed to expect of me.

My writing-master, M. Després, who wore a pig-tail, was no more satisfied with me than were my parents; he was eternally making me copy, from a slip in his own writing, the following couplet, which I came to detest, not by reason of any error of construction that it may contain:

> C'est à vous, mon esprit, à qui je veux parler:
> Vous avez des défauts que je ne puis celer.[1]

He accompanied his reprimands with cuffs in my neck, calling me *tête d'achôcre:* did he mean *ἀχὼρ* ?[2] I do not know what a *tête d'achôcre* is, but I take it to be something frightful.

Saint-Malo is a mere rock. Originally rising from the middle of a salt marsh, it became an island in 709 through an incursion of the sea, which hollowed out the gulf and set Mont Saint-Michel amid the waves. Nowadays the rock of Saint-Malo is attached to the mainland only by a causeway poetically designated as the Sillon, or Furrow. The Sillon is on one side assaulted by the open sea, and on the other washed by the flowing tide, which turns to enter the harbour. In 1730 it was almost entirely destroyed by a storm. At ebb-tide the harbour is dry, displaying on its edge east and north of the sea a beach of the most beautiful sand. It is then possible to walk round my paternal nest. Near and far are strewn rocks, forts, uninhabited islets: the Fort-Royal, the Conchée, Césembre, and the Grand-Bé, where my tomb will be. I unwittingly made a good choice: *bé*, in Breton, means tomb.

At the end of the Furrow, a Calvary stands upon a sandy knoll jutting out into the open sea. This knoll is called the Hoguette; it is crowned with an old gallows: we used to play puss-in-the-corner between its posts, disputing their possession with the birds of the sea-shore. It was not, however, without a certain sense of fright that we stopped in that place.

There, too, are the Miels, downs on which the sheep used to graze; to the right are meadows below Paramé, the posting-road to Saint-Servan, a Calvary, and wind-mills standing on rising ground, like those on Achilles' Tomb at the entrance to the Hellespont.

---

[1] "To you, my mind, I wish to remark,
    You have many faults which I cannot keep dark."—T.
[2] 'Aχὼρ, scurf.—*Author's Note.*

I reached my seventh year; my mother took me to Plancoët, to be released from my nurse's vow; we stayed at my grandmother's. If ever I have known happiness, it was certainly in that house.

My grandmother lived in the Rue du Hameau-de-l'Abbaye, in a house whose gardens ran terrace-wise into a dale, at the bottom of which was a spring surrounded by willows. Madame de Bedée could no longer walk, but with this exception she suffered from none of the inconveniences attendant upon her age. She was a pleasant old woman, fat, white-haired, neat, with the grand air and fine and noble manners. She wore old-fashioned plaited gowns and a head-dress of black lace fastened under her chin. Her mind was cultivated, her conversation grave, her mood was serious. She was cared for by her sister, who resembled her only in kind-heartedness. Mademoiselle de Boisteilleul was a little lean person, sprightly, talkative, addicted to raillery. She had been in love with a certain Comte de Trémigon, and the said count, after becoming engaged to her, had broken his promise. My great-aunt had consoled herself by singing her love, for she was poetically inclined. I remember often hearing her hum, in snuffling fashion, with her glasses on her nose, while embroidering double-rowed ruffles for her sister, an apologue commencing :

> Un épervier aimait une fauvette
> Et, ce dit-on, il en était aimé,[1]

which I always thought strange for a sparrow-hawk.
The song ended with this refrain :

> Ah ! Trémigon, la fable est-elle obscure?
> Ture, lure.[2]

How many things in this world end, like my aunt's love, in "Derry down !"

My grandmother left the housekeeping to my sister. She dined at eleven o'clock in the morning, took her *siesta*, woke up at one; she was carried down the garden terraces and placed under the willows near the spring, where she sat knitting, surrounded by her sister, her children, and grandchildren. At that time old age was a distinction; nowadays it is an

---

[1] " A sparrow-hawk loved a warbler fair,
    And, it is said, was loved by her."—T.

[2] " Is the fable obscure, Tremigon?
    Derry down !"—T.

encumbrance. At four o'clock, my grandmother was carried back to her drawing-room; Pierre, the man-servant, set out a card-table; Mademoiselle de Boisteilleul knocked with the tongs against the back of the fire-place, and a few minutes later three other old maids would walk in, who had come from the next house in obedience to my aunt's summons.

These three sisters were called the Demoiselles Vildéneux ;[1] they were the daughters of a poor gentleman, and instead of dividing his slender inheritance, they had enjoyed it in common, had never left one another, had never been out of their natal village. They had been intimate with my grandmother since childhood, lived next door to her, and came every day, at the preconcerted signal in the chimney, to make up their friend's party at quadrille. The game began; the good ladies quarrelled; it was the only incident in their lives, the only moment that spoiled the evenness of their temper. At eight o'clock, supper restored their serenity. Often my uncle de Bedée,[2] with his son and his three daughters, would be present at my grandmother's supper. The latter would tell a thousand stories of the old days; my uncle, in his turn, would describe the battle of Fontenoy, at which he was present, and crown his boasting with stories which were a little free and which made the worthy spinsters die with laughing. At nine o'clock, supper over, the servants entered; all went on their knees, and Mademoiselle de Boisteilleul said prayers aloud. At ten o'clock all in the house slept, except my grandmother, who made her waiting-woman read to her till one in the morning.

This society, which was the first I saw in my life, was also the first to disappear from my eyes. I saw death enter that abode of peace and bliss, making it gradually lonely, closing first one room and then another which were never reopened. I saw my grandmother obliged to forego her quadrille, for want of her accustomed partners; I saw the number of her constant friends diminish until the day came when my grandmother was the last to fall. She and her sister had promised to call each other so soon as one had preceded the other; they kept their word, and Madame de Bedée survived Mademoiselle de Boisteilleul but a few months. I am perhaps the only man living that knows that these persons existed. Twenty times since that period I have made the same remark; twenty times

---

[1] Their correct name was Loisel de La Villedeneu.—B.
[2] Marie Antoine Bénigne de Bedée, Comte de La Bouëtardais (1727-1807), younger brother to Madame de Chateaubriand.—B.

have societies been formed and dissolved around me. The impossibility of long duration in human relations, the profound forgetfulness that pursues us, the invincible silence that takes possession of our tomb and spreads thence over our house, constantly recall me to the necessity of isolation. Any hand will serve to give us the glass of water which we may need in the fever preceding death. Ah, that it may not be too dear to us! For how can one forsake without despair the hand which he has covered with kisses, and which he would like to hold to his heart for ever?

The Comte de Bedée's house [1] was a league away from Plancoët, in a high and cheerful position. Everything about it breathed gladness: my uncle's gaiety was inexhaustible. He had three daughters, Caroline, Marie and Flore, and one son, the Comte de La Bouëtardais, a counsellor to the Parliament, all of whom shared his light-heartedness. Monchoix was filled with cousins from the neighbourhood; they made music, danced, hunted, and revelled from morning till night. My aunt, Madame de Bédee,[2] who saw my uncle gaily squandering his capital and his income, was very properly vexed; but no one listened to her, and her ill-humour but increased the good-humour of her family, the more so as my aunt herself displayed a number of eccentricities: she always had a great snarling hound lying in her lap, and was followed by a tame boar, which filled the house with its grunts. When I came from my father's house, so sombre and so silent, to this house of noise and merry-making, I felt myself in a genuine paradise. The contrast became more striking when my family were settled in the country: the change from Combourg to Monchoix was a change from the wilderness to the world, from the castle-keep of a mediæval baron to the villa of a Roman prince. ·

On Ascension Day 1775, I set out from my grandmother's house to go to Our Lady of Nazareth, accompanied by my mother, my aunt de Boisteilleul, my uncle de Bedée and his children, my nurse, and my foster-brother. I wore a white surtout, white shoes, gloves, and hat, and a blue silk sash. We went up to the Abbaye at ten o'clock in the morning. The convent, which stood by the road-side, derived

[1] The Château de Monchoix is in the parish of Pluduno, now one of the communes of the Canton of Plancoët, Arrondissement of Dinan, and is inhabited by M. du Boishamon, the Comte de Bedée's great-grandson.—B.

[2] Marie Angélique Fortunée Cécile Ginguené (1729-1823), daughter of Écuyer François Ginguené and of Dame Thérèse Françoise Jean. She married the Comte de Bedée on the 23rd of November 1756.—B.

an appearance of age from a quincunx of elms dating back to John V. of Brittany.[1] The quincunx led to the cemetery; it was only through the region of the tombstones that the Christian could reach the church: it is death which admits to the presence of God.

The monks were already seated in their stalls; the altar was lighted with a multitude of candles; lamps hung from the different arches: Gothic edifices offer successive distances and, as it were, horizons. The bedels met me at the door, in state, and conducted me to the choir. Three seats had been prepared; I sat down upon the middle one, my nurse placed herself on my left, my foster-mother on my right.

The mass commenced; at the Offertory, the celebrant turned to me and read some prayers; after which my white clothes were taken off and hung as an *ex voto* beneath a picture of the Virgin. They then dressed me in a violet-coloured frock. The Prior delivered a discourse upon the efficacy of vows; he recalled the history of the Baron of Chateaubriand who had gone to the East with St. Louis; he told me that perhaps I, too, should go to Palestine and visit that Virgin of Nazareth to whom I owed my life, thanks to the prayers of the poor, which were always powerful with God. This monk, who told me the history of my family as Dante's grandfather told him the history of his ancestors, might also, like Cacciaguida, have added to it by predicting my exile.[2]

Since the Benedictine's exhortation, I always dreamt of the pilgrimage to Jerusalem, and I ended by accomplishing it.

I was consecrated to religion: the wardrobe of my innocence has lain upon its altars: it is not my garments that should to-day be hung within its temples, but my misfortunes.

I was taken back to Saint-Malo. Saint-Malo is not the Aleth of the *Notitia Imperii:* Aleth was better placed by the Romans in what is now the suburb of Saint-Servan, in the military port known as Solidor, at the mouth of the Rance. Facing Aleth was a rock, *est in conspectu Tenedos,*[3] not the refuge of the perfidious Greeks, but the retreat of Aaron the Hermit,[4] who took up his abode on that island in 507, the date of the victory of Clovis over Alaric:[5] one founded a little

---

[1] 1339-1442.—T.
[2] I omit eleven lines of quotation and their translation.—T.
[3] VIR., Æn. I. 184.—T.
[4] St. Aaron the Hermit is honoured on the 22nd of June.—T.
[5] At the battle of Vouillé, where Clovis killed Alaric II., King of the Visigoths, with his own hand.—T.

convent, the other a great monarchy, two edifices both of which
have perished.

Malo, in Latin Maclovius, Macutus, or Machutes, became
Bishop of Aleth in 541, and, attracted as he was by Aaron's
fame, visited him.   As chaplain of the hermit's oratory, after
the saint's death he raised a cenobitical church, *in prædio
Machutis*.   Malo's name was given to the island, and subsequently to the town, Maclovium, Maclopolis.

Between St. Malo, first Bishop of Aleth, and Blessed John
surnamed "of the Gridiron," who was consecrated in 1140 and
built the cathedral, came five-and-forty bishops.   Aleth was
already almost wholly abandoned, and John of the Gridiron
transferred the episcopal see from the Roman to the Breton
city which was spreading over Aaron's rock.

Saint-Malo suffered greatly in the wars waged between the
Kings of France and England.   The Earl of Richmond, later
Henry VII. of England, in whom ended the Wars of the
Roses, was taken to Saint-Malo.   He was handed over by the
Duke of Brittany to the ambassadors of Richard, who carried
him to London to be put to death.   He escaped from his
guards, and took refuge in the cathedral, *asylum quod in eâ
urbe est inviolatissimum :* the right of sanctuary dated back to
the Druids, the first priests of Aaron's isle.

A Bishop of Saint-Malo was one of the three favourites
(the others were Arthur de Montauban and Jean Hingant)
who killed the unfortunate Giles of Brittany, as may be read
in the *Histoire lamentable de Gilles, seigneur de Chateaubriand
et de Chantocé, prince du sang de France et de Bretagne,
étranglé en prison par les ministres du favori, le* 24 *avril*
1450.

There exists a fine capitulation between Henry IV. and
Saint-Malo : the city treats as between Power and Power,
protects those who have taken refuge within its walls, and
retains the right, by an order of Philibert de La Guiche, grand-
master of artillery of France, to cast one hundred pieces of
cannon.   Nothing more closely resembled Venice (failing the
sun and the pursuit of the arts) than did this little commonwealth of Saint-Malo in religion, wealth, and prowess at sea.
It supported Charles V.'s expedition to Africa and came to
the aid of Louis XIII. at the Rochelle.   It flew its ensign over
all the seas, maintained relations with Mocha, Surat, Pondicherry ; a company formed in its midst explored the South Sea.

From the reign of Henry IV. onwards, my native city
distinguished itself for its devotion and fidelity to France.

The English bombarded it in 1693; on the 29th of November in that year, they launched against it an infernal machine, in the wreck of which I have often disported myself with my play-fellow. . They bombarded it again in 1758.

The Malouins lent considerable sums of money to Louis XIV. during the war of 1701; in recognition of this service, he confirmed them in their privilege of guarding their own city, and ordered that the crew of the first ship in the Royal Navy should consist exclusively of sailors drawn from Saint-Malo and its territory. In 1771, the Malouins repeated their sacrifice and lent thirty millions to Louis XV.

The famous Admiral Anson[1] landed at Cancale in 1758, and burnt Saint-Servan. In Saint-Malo Castle, La Chalotais wrote upon rags, with the aid of a tooth-pick, soot and water, the Memoirs which made so much noise and which nobody remembers. Events efface events; they are but inscriptions traced upon other inscriptions, making pages of palimpsestic history.

Saint-Malo furnished the Royal Navy with its best sailors; the complete roll may be found in a folio volume published in 1682 with the title: *Rôle général des officiers, mariniers et matelots de Saint-Malo.* There is a *Coutume de Saint-Malo*, printed in the collection of the Customary-General. The city archives contain a fair number of charters useful to the study of history and maritime law.

Saint-Malo gave birth to Jacques Cartier,[2] the French Christopher Columbus, who discovered Canada. At the other extremity of America the Malouins marked out the islands to which they gave their name: Îles Malouins.[3] It is the native city of Duguay-Trouin,[4] one of the greatest seamen ever known, and more recently, of Surcouf.[5] The celebrated Mahé de La Bourdonnais,[6] Governor of the Isle of France, was born at Saint-Malo, as were La Mettrie,[7] Maupertuis, the Abbé

---

[1] George Anson, Lord Anson (1697–1762). He received his promotion and peerage after defeating La Jonguère in 1747.—T.

[2] Jacques Cartier (1494–*circa* 1554), discovered the St. Lawrence in 1534–35, following this up by exploring the greater part of Canada.—T.

[3] The Falkland Islands.—T.

[4] René Duguay-Trouin (1673–1736), the hero of a number of brilliant naval expeditions, of which the most famous is the capture of Rio de Janeiro in 1711.—T.

[5] Robert Surcouf (1773–1827), the celebrated corsair, said to have been descended on the mother's side from Duguay-Trouin.—T.

[6] Bertrand François Mahé de La Bourdonnais (1699–1753), Governor-General of the Isle of France (Mauritius) and Bourbon from 1734 to 1743, when he went to India, defeating the English in Madras in 1746.—T.

[7] Offroy de La Mettrie (1709–1752), the author of a number of works of per-

Trublet, of whom Voltaire made sport: all this is not bad for an area not so large as that of the Tuileries Gardens.

Far ahead of these smaller literary lights of my birthplace stands the Abbé de Lamennais.[1] Broussais[2] also was born at Saint-Malo, as well as my noble friend, the Comte de La Ferronnays.[3]

Finally, so as to omit nothing, I will mention the mastiffs which formed the garrison of Saint-Malo. They were descended from the famous dogs which were regimental pets under the Gauls, and which, according to Strabo, fought by their masters' side in pitched battles against the Romans. Albertus Magnus, a monk of the Dominican Order, and as serious a writer as the Greek geographer, declares that at Saint-Malo "the safety of this important place was entrusted nightly to the faithful care of certain dogs, which patrolled well and trustily." They were condemned to capital punishment for having had the misfortune inconsiderately to bite a gentleman's legs; which gave rise in our days to the song, *Bon voyage:* people will laugh at anything. The criminals were imprisoned; one of them refused to take his food from the hands of his keeper, who wept; the noble animal elected to die of hunger: dogs, like men, are punished for their fidelity. In addition to this, the Capitol was, like my own Delos, guarded by dogs, which did not bark when Scipio Africanus came to say his morning prayer.

Saint-Malo is an enclosure of walls of different periods, divided into "great" and "little" walls, which form walks, and is defended besides by a castle of which I have spoken, and which the Duchess Anne fortified with towers, bastions, and moats. Seen from the outside, the island city resembles a granite citadel.

The children's meeting-place is the strand of the open sea, between the Castle and the Fort-Royal; here I was reared, the companion of the waves and winds. One of my earliest delights was to fight with the storms, to play with

verted philosophy. Frederic II. appointed him his reader and composed a eulogy upon his death, which occurred from indigestion.—T.

[1] The Abbé Félicité Robert de Lamennais (1782–1854), a religious and royalist writer until the Revolution of 1830, which converted him to demagogy and irreligion. His later works were condemned by the Holy See, and he was buried, by his own desire, without funeral rites.—T.

[2] François Joseph Victor Broussais (1772–1832), a distinguished physician and adversary of the spiritualistic sects.—T.

[3] Pierre Louis Auguste Ferron, Comte de La Ferronnays (1772–1842), occupied a number of prominent diplomatic posts under the Restoration. He was one of the most honest Frenchmen of his time.—T.

the waves which retired before me or chased me across the beach. Another diversion was, with the sand on the sea-shore, to build edifices which my play-fellows called "ovens." Since that time I have often seen castles, built for eternity, that have crumbled more swiftly than my sand palaces.

My lot being irrevocably fixed, I was left to pass an idle childhood. A few notions of drawing, English, hydrography and mathematics seemed more than sufficient for the education of a little boy destined beforehand for the rough life of a sailor.

I grew up in my family without lessons. We no longer occupied the house in which I was born: my mother lived in a large house in the Place Saint-Vincent, almost facing the gate which leads to the Sillon. The ragamuffins of the town had become my dearest friends: I filled the yard and the staircases of the house with them. I resembled them in all things: I spoke their language; I had their ways and their walk; I was dressed like them, my clothes were as indecent and undone as theirs; my shirts fell to rags; I had never a pair of stockings but it was full of holes; I shuffled about in shabby shoes, down at heel, falling off my feet at every step; I often lost my hat and sometimes my coat. My face was smudged, scratched, bruised; my hands black. So strange was my appearance that my mother, in the midst of her anger, could not keep from laughing and exclaiming, "How ugly he is!"

Nevertheless I loved, and I have always loved, cleanliness and elegance. At night I tried to mend my rags. Kind Villeneuve and my Lucile assisted in repairing my clothes, to save me from scoldings and punishments; but their patching only served to make my outfit the odder. I was particularly disconsolate when I appeared in tatters among children proud of their new clothes and of their finery.

There was something about my fellow-townsmen that was foreign and suggested Spain. Families from Saint-Malo had settled at Cadiz; families from Cadiz lived at Saint-Malo. Saint-Malo's insular position, its embankment, its architecture, its houses, its tanks, and its granite walls give it a certain resemblance to Cadiz; when I saw the latter town it often reminded me of the former.

Locked up at night in their city under the same key, the Malouins formed but one family. So primitive were the habits of the place, that young women who sent to Paris for their ribbons and muslins were looked upon as worldly creatures from whom their startled acquaintances held aloof. A frailty was a thing unknown : suspicion having fallen upon a certain Comtesse d'Abbeville, the result was a ballad in singing which people crossed themselves. Nevertheless the poet, faithful, in spite of himself, to the troubadour tradition, took sides against the husband, whom he called "a barbarous monster."

On certain days of the year, the townsmen and the country-people met at fairs called "assemblies," which were held upon the islands and forts surrounding Saint-Malo; these were reached on foot when the sea was low, by boat when it was high. The crowd of sailors and peasants; the covered carts; the caravans of horses, donkeys and mules; the concourse of dealers; the tents lining the sea-shore; the processions of monks and brotherhoods winding with their banners and crosses amid the crowd; the rowing- and sailing-boats flitting to and fro; the ships entering harbour or heaving anchor in the roads; the salutes of artillery, the pealing of the bells, all combined to fill these gatherings with noise, movement and variety.

I was the only witness of these holidays who did not share in the general gaiety. I had no money to buy toys and cakes. In order to avoid the scorn attached to ill-fortune, I sat far from the crowd, near those pools of water which the sea keeps up and replenishes in the hollows of the rocks. There I amused myself by watching the flight of the gulls and seamews, staring at the blue expanse of sky, gathering shells, listening to the refrain of the waves among the rocks. At night, at home, I was but little happier; I disliked certain dishes: I was forced to eat them. I cast beseeching glances at La France, who cleverly whipped away my plate when my father's head was turned. In the matter of the fire, the same harshness: I was not permitted to go near the chimney. It is a far cry from those severe parents to the spoil-children of to-day.

But if I had troubles unknown to modern children, I had some pleasures also of which they know nothing. The very meaning has been forgotten of those religious and domestic solemnities in which the whole country and the God of that country seemed to rejoice. Christmas, New Year's Day, Twelfth Night, Whitsuntide, Midsummer were prosperous days for me. Possibly the influence of my native rock worked upon my sentiments and studies. In the year 1015 the Malouins vowed to assist "with their hands and means" to build the steeples of the cathedral at Chartres: have I too not laboured with my hands to rebuild the stricken spire of the ancient Christian basilica? "The sun," says Père Maunoir, "never shone upon canton where more constant and invariable fidelity to the true Faith was shown than in Brittany. For thirteen centuries no heresy has stained the tongue which has served as an organ for preaching Jesus Christ, and the man is as yet unborn who has seen a Breton of Brittany preach any religion other than the Catholic."

On the feast-days which I have mentioned, I was taken with my sisters to perform my stations at the various sanctuaries in the town, at St. Aaron's Chapel or the Convent of Victory; my ear was struck by the sweet voices of a hidden choir of women; the harmony of their chant mingled with the roar of the billows. When, in the winter, at the hour of Benediction, the Cathedral was filled by the multitude; when old sailors upon their knees, young women and children read their Hours with lighted tapers in their hands; when the congregation at the Benediction joined in singing the *Tantum Ergo*; when, in the intervals between the hymns, the Christmas squalls dashed against the panes of the Cathedral and shook the arches of the nave which had resounded with the manly tones of Jacques Cartier and Duguay-Trouin, I experienced an extraordinary feeling of religion. I had no need to be told by Villeneuve to fold my hands and invoke God by all the names which my mother had taught me; I saw the heavens opening, the angels offering up our incense and our prayers; I bowed my forehead: it was not yet laden with those cares which weigh upon us so terribly that we are tempted not to raise our heads after bending them at the foot of the altar.

One sailor, the function concluded, would set sail all fortified against the night, while another would return to harbour and turn his steps to the illuminated dome of the church: thus religion and danger were constantly in sight one of the other, and their features were inseparable in my thoughts. I was hardly born before I heard speak of death: in the evening, a man went from street to street with a bell, calling upon Christians to pray for a brother deceased. Scarcely a year passed but vessels went under before my eyes, and as I played upon the beach the sea rolled to my

feet the corpses of foreign men who had expired far from
their native land. Madame de Chateaubriand said to me, as
St. Monica said to her son: *Nihil longe est a Deo.* My
education had been entrusted to Providence, which spared
me none of its lessons.

Vowed as I was to the Virgin, I knew and loved my
Protectress, whom I confused with my Guardian Angel:
her portrait, which had cost my kind Villeneuve a half sou,
was fastened with four pins over the head of my bed. I
ought to have lived in the times when one said to Mary:
"Sweet Lady of Heaven and Earth, Mother of Pity, Fountain
of all Good, that carried Jesus Christ in thy precious womb,
fair and most sweet Lady, I thank thee and entreat thee."

The first thing I knew by heart was a sailors' hymn,
which began:

> Je mets ma confiance,
> Vierge, en votre secours ;
> Servez-moi de défense,
> Prenez soin de mes jours ;
> Et quand ma dernière heure
> Viendra finir mon sort,
> Obtenez que je meure
> De la plus sainte mort.[1]

I have since heard this hymn sung in a shipwreck. To
this day I can repeat these bad rhymes with as much pleasure
as Homer's verses. A statue of Our Lady, adorned with a
Gothic crown and clad in a robe of blue silk trimmed with
a silver fringe, inspires me with more devotion than one of
Raphael's Virgins.

If at least that peaceful *Stella maris* had been able to
calm my troubled life ! But I was doomed to agitation even
in my childhood. I was like the Arab's date-tree: scarce
had my stem issued from the rock before it was stricken by
the wind.

I have told how my premature revolt against Lucile's
mistresses began my bad reputation : a play-fellow completed it.

[1] " To thee, O Mother-Maid,
   My song of hope I raise ;
Be thou my constant aid,
   Watch over all my ways ;
And when Death's hour is nigh,
   When life's long toil shall cease,
Pray, Mother, that I die
   In holiness and peace."—T.

My uncle, M. de Chateaubriand du Plessis, lived at Saint-Malo like his brother, and had, like him, four girls and two boys. Of my two cousins, Pierre and Armand, who were my first companions, Pierre became one of the Queen's pages, Armand was sent to college as being destined for the ecclesiastical state. Pierre, his service as a page ended, entered the navy and was drowned off the coast of Africa. Armand, after a long stay at college, left France in 1790, served throughout the emigration, made a score of intrepid descents in a small vessel upon the coast of Brittany, and at last, on Good Friday 1809,[1] gave his life for the King on the Plaine de Grenelle, as I have already stated and as I shall repeat once more when I come to relate the catastrophe.[2]

Deprived of the society of my two cousins, I made up for it by a new connection. On the second floor of the house in which we lived, resided a gentleman called Gesril, who had a son and two daughters. This son had been brought up differently from myself; a spoilt child, all he did was thought charming. His one pleasure consisted in fighting, and especially in raising quarrels in which he appointed himself referee. He played practical jokes on nursemaids taking children out walking, and nothing was talked of save his pranks, which were transformed into the blackest crimes. The father laughed at everything, and "Joson" was but the more petted for it.

Gesril became my intimate friend, and acquired an incredible ascendency over me: I was his apt pupil, although my character was the entire opposite of his. I liked solitary games, and sought quarrels with nobody: Gesril doted on pleasures and crowds, and revelled in childish squabbles. When some ragamuffin addressed me, Gesril would ask, "Do you allow that?" Thereupon I thought my honour at stake, and struck out at the rash one's eyes; his age and height made no difference. My friend would watch the fight and applaud my courage, but did nothing to assist me. Sometimes he levied an army of all the gutter-snipes he knew, divided his recruits into two bands, and we skirmished on the sands with the aid of stones.

Another game invented by Gesril was still more dangerous.

---

[1] This should be 1810 : *vide supra.*—T.

[2] He left a son, Frédéric, for whom I first obtained a post in the Guards of Monsieur, and who afterwards joined a regiment of Cuirassiers. He married, at Nancy, Mademoiselle de Gastaldi, by whom he has had two sons, and retired from the service. Armand's elder sister, my cousin, has for many years been a superior of the Trappist nuns.—*Author's Note* (Geneva, 1831).

At high-tide, when there was a storm, the waves, beating at the foot of the Castle, on the side of the long beach, would leap to the level of the great towers. Twenty feet above the base of one of these towers ran a granite parapet, narrow, sloping, and slippery, leading to the ravelin which defended the moat. The trick was to seize the moment between two waves and clear the dangerous spot before the surge broke and covered the tower. You saw a mountain of water approach you, roaring as it came, which, if you delayed a minute, must either drag you with it or crush you against the wall. Not one of us refused the venture, but I have seen children turn pale before attempting it.

This inclination to urge others to encounters of which he remained a spectator would lead one to think that, in after life, Gesril did not display great generosity of character; and yet, although on a smaller stage, he succeeded perhaps in surpassing the heroism of Regulus: his glory only needed Rome and Titus Livy. He became a naval officer, and he was taken prisoner in the engagement of Quiberon.[1] When the action was decided, seeing that the English continued to fire upon the Republican troops, Gesril[2] sprang into the sea, swam out to the ships, and told the English to cease fire, informing them of the disaster and of the capitulation of the Emigrants. They tried to save him by throwing a rope to him, and urged him to come on board. "I am a prisoner on parole," he cried, from the midst of the waves, and swam back to land: he was shot with Sombreuil and his companions.[3]

Gesril was my first friend; both of us were misunderstood in childhood, and we became intimate through an instinct that told us what we might some day be worth.

Two adventures put an end to this first part of my story, and produced a noteworthy change in the system upon which my education was conducted. We were one Sunday on the beach, in the "fan" of the Porte Saint-Thomas and along the Sillon, where great stakes sunk into the sand protect the walls against the swell of the sea. We would generally climb to the top of these stakes to watch the first waves of the rising tide flow beneath us. We had taken our places as usual; several little girls were among us small boys. I was the

---

[1] 21 July 1795.—T.

[2] Joseph François Anne Gesril du Papeu (1767-1795) fought in the American War of Independence as a lad of fourteen.—B.

[3] 27 August 1795. The Republicans denied the capitulation. But M. Biré gives a list of nine names which all bear witness to the fact that Sombreuil and his men laid down their arms only after capitulating.—T.

furthest out at sea, having none in front of me save a pretty little thing called Hervine Magon, who was laughing with pleasure and crying with fear.   Gesril was at the further end inland.

The tide rose; it was blowing; already the nurses and footmen were crying: "Come down, miss! Come down, sir!" Gesril waited for a big wave, and as it dashed between the stakes, he pushed the child seated next to him.   This one fell against another, that against a third; the whole row fell flat like "friars" of cards, but each was saved by his neighbour; the only exception was the little girl at the extreme end of the row, against whom I was upset, with the result that, having no one to support her, she fell off.   She was dragged away by the reflux; a thousand cries arose; all the nurses tucked up their skirts and waded into the sea, each catching hold of her brat and giving it a smack.   Hervine was fished out, and declared that François had thrown her down.   The nurses made a rush for me; I escaped from them, and ran and shut myself in the cellar at home, whither the army of females pursued me.   Fortunately my father and mother had gone out.   Villeneuve valiantly defended the door, and boxed the ears of the enemy's van-guard.   The real author of the mischief, Gesril, lent me his aid: climbing to his own floor, with his two sisters he threw pots of water and baked apples at my assailants from the windows.   They raised the siege at nightfall; but the news spread through the town, and the nine-year-old Chevalier de Chateaubriand was reputed a monster of iniquity, a survival of those pirates whom St. Aaron had driven from his rock.

The other adventure was this: I went with Gesril to Saint-Servan, the suburb divided from Saint-Malo by the merchant harbour.   In order to reach it at low water, you cross certain currents by means of low and narrow stepping-stones, which are covered when the sea rises.   The footmen who escorted us had loitered some way behind.   At the end of one of these bridges of stones we saw two ship's lads coming in our direction.   Gesril said to me: "Are we to let those beggars pass?" and shouted to them: "Into the water, ducks!"   Like true salts, refusing to take chaff, they came on; Gesril retreated; and stationing ourselves at one end of the bridge, we caught up some pebbles and threw them at the ship-boys' heads.   They rushed upon us, forced us to fall back, armed themselves with pebbles in their turn, and drove us back, fighting, upon our reserves, in other words, our servants.   I was not, like Horatius, hit in the eye; but a stone caught me so violently that my left ear was cut in two and hung down upon my shoulder.

I did not think of my hurt, but of my return home. When my friend came back from his excursions with a black eye and a torn coat, he was pitied, pampered, codled, dressed up again; while I, under similar circumstances, was promptly punished. The wound I had received was dangerous, but La France was unable to persuade me to come indoors, such was my fright. ¶I went and hid on the second floor with Gesril, who bound up my head in a napkin. This napkin set him going: it suggested a mitre to him; he turned me into a bishop and made me sing High Mass with him and his sisters until supper-time. The dignitary of the Church was at last obliged to go downstairs: my heart beat. Taken aback by my face disordered and smeared with blood, my father said not a word; my mother screamed; La France told my piteous case, and tried to excuse me; I was nevertheless rated for it. They dressed my ear, and Monsieur and Madame de Chateaubriand resolved to separate me from Gesril as soon as possible.[1]

I am not sure that it was not in this year that the Comte d'Artois[2] visited Saint-Malo: a sham fight was arranged for him in the roads. From the top of the bastion of the powder-magazine I watched the young Prince standing among the crowd on the beach: in his splendour and in my obscurity how many unknown destinies lay hidden! Thus, if my memory do not fail me, Saint-Malo has seen two Kings of France only: Charles IX. and Charles X.

There you have the picture of my early childhood. I do not know whether the harsh education I received be sound in principle, but it was adopted by my relations without purpose and as the natural outcome of their temperament. What is certain is that it imbued me with ideas different from those of other men; what is still more certain is that it impressed upon my sentiments a character of melancholy which arose from the habit of suffering acquired in the age of weakness, improvidence and mirth.

---

[1] I have already spoken of Gesril in my other works. One of his sisters, Angélique Gesril de La Trochardais wrote to ask me to obtain leave for her husband and her sister's husband to add the name of Gesril to their surnames: I failed in my negociation.—*Author's Note* (Geneva, 1831).

[2] Charles Philippe, Comte d'Artois (1757–1836), afterwards King Charles X. His visit to Saint-Malo took place on the 11th of May 1777, and lasted three days.—T.

Is it suggested that the manner of my bringing-up might have led me to abhor the authors of my being? Not at all: the remembrance of their sternness is almost pleasant to me; I value and honour their great good qualities. When my father died, my comrades in the Navarre Regiment witnessed my regret. From my mother I derive the consolation of my life, since it was she who taught me my religion; I gathered the Christian verities that issued from her mouth, as Pierre de Langres studied at night in church, by the light of the lamp burning before the Blessed Sacrament. Would my intelligence have received a greater development had I been set earlier to my studies? I doubt it: the waves, the winds, the solitude which were my first masters were probably better suited to my native disposition; possibly I owe to those wild tutors virtues which might have remained unknown to me. The truth is that no system of education is in itself to be preferred to any other system: do children love their parents better nowadays when they say *tu* and *toi* to them and no longer fear them? Gesril was spoilt in the same house in which I was scolded: we have both been honest men and loving and respectful sons. This thing which you think bad brings out your child's gifts; that other which you think good would stifle those same gifts. What God does is well done: it is Providence that guides us, when it destines us to play a part upon the world's stage.

BOOK II[1]

ON the 4th of September 1812,[2] I received the following note
from M. Pasquier,[3] the Prefect of Police:

"PREFECT'S OFFICE.

"The Prefect of Police begs M. de Chateaubriand kindly to
call at his office, either at about four o'clock this afternoon or
at nine o'clock to-morrow morning."

The object of Prefect of Police in sending for me was to
serve an order on me to leave Paris. I withdrew to Dieppe,
which was first called Bertheville and more than a hundred
years ago changed its name to Dieppe, from the English
word "deep."[4] In 1788, I was in garrison here with the

---

[1] This book was written at Dieppe in September and October 1812 and at
the Vallée-aux-Loups in December 1813 and January 1814, and was revised in
June 1846.—T.

[2] The author's forty-fourth birthday.—B.

[3] Étienne Denis Duc Pasquier (1767–1862), became Prefect of Police under
Bonaparte in 1810, President of the Chamber of Deputies under Louis XVIII.
in 1816, Foreign Minister in 1819. In 1821, on the fall of the Villèle Ministry,
Pasquier received his peerage. Louis-Philippe made him President of the
Chamber of Peers in 1830, Chancellor in 1837, and created him a duke in 1844.
In his capacity as a peer, therefore, and also as an Academician, he eventually
became Chateaubriand's colleague.—T.

[4] The River Arques, which discharges itself at Dieppe, was formerly called
the Deep.—T.

second battalion of my regiment: to dwell in this town of red-brick houses and ivory-white shops, this town of clean streets and clear atmosphere, was to take shelter in the days of my youth. When I walked out, I came across the ruins of Arques Castle, standing in the midst of its rubbish-heaps. It will be remembered that Dieppe was the birthplace of Duquesne.[1] When I stayed indoors, the sea lay spread before my view; from the table at which I sat I gazed upon the sea which saw me born and which bathes the shores of Great Britain, where I underwent so long an exile: my eyes surveyed the billows which carried me to America, cast me back upon Europe, and again bore me to the coasts of Africa and Asia. Hail, O sea, my cradle and my image! I will relate to thee the sequel of my story: if I lie, thy waves, commingled with all my days, shall accuse me of imposture to the generations to come.

My mother had constantly desired that I should be given a classical education. The career of a sailor, for which I was intended, "would perhaps," she said, "not be to my taste;" she thought that, in any event, it would be well to make me capable of following another profession. Her piety led her to hope that I should decide in favour of the Church. She therefore proposed to send me to a college where I should learn mathematics, drawing, fencing and English; she did not mention Greek or Latin for fear of scaring my father; but she intended to have me taught them, at first in secret, and later openly, when I should have made progress. My father accepted her proposal: it was arranged to send me to the college at Dol. This town was selected because it lay upon the road from Saint-Malo to Combourg.

In the very cold winter immediately preceding my school-days, the house in which we lived took fire: I was saved by my eldest sister, who carried me through the flames in her arms. M. de Chateaubriand, who had gone to his castle, sent for his wife to join him there: we did so in the spring.

Spring in Brittany is milder than in the country round Paris, and the trees bud three weeks earlier. The five birds that herald its coming, the swallow, the loriot, the cuckoo, the quail, and the nightingale, come with the breezes that nestle in the gulfs of the Armorican Peninsula. The earth grows as thick with

---

[1] Abraham Marquis Duquesne (1610-1688), the famous sailor. His religion—he was a Huguenot—prevented Louis XIV. from making him an admiral; the highest rank he obtained was that of lieutenant-general. A statue of Duquesne was erected at Dieppe in 1844.—T.

daisies, pansies, jonquils, narcissuses, hyacinths, ranunculuses, anemones as the neglected spaces around the churches of St. John Lateran and the Holy Cross of Jerusalem in Rome. Glades deck themselves with tall and graceful ferns ; fields of broom and furze glow with flowers gay as golden butterflies. The hedgerows at whose feet strawberries, raspberries and violets abound are adorned with hawthorn, honeysuckle and brambles, whose brown and twisted shoots bear glorious fruit and leaves. The country is alive with bees and birds; swarms and nests greet the children at every step. In sheltered nooks, myrtle and oleander grow in the open as in Greece; the fig-tree ripens as in Provence; each apple-tree, with its carmine-tinted blossoms, resembles the large nosegay of a village bride.

In the twelfth century, the cantons of Fougères, Rennes, Bécherel, Dinan, Saint-Malo and Dol were covered by the Forest of Brécheliant, which had served as a battlefield to the Francs and the races peopling the Domnonée. Wace[1] tells of the wild man seen there, of the fountain of Berenton, and a golden basin. An historic document of the fifteenth century, the *Usemens et coutumes de la forêt de Brécilien*, confirms the statement of the *Roman du Rou*: it is, say the *Usemens*, of great and wide extent: "there are four castles, a very great number of fair pools, fine chaces where are found no venemous beasts nor insects, two hundred woods, as many springs, notably the fountain of Belenton, near which Sir Pontus wrought his feats of arms."

To this day the country-side retains traces of its origin: intersected by wooded ditches, it presents at a distance the aspect of a forest, and reminds one of England; it was the abode of the fairies, and you shall see that I did, in fact, meet a sylph there. Narrow dales are watered by shallow rivulets. These dales are separated by moors and by tufts and clusters of holly-trees. The coast presents an array of beacons, lookouts, dolmens, Roman structures, ruins of mediæval castles, Renascence steeples: all bordered by the sea. · Pliny calls Brittany, *Peninsula Oceani spectatrix.*[2]

Between the sea and the land stretch pelagian plains, the fickle frontier of the two elements: there the field-lark flies

[1] Robert Wace, a native of Jersey, author of the *Brut d'Angleterre* or *Artus de Bretagne*, the *Roman du Rou* (Rollo Duke of Normandy), and the *Chronique ascendante des ducs de Normandie*. He was reading-clerk to Henry I. and Henry II., later a canon of Bayeux, and died in England *circa* 1184.—T.
[2] PLINY, III. x. 15.—T.

with the sea-lark; the plough and the bark furrow the earth
and the water at a stone's throw one from the other. The
sailor and the shepherd borrow each other's language: the
seaman says, "The waves are fleecy;" the herd speaks of
"fleets of sheep." Sands of changing colours, banks varie-
gated with shells, wreckage, fringes of silver foam line the
green or yellow edge of the corn-fields. I cannot recall the
name of the island in the Mediterranean in which I saw a
bas-relief representing nereids decorating with festoons the
hem of Ceres' robe.

But what is most admirable in Brittany is to see the moon
rising on land and setting upon the sea. The moon, by divine
creation governess of the deep, has her clouds, her mists, her
beams, her projected shadows like the sun; but, unlike the
latter, she does not set alone: a retinue of stars accompanies
her. As, upon my native coast, she descends the vault of
heaven, she extends her silence, and communicates it to the
sea; soon she sinks to the horizon, intersects it, shows but
the half of her forehead, which diminishes, dips, and disappears in the yielding intumescence of the waves. The stars
attendant upon their queen, before plunging in her train, seem
to pause suspended upon the crest of the billows. No sooner
has the moon set, than a gust of wind from the open sea
shatters the picture of the stars, like candles extinguished after
a celebration.

I was to accompany my sisters to Combourg: we set out
in the first fortnight in May. We left Saint-Malo at sunrise, my mother, my four sisters and I, in a huge, antiquated
berlin, with double-gilt panels, outside steps, and purple
tassels at the four corners of the roof. To this were
harnessed eight horses caparisoned like the mules in Spain,
with bells at their collars and bridles, and housings and
fringes of wool of many colours. While my mother was
sighing and my sisters talking themselves out of breath, I
looked with all my eyes, listened with all my ears, was
wonderstruck at each turn of the road: the first steps of a
Wandering Jew who was never to stop. Even then, if man
changed only his surroundings! But his days change, and
his heart.

Our horses were rested at a fishing-village on Cancale
Beach. We next went through the marshes and the fever-
stricken town of Dol, and after passing the gate of the
college to which I was soon to return, we plunged inland

For four mortal hours we saw nothing but heaths wreathed with woods, wastes scarce touched with the hoe, fields sown with poor, black, stunted corn, and poverty-stricken patches of oats. Charcoal-burners led teams of small horses with long and shaggy manes; lank-haired peasants in goat-skin great-coats drove lean bullocks with shrill cries or tramped behind a heavy plough, like labouring fauns. At last we caught sight of a valley at the bottom of which, not far from a pond, ascended the spire of a village church; the towers of a feudal castle rose amid the trees of a wood illumined by the setting sun.

I have been obliged to stop: my heart was beating so violently as almost to push back the table at which I am writing. The recollections awakened in my memory overpower me with their number and their force: and yet, what are they to the rest of the world?

After descending the hill, we forded a stream, drove on for half-an-hour, and then turned out of the high-road. The carriage rolled along a quincunx in an avenue of yoke-elms, whose crowns were interwoven above our heads: I still remember the moment at which I entered their shade and the feeling of affrighted gladness which I experienced.

On emerging from the darkness of the woods, we crossed a fore-court planted with walnut-trees, adjoining the house and garden of the steward; thence we passed, through a stone gateway, into a grassy court called the *Cour Verte*. On the right were a long row of stables and a clump of chesnut-trees; on the left, another clump of chesnut-trees. At the end of the court-yard, the lawn of which sloped imperceptibly upwards, appeared the castle between two clusters of trees. Its severe and gloomy frontage presented a curtain crowned with a machicolated, crenulated, covered gallery. This curtain connected two towers unlike in age, materials, height and thickness, which ended in battlements surmounted by a peaked roof, like a cap placed upon a Gothic crown.

Here and there, grated windows broke the bareness of the walls. A wide flight of steps, straight and steep, twenty-two in number, without balusters or hand-rail, took the place of the drawbridge across the moat, which was now filled up: it led to the door of the castle, pierced in the middle of the curtain. Above the door one saw the arms of the Lords of Combourg and the apertures through which had formerly issued the shafts and chains of the drawbridge.

The carriage drew up at the foot of the steps; my father

came down to welcome us. The meeting with his family so greatly softened his mood for the moment, that he favoured us with his most gracious looks. We climbed the steps and entered a resonant vestibule, with a pointed arch, through which we passed into a small inner court-yard. From this yard we entered the building looking south over the pond, and joined to the two smaller towers. The whole castle had the shape of a four-wheeled cart. We found ourselves on the same floor in a room formerly known as the Guard-room. A window opened out at either end; two others were cut into the side-wall. To enlarge these four windows, it had been necessary to excavate walls of eight to ten feet in thickness. Two sloping galleries, like the gallery in the Great Pyramid, issued from the two outer angles and led to the small towers. A winding staircase in one of these towers formed a communication between the Guard-room and the upper storey. Such was this portion of the building.

That contained within the frontage of the tall and of the thick tower, commanding a north aspect over the Cour Verte, consisted of a sort of square and sombre dormitory used as a kitchen, in addition to the vestibule, the steps, and a chapel. Above these apartments was the Rolls Hall, or Armoury, or Hall of Birds, or Knights' Hall, so called from a ceiling strewn with blazoned coats-of-arms and painted birds. The embrasures of the narrow trefoil windows were so deep as to form recesses, around which ran a granite seat. Add to this, in different parts of the building, secret passages and staircases, dungeons and cells, a labyrinth of covered and open galleries, and walled-up underground passages, the ramifications of which were unknown; on all sides gloom, silence, and a face of stone: and you see Combourg Castle.

A supper served in the Guard-room, at which I ate without constraint, ended the first happy day of my life. True happiness costs little; when it is dear, it is not the real metal.

So soon as I awoke the next morning, I set out to visit the castle grounds and to celebrate my advent to solitude. The steps faced north-west. Seated in the centre of the top step, one saw before him the Cour Verte, and beyond this court a kitchen-garden stretching out between two belts of trees: one, on the right, the quincunx by which we had come, was called the Little Mall; the other, on the left, the Great Mall: the latter was a wood of oaks, beeches, sycamores, elms, and chesnuts. Madame de Sévigné extolled those old shades in her day: since that time, one hundred and forty years had added to their beauty.

In the other direction, south and east, the landscape offered a quite different view: through the windows of the great hall one saw the houses of Combourg, a pond, the embankment of the pond along which ran the Rennes highroad, a water-mill, a meadow covered with herds of cows and separated from the pond by the embankment. Along the edge of this meadow stretched a hamlet forming a dependency of a priory founded in 1149 by Rivallon, Lord of Combourg, and containing his mortuary statue, recumbent in a knight's armour. Beyond the pond, the ground rose gradually and formed an amphitheatre of trees, whence issued village belfries and the turrets of country-houses. On the far horizon, between the west and the south, were outlined the heights of Bécherel. On that side, a terrace lined with large coppices skirted the foot of the castle, passed behind the stables, and repeatedly joined the fountain garden which communicated with the Great Mall.

If, after this too long description, a painter were to take up his pencil, would he produce a sketch resembling the castle? I do not think so; and yet the subject lives in my memory as though I had it before my eyes: so great is the power of recollection, so small the power of words in the expression of material things. When I begin to speak of Combourg, I quote the first couplets of a ballad which will charm none but myself: ask the Tyrolean herd why he finds pleasure in the three notes or four which he sings to his goats, notes of the mountain, flung from echo to echo to resound from one side of a torrent to the other.

My first appearance at Combourg lasted but a short while. When a fortnight had passed, the Abbé Porcher arrived, the principal of Dol College; I was handed over to him, and followed him despite my tears. I was, in a fashion, connected with Dol; my father was a "canon" of the town, as the descendant and representative of the house of Guillaume de Chateaubriand, Lord of Beaufort, who in 1529 founded one of the first stalls in the cathedral choir. The Bishop of Dol was M. de Hercé, a friend of my family, and a prelate of great moderation in politics, who, kneeling, and crucifix in hand, was shot at Quiberon on the Champ du Martyre, together with his brother, the Abbé de Hercé.[1] On reaching

---

[1] Urbain René de Hercé (1726-1795), consecrated Bishop of Dol in 1757, was shot not at, but after, Quiberon, at Vannes, 28 July 1795, together with Sombreuil and fourteen other victims, including his brother, François de Hercé (1733-1795), Grand-Vicar of Dol, and Gesril (vide supra).—B.

the college, I was entrusted to the special care of M. l'Abbé Leprince, professor of rhetoric and a thorough geometrician, a man of intelligence, handsome, devoted to the arts, and a fair portrait-painter. He undertook to teach me my Bezout;[1] the Abbé Égault, master of the third form, became my Latin master: I studied mathematics in my own room, Latin in the common school-room.

It took some time for an owl of my species to grow accustomed to a school cage and to measure its flight by the sound of a bell. I was not able to make those quick friends with whom fortune supplies one, for there was nothing to be made out of a poor urchin who was not even endowed with pocket - money; nor did I join any set of hangers-on, for I hated protectors. In our games, I did not claim to lead others, but neither did I wish to be led: I was fitted to be neither a tyrant nor a slave, and so I have always remained.

And yet it happened that I soon became the centre of a set; later, in my regiment, I exercised the same power: plain ensign though I were, the older officers spent their evenings with me, and preferred my quarters to the coffee-house. I do not know whence this came, unless it were due to the ease with which I entered into the minds and adopted the manners of others. I was as fond of hunting and coursing as of reading and writing. To this day, it is a matter of indifference to me whether I speak of the most commonplace things or discuss the loftiest subjects. I am very little attracted by cleverness, and find it almost disagreeable, although I am not a fool. No imperfection offends me, except mockery and self-conceit, which I have great difficulty in not defying. I find that others are always my superiors in some respect, and if perchance I feel myself to have an advantage, I am quite embarrassed in consequence.

Qualities which my early training had allowed to lie dormant were awakened at college. My aptitude for work was remarkable, my memory extraordinary. I made rapid progress in mathematics, to which I brought a clearness of apprehension that astonished the Abbé Leprince. At the same time, I displayed a decided taste for languages. The rudiments, the torture of school - boys, cost me no trouble to learn; I awaited the time of the Latin lessons with a

---

[1] Étienne Bezout (1730–1783), author of a number of mathematical works employed in schools in the eighteenth century.—T.

sort of impatience, as a relief from my figures and geometrical problems. In less than a year, I was well ahead in the fifth form. In an odd manner, my Latin sentences shaped themselves so naturally into pentameters that the Abbé Égault called me the Elegist, a nickname which long clung to me among my schoolfellows.

I can quote two instances of my power of memory. I learnt my tables of logarithms by heart : that is to say, a number being given in geometrical proportion, I could quote from memory its exponent in arithmetical proportion, and *vice versâ*.

After evening prayers, which were said in public in the college chapel, the principal used to read to us. One of the boys, taken at random, had to give an account of what had been read. We came to prayers from our games tired and very sleepy ; we flung ourselves upon the forms, trying to hide in a dark corner so as not to be seen and consequently questioned. There was a confessional, in particular, which we fought for, as offering a safe retreat. One evening I had the good fortune to gain this harbour and thought myself safe from the principal ; unluckily he perceived my stratagem, and resolved to make an example. Slowly and at great length he read the second head of a sermon ; every one went to sleep. By mere chance, I remained awake in my confessional. The principal, who could only see the tips of my feet, thought that I had dropped off like the rest, and suddenly called me by my name and asked me what he had been reading.

The second head of the sermon contained an enumeration of the various ways in which it is possible to offend against God. I not only related the substance of the matter, but repeated the divisions in their proper order, and recited almost word for word several pages of mystical prose, devoid of meaning to a child. A murmur of applause ran through the chapel: the principal called me to him, gave me a tap on the cheek, and in reward allowed me to stay in bed next morning till breakfast-time. I modestly withdrew from my schoolfellows' admiration, and took good care to avail myself of the favour accorded me. This memory for words, which I have partly lost, has been replaced in my case by another and more singular kind of memory, of which I shall perhaps have occasion to speak.

One thing I find humiliating: memory is often the one accomplishment that accompanies stupidity ; it belongs generally to ponderous minds, which it makes yet heavier with the luggage with which it overcharges them. And yet, without memory, where should we be? We should forget our friendships, our loves, our pleasures, our business; genius would be unable to collect its ideas; the fondest heart would lose its tenderness, if it lost its memory; our existence would be reduced to the successive moments of an incessantly gliding present; there would be no longer a past. Alas, unhappy that I am! Our life is so vain as to be but a reflex of our memory.

I went to Combourg for the holidays. Country-house life in the neighbourhood of Paris can give no idea of country-house life in a distant province. The Combourg property consisted, as its sole domain, of moorland, a few mills, and the two forests of Bourgouët and Tanoërn, in a district where timber is of almost no value. But Combourg was rich in feudal rights. These rights were of different kinds: some fixed certain dues in exchange for certain concessions, or established customs sprung from the ancient order of politics; others seemed from the first to have been sports and nothing more.

My father had revived some of the latter rights, so as to prevent their lapsing by prescription. When the whole family were together, we took part in these Gothic amusements: the three principal were the Fishermen's Leap, the Quintain, and a fair called the Foire Angevine. Peasants in clogs and breeches, men of a France that is past, watched these sports of a France that is past. There were prizes for the winners, forfeits for the beaten.

The Quintain kept up the tradition of the tournaments: it had doubtless some connection with the old military service of the fiefs. It is very well described in Du Cange[1] (*voce* QUINTANA). The forfeits had to be paid in old copper money, up to the value of two *moutons d'or à la couronne* of 25 *sols Parisis* each.[2]

---

[1] Charles Dufresne Ducange (1610–1688), a learned expert in historical research, author of the *Glossarium mediæ et infimæ Latinitatis*, in which the description of the quintain occurs, and a number of other works of value.—T.

[2] The Manuscript of 1826 here contains a short description of the sport of the quintain: "All the bridegrooms of the year within the holding of Combourg were obliged, in the month of May, to come and break a wooden lance against a post placed in a sunk road that ran above the Great Mall. The tilters were on horseback; the bailiff, who acted as lord of the lists, examined the lance, and declared that there was no fraud nor guile in the arms: it was allowed to tilt three times at the post, but at the third time, if the lance was not broken, the jibers of the rustic tournament covered the awkward tilter with pleasantries, who paid a crown-piece to the liege lord."—T.

The Angevin Fair was held in the meadow by the pond on the 4th of September of each year, my birthday. The vassals had to take up arms and come to the castle to raise the liege lord's banner; thence they went to the fair to establish order and enforce the collection of a toll due to the Counts of Combourg on each head of cattle, a sort of royalty. During that time my father kept open house. We danced for three days: the gentry in the great hall, to the scraping of a fiddle; the vassals in the Cour Verte, to the squealing of a bag-pipe. We sang, cheered, fired off arquebuses. These noises mingled with the lowing of the droves at the fair; the crowd wandered through the woods and gardens, and at least once in the year one saw at Combourg something akin to merriment.

Thus have I been so singularly placed in life as to have assisted at the tilting at the Quintain and at the proclamation of the Rights of Man; to have beheld the train-bands of a Breton village and the National Guard of France, the banner of the Lords of Combourg and the flag of the Revolution. I am as it were the last surviving witness of the feudal customs.

The visitors whom we received at the castle consisted of the inhabitants of the market-town and the neighbouring gentry: these good people were my first friends. Our vanity attaches too much importance to the part we play in the world. The citizen of Paris laughs at the citizen of a small town; the Court noble scoffs at the provincial noble; the well-known scorns the unknown man, without reflecting that time does equal justice to their pretensions, and that they are all equally ridiculous or insignificant in the eyes of successive generations.

The principal resident of the place was a M. Potelet,[1] a retired ship's captain of the Indian Company's service, who told us long stories about Pondicherry. He related them with his elbows resting on the table, and my father always had a mind to throw his plate in his face. Next came the bonder of tobacco, M. Launay de La Billardière,[2] the father of a family of twelve, like Jacob, nine girls and three boys, of whom the youngest, David, was my playmate.[3] The worthy man bethought himself of aspiring to nobility in 1789: he chose a

---

[1] Noble Maître François Jean Baptiste Potelet, Seigneur de Saint-Mahé et de La Durantais.—B.

[2] Gilles Marie de Launay, Sieur de La Billardière, successively procurator-fiscal of Bécherel, *sénéchal des juridictions* of the Vauruffier, the Viscounty of Besso and the Marquisate of Caradenc, and bonder of the King's tobacco taxes at Combourg.—B.

[3] I have met my friend David again since: I shall tell when and how.— *Author's Note* (Geneva, 1832).

good time! In that house there was plenty of gaiety and many debts. Gesbert[1] the seneschal, Petit[2] the procurator-fiscal, Corvaisier[3] the receiver, and the Abbé Chalmel,[4] the chaplain, formed the society of Combourg. I did not at Athens meet persons more celebrated than these.

Messieurs du Petit-Bois,[5] de Château d'Assie,[6] de Tinténiac, and one or two other noblemen would come on Sundays to hear Mass in the parish church, and afterwards to dine with the owner of the castle. We were more intimately acquainted with the Trémaudan family, consisting of the husband,[7] the wife, who was extremely beautiful, a natural sister, and several children. This family lived on a small farm, with a dove-cote for sole evidence of nobility. The Trémaudans are still living. Wiser and happier than I, they have not lost sight of the turrets of the castle which I left thirty years ago; they are still doing what they did when I went to eat brown bread at their table; they have never left the port to which I shall never return. Perhaps they are speaking of me at the very moment at which I write this page: I reproach myself for dragging their name from its protective obscurity. They long hesitated to believe that the man of whom they heard speak was "the little chevalier." The rector or curate of Combourg, the Abbé Sévin,[8] to whose sermons I used to listen, at first displayed the same incredulity: he could not persuade himself that the urchin, the peasants' friend, was the same as the defender of religion; he ended by believing it, and quotes me in his sermons, after having held me on his knees. Would these good people, who import no foreign idea into their image of me, who see me as I was in my childhood and in my youth, would they recognize me to-day through the disguise of time? I should be obliged to tell them my name before they would feel a wish to press me in their arms.

I bring bad luck to my friends. A game-keeper called \

<hr>

[1] Jean Baptiste Gesbert, Seigneur de La Noé-Sécho, seneschal of the manorial jurisdiction of Combourg.—B.

[2] Maître René Petit, procurator-fiscal of the County of Combourg.—B.

[3] Maître Julien Corvaisier or Le Corvaisier, notary and attorney of the jurisdiction.—B.

[4] The Abbé Jean François Chalmel, chaplain of Combourg Castle.—B.

[5] Jean Anne Pinot du Petitbois (1737–1789) lived in the Château du Grandval at Combourg, still occupied by his descendants.—B.

[6] Michel Charles Locquet, Comte de Château-d'Assis, lived in the Château de Triaudin, Combourg, now owned by the Vicomte Roger du Petitbois.—B.

[7] Nicolas Pierre Philippes, Seigneur de Trémaudan.—B.

[8] René Malo Sévin, rector of the parish of Combourg in 1776, refused to subscribe to the civil constitution of the clergy, and went to Jersey in 1792. He returned in 1797, was reinstated in his parish in 1803, and died at Combourg in 1817.—B.

Raulx, who was attached to me, was killed by a poacher. The murder made an extraordinary impression upon my mind. What a strange mystery lies in human sacrifice! Why should it be both the greatest crime and the greatest glory to shed the blood of man? My imagination pictured Raulx holding his entrails in his hands as he dragged himself to the cottage where he expired. I conceived the idea of vengeance; I should have liked to fight his murderer. In this respect I am curiously constituted: at the first moment of an offence, I hardly feel it; but it becomes imprinted on my memory; the recollection of it grows stronger, rather than fainter, with time; it sleeps within my heart for months, for whole years, and then awakens at the least circumstance with renewed force, and my wound becomes more painful than on the first day. But if I do not pardon my enemies, I do them no harm: I bear ill-will, but am not vindictive. If ever I have the power to revenge myself, I lose the wish: I should be dangerous only in misfortune. Those who have tried to make me yield by oppressing me have deceived themselves; adversity is to me what the earth was to Antæus: I gather fresh strength in my mother's bosom. If ever Good Fortune had taken me in her arms, she would have stifled me.

I returned to Dol, much to my regret. The next year, a plan was formed for a descent upon Jersey, and a camp was established at Saint-Malo. Troops were quartered at Combourg; M. de Chateaubriand, through courtesy, entertained in succession the colonels of the Touraine and Conti Regiments. One was the Duc de Saint-Simon,[1] the other the Marquis de Causans.[2] A score of officers were invited daily to my father's table. The jokes of these strangers displeased me; their walks disturbed the peacefulness of my woods. It was from seeing the lieutenant-colonel of the Conti Regiment, the Marquis de

---

[1] Claude Anne, successively Vicomte, Marquis, and Duc de Saint-Simon, emigrated to Spain, entered the Spanish service, and became Captain-General of Old Castile. King Charles IV. created him a grandee of Spain, King Ferdinand VII. a duke. He died in Madrid in 1819. In 1808, on the capture of Madrid by the French, he was sentenced to death by court-martial; the sentence was commuted to imprisonment for life, and he was confined in the Citadel of Besançon until the fall of the Empire in 1814.—B.

[2] It gave me a genuine pleasure to renew my acquaintance, during the Restoration, with this gallant officer, so distinguished for his loyalty and his Christian virtues.—*Author's Note* (Geneva, 1831).

Jacques Vincent Marquis de Causans de Mauléon (1751-1824), was promoted to the rank of lieutenant-general in 1814, and sat in the Chamber of Deputies as member for Vaucluse from 1815 until his death.—B.

Wignacourt,[1] gallop under the trees that the idea of travelling first passed through my mind.

When I heard our guests speak of Paris and the Court, I became sad; I tried to imagine what society was: I discovered a confused and distant something; but soon I turned giddy. Casting my eyes upon the world from the tranquil region of innocence, I had a swimming in the head, as when one looks down upon the earth from the top of a tower lost in the sky.

One thing, nevertheless, delighted me: the parade. Every day the soldiers going on guard marched past, to the sound of the drum and band, at the foot of the steps in the Cour Verte. M. de Causans offered to show me the camp on the coast: my father gave his leave. I was taken to Saint-Malo by M. de La Morandais,[2] a gentleman of very good family, whom poverty had reduced to accept the stewardship of the Combourg property. He wore a coat of grey camlet, with a little silver lace at the collar, and a helmet-shaped peaked cap with flaps. He set me astride behind him, on the crupper of his mare Isabelle. I held fast by the belt of his hunting-knife, which he wore outside his coat: I was delighted. When Claude de Bullion and the father of the Président de Lamoignon, as children, went to the country, " they were both carried by the same donkey, in panniers, one on one side, the other on the other, and a loaf of bread was placed on Lamoignon's side because he was lighter than his fellow, to keep the balance." (*Mémoires du président de Lamoignon.*)[3]

M. de La Morandais took cross-roads:

> Moult volontiers, de grand' manière,
> Alloit en bois et en rivière :
> Car nulles gens ne vont en bois
> Moult volontiers comme François.[4]

We stopped for dinner at a Benedictine abbey which, for want of a sufficient number of monks, had just been incorpo-

---

[1] Antoine Louis Marquis de Wignacourt, Knight of St. Louis.—B.

[2] François Placide Maillard, Seigneur de La Morandais. The Maillards de La Morandais delivered proofs of eight generations of nobility in 1670. Those who had settled at Combourg had degenerated through poverty.—B.

[3] Guillaume de Lamoignon (1617-1677), First President of the Parliament of Paris, founder of a most distinguished legal family, and great-grandfather of Lamoignon de Malesherbes.—T.

[4] " Right gladly and in brave array,
By wood and river made his way :
For no folk through the woods advance
Right gladly like the folk of France."—T.

rated in one of the chief communities of the order. We found only the father procurator, who had been left behind to dispose of the chattels and sell the timber. He ordered an excellent fish dinner to be served for us, in what was formerly the prior's library: we ate a quantity of new-laid eggs with huge pikes and carps. Through the arch of a cloister, I saw tall sycamores at the edge of a pond. The woodman's axe struck at their feet, their tops trembled in the air, and they fell to make a show for us. Carpenters, come from Saint-Malo, sawed off green branches, which dropped to the ground like the hair of a child cut for the first time, or squared the felled trunks. My heart bled at the sight of those impaired woods and that dismantled monastery. The general sack of the religious houses has since called up to my mind the spoliation of the abbey which was to me an omen.

I found the Marquis de Causans at Saint-Malo, and went through the streets of the camp under his escort. The tents, the stacked arms, the picketed horses made a fine spectacle in conjunction with the sea, the ships, the walls, and the distant steeples of the town. I saw gallop past me at full speed, in an hussar's uniform and mounted on a Barbary horse, one of those men who marked the end of a world, the Duc de Lauzun.[1] The Prince de Carignan[2] had come to the camp, and married the daughter of M. de Boisgarein, a charming creature, though a little lame: this caused a great sensation and gave rise to a law-suit in which M. Lacretelle[3] the Elder is pleading to this day. But what have these things to do with

---

[1] Armand Louis de Gontaut de Biron, Duc de Lauzun (1747-1793), and Duc de Biron on the death of his father in 1788. He was one of the handsomest men at the Court of Louis XVI. In 1789 he joined the party of the Duc d'Orléans, and served as a general in the Republican army, but was guillotined on the last day of December 1793.—T.

[2] Prince Eugène de Savoie-Carignan (1753-1785), younger son of Prince Louis Victor de Savoie-Carignan, and brother of the Princesse de Lamballe. A scion of the younger branch of the Royal House of Savoy, he entered the French service under the title of Count of Villafranca, and was made colonel of the Villefranche Regiment. In 1781 he married Elizabeth Anne, daughter of Jean François Nicolas Magon, Seigneur de Boisgarein; but the marriage was annulled by parliament upon the petition of the Prince's parents. He struggled desperately to obtain a revision of the decree of annulment. On the accession of the younger branch to the throne of Sardinia in 1831, the grandson of Prince Eugène and Mademoiselle de Boisgarein was restored to his ancestral rank, and in 1888 his morganatic children received from the late King of Italy the name of Villafranca-Soisson, with the title of count.—B.

[3] Pierre Louis Lacretelle (1751-1824), known as Lacretelle the Elder, to distinguish him from his brother, Charles Joseph Lacretelle, the Younger. He was a member of the French Academy, and author of a number of legal works and political and philosophical treatises.—T.

my life? "It is pitie," says Montaigne; "I have assayed by the trial of some of my private friends: according as their memory hath ministered to them a whole and perfect matter, who recoil their narration so farre-backe, and stuff it with so many vaine circumstances, that if the story bee good, they smoother the goodnesse of it: if bad you must needs either curse the good fortune of their memorie, or blame the misfortune of their judgement. . . . I have heard some very pleasant reports become most irksome and tedious in the mouth of a certaine Lord." [1] I am afraid of being that certaine Lord.

My brother was at Saint-Malo when M. de La Morandais set me down there. One evening he said to me:

" I am taking you to the play: get your hat."

I lost my head; I ran straight to the cellar to fetch my hat which was in the garret. A company of travelling play-actors had just arrived. I had seen a Punch and Judy show, and presumed that the puppets at the theatre were much finer than those in the street. With beating heart I reached a wooden building in an unfrequented street in the town. I went through dark passages, not without a certain movement of dread. A small door was opened, and I found myself with my brother in a half-full box.

The curtain was up, and the piece had commenced: they were playing the *Père de famille*.[2] I saw two men walk about the stage talking, while everybody looked on. I took them for the managers of the puppet-show, chatting before the time came for Madame Gigogne to tumble head over heels, awaiting the arrival of the audience: I was only surprised that they should discuss their business so loudly, and that they were listened to in silence. My amazement increased when other persons came upon the stage and began to make great gestures and shed tears, and when everybody began to cry in sympathy. The curtain fell without my having understood a word of all this. My brother went down to the green-room between the acts. I remained in the box among strangers, in an agony of shyness, and wished myself back at school. That was the first impression which I received of the art of Sophocles and Molière.

The third year of my life at Dol was marked by the

---

[1] Florio's MONTAIGNE, Booke I. chap. 9: *Of Lyers.*—T.

[2] By Diderot; printed in 1758, and first performed at the Comédie Française ten years after, when it met with indifferent success, attaining a total of seven performances.—B.

wedding of my two eldest sisters: Marianne married the
Comte de Marigny, and Bénigne the Comte de Québriac.
They accompanied their husbands to Fougères: the first signal
for the dispersion of a family whose members were soon to
part. My sisters received the nuptial benediction at Combourg on the same day, at the same hour, at the same altar,
in the castle chapel.[1] They wept, my mother wept; I was
astonished at their grief: I understand it now. I never
assist at a christening or a wedding without smiling bitterly
or feeling anguish of heart. After the misfortune of being
born, I know none greater than that of giving birth to a human
being.

In this same year began a revolution, not only in my family,
but in my own person. Chance caused to fall into my hands
two very different books: an unexpurgated Horace and a
history of *Confessions mal faites*. An incredible perturbation
of ideas was produced in my mind by these two books: an
unknown world arose around me. On the one side, I suspected
the existence of secrets incomprehensible to one of my age,
of a manner of living different from mine, of pleasures beyond
my vision, of charms of an unknown nature in a sex in which
I had only met a mother and sisters; on the other side,
spectres dragging chains and vomiting flames threatened me
with eternal torture for one sin concealed. I could not sleep;
at night I thought I saw black hands and white pass by turns
through the curtains of my bed: I began to imagine that
the latter hands were cursed by religion, and this idea increased
my terror of the infernal shades. In vain I sought in Heaven
and Hell for the explanation of a two-fold mystery. Smitten
at one and the same time in my moral and physical being, I
continued to struggle with my innocence against the storms of
premature passion and the terrors of superstition.

Thenceforward I felt escape from me some sparks of that
fire which is the transmission of life. I was construing the
fourth book of the *Æneid* and reading *Télémaque*: suddenly
I discovered in Dido and Eucharis beauties that delighted me;
I felt the harmony of those admirable verses and of that classic
prose. One day I translated Lucretius'

Æneadum genitrix, hominum divinumque voluptas[2]

---

[1] 11 January 1780, Marie Anne Françoise married Jean Joseph Geffelot, Comte
de Marigny; Bénigne Jeanne married Jean François Xavier Comte de Québriac,
Seigneur de Patrion.—B.

[2] LUCRETIUS, L. I.—T.

at sight, with such spirit that M. Égault snatched the poem from my hands and set me to do my Greek roots. I stole a Tibullus: when I came to the

Quam juvat immites ventos audire cubantem,[1]

these expressions of voluptuous melancholy seemed to reveal to me my own nature. The volumes of Massillon[2] which contained the sermons on the *Pécheresse* and the *Enfant prodigue* never left my side. I was allowed to read them, for no one suspected what I found in them. I stole short candle-ends from the chapel to enable me at night to read those alluring descriptions of the disorders of the soul. I fell asleep stammering incoherent phrases, in which I strove to employ the sweetness, the rhythm, and the grace of the writer who has been most successful in transmitting to prose the euphony of Racinian verse.

If, later, I have with some measure of truthfulness depicted the impulses which, mingled with Christian remorse, sway the heart, I am convinced that I owe this success to the chance which made me acquainted at the same moment with two hostile empires. The ravages made in my imagination by a bad book found their antidote in the terrors with which another book inspired me, and the latter were as it were allayed by the enervating thoughts drawn from pictures of the unveiled.

Misfortunes are said never to come singly, and the same may be said of passions: they come together, like the Muses or the Furies. With the propensity which began to torture me, there was born in me the sense of honour, an exaltation of the soul which preserves the heart uncorrupted in the midst of corruption, a sort of restorative principle placed beside a devouring principle, as the inexhaustible source of the prodigies which love demands of youth and of the sacrifices which it imposes.

When the weather was fine, the college boarders went out on Thursdays and Sundays. We were often taken to Mont Dol, on the top of which were some Gallo-Roman ruins: from the summit of this isolated eminence, the eye looks down on the sea and on marshes over which by night hovers the will o' the wisp, the wizard's light that burns in our lamps to this day. Another object of our walks was the fields

---

[1] TIBULLUS, I. I. 45.—T.

[2] Jean Baptiste Massillon (1663–1742), Bishop of Clermont, and a famous Catholic preacher. He left nearly a hundred sermons, in addition to a great number of other religious works. Massillon was elected an Academician in 1789.—T.

in which stood a seminary of Eudists, after Eudes, brother of Mézeray the historian [1] and founder of their congregation. One day in May, the Abbé Égault, the prefect of the week, had taken us to this seminary. We were allowed full liberty in our games; only we were expressly forbidden to climb the trees. The master left us in a grassy lane, and walked away to say his breviary.

The lane was bordered by elms: right at the top of the tallest, a magpie's nest was clearly visible. We were all agog at the sight, pointing out to each other the mother sitting on her eggs, and smitten with the keenest longing to capture that superb prize. But who would dare to make the attempt? The orders were so strict, the prefect so near, the tree so high! Every hope was turned upon me; I climbed like a cat. I wavered, and then love of glory carried the day: taking off my coat, I flung my arms around the elm and began the ascent. The trunk had no branches, except at two-thirds of its height, where it split into a fork, one of whose extremities bore the nest.

Gathered beneath the tree, my friends applauded my efforts, looking up at me, looking in the direction whence the prefect might come, stamping with joy in their hope of the eggs, trembling with fear in their expectation of punishment. I approached the nest; the magpie flew away; I seized the eggs, put them inside my shirt, and began to climb down. Unfortunately, I slipped between the twin sections of the trunk and remained seated astraddle. The tree had been pruned, I could find no foothold on either side by which to raise myself and recover the outer limb, and I remained hanging in mid-air, fifty feet from the ground.

Suddenly a cry arose of "The prefect is coming!" and I saw myself incontinently abandoned by my friends, as always happens. One boy alone, called Le Gobbien, tried to assist me, and was soon obliged to relinquish his generous attempt. There was only one way to extricate myself from my painful position, which was to hang on outside, by my hands, to one of the two teeth of the fork, and to try, with my feet, to seize the trunk below the place where it split in two. I carried out this operation at the risk of my life. In the midst of my tribulations, I had not let go of my prize; I should have done better to fling it away, as I have since done with so many

---

[1] François Eudes de Mézeray (1610–1683). The Eudists, founded by Jean Eudes, have still a house at Rennes. The community is also known as the Congregation of Jesus and Mary.—T.

others. In sliding down the trunk, I rubbed the skin off my hands, bruised my legs and chest, and smashed the eggs: this last proved my ruin. The prefect had not seen me in the tree; I contrived to hide the traces of blood, but there was no concealing the brilliant yellow with which I was smeared.

"Very well, sir," he said, "you shall have the cane."

If that man had stated that he would commute this sentence to one of death, I should have experienced a thrill of joy. The notion of shame had never yet presented itself to one of my untrammelled upbringing : at no period of my life would I not have preferred any punishment to the horror of having to blush before a living creature. My heart filled with indignation; I answered the Abbé Égault, in the accents not of a child but of a man, that neither he nor any other should ever lay a hand upon me. This reply incensed him; he called me a rebel and promised to make an example of me.

"We shall see," I retorted, and began to play at ball with a coolness which confounded him.

We returned to the college; the prefect took me to his room and ordered me to prepare for punishment. My exalted sentiments gave place to floods of tears. I represented to the Abbé Égault that he had taught me Latin; that I was his scholar, his disciple, his child; that he could not wish to dishonour his pupil and make the sight of my schoolfellows unbearable to me; that he could lock me up on bread and water, stop my recreations, set me impositions; that I would thank him for his clemency and love him the more for it. I fell upon my knees, I folded my hands, I besought him in the name of Jesus Christ to spare me; he remained deaf to my entreaties. I rose in a fit of fury, and aimed at his legs a kick so violent that he yelled. He limped to the door of his room, locked it, and came back to me. I entrenched myself behind the bed; he struck out at me across the bed with a cane. I rolled myself in the bed-clothes and, heated with the fray, exclaimed :

Macte animo, generose puer ! [1]

This brattish erudition made my enemy laugh in spite of himself; he suggested an armistice: we concluded a treaty; I agreed to refer the matter to the arbitration of the principal. Without giving his award in my favour, the principal consented to cancel the punishment which I had refused to take.

[1] STAT., *Th.* vii. 280.—T.

When the excellent priest pronounced his acquittal, I pressed my lips to the sleeve of his gown with so great a display of heartfelt gratitude that he could not refrain from giving me his blessing. Thus ended the first combat which restored to me the honour which has been the idol of my life and which has so often cost me my repose, my pleasure, and my fortune.

The holidays in the course of which I entered upon my twelfth year were sad ones. The Abbé Leprince accompanied me to Combourg. I went out only with my tutor; we took long rambles together. He was dying of consumption, and was silent and melancholy; I myself was not much livelier. We walked for hours without saying a word. One day we lost our way in the woods; M. Leprince turned to me and asked:

"Which way shall we go?"

I answered without hesitation:

"The sun is setting; it is now striking the window in the big tower; let us go that way."

M. Leprince the same evening told the incident to my father: the future traveller showed himself in that decision. Many a time, when I saw the sun set in the forests of America, have I recalled the woods of Combourg: my memories are echoes one of the other.

The Abbé Leprince wanted them to give me a horse; but according to my father's notions, the only thing a naval officer need know how to steer was his ship. I was reduced, therefore, to riding two fat coach-horses or a big piebald by stealth. The latter was not, like Turenne's *Pie*, one of those steeds which the Romans called *desultorii equi*[1] and trained to aid their masters; it was a moon-eyed Pegasus, which overreached in trotting, and bit my legs when I set it at a ditch. I never cared much about horses, although I have led the life of a Tartar; and, contrary to the effect which my early training should have produced, I ride with an elegant rather than a firm seat.

A tertiary fever, the germs of which I had brought with me from the marshes of Dol, rid me of M. Leprince. A quack passed through the village; my father, who did not believe in doctors, believed in charlatans: he sent for the empiric, who undertook to cure me in twenty-four hours. He returned the next day, in a green, gold-laced coat, a huge, powdered wig, wide ruffles of dirty muslin, false diamonds on his fingers, worn black satin breeches, bluey-white silk stockings, and shoes with enormous buckles. He pulled back my curtains, felt my pulse, made

---

[1] SUET., *Cas.* 39.—T.

me put out my tongue, jabbered a few words with an Italian accent on the necessity for purging me, and gave me a little piece of burnt sugar to eat. My father approved of the treatment, for he maintained that all sickness came from indigestion, and that for every kind of ill you should purge your man till the blood came.

Half-an-hour after swallowing the caramel, I was seized with a terrible vomiting; they sent to tell M. de Chateaubriand, who wanted to throw the poor wretch from the window of the tower. The latter, terrified, took off his coat, tucked back his shirt-sleeves, and made the most grotesque gestures. At each movement, his wig turned in every direction; he repeated my cries, adding after each: "*Che, Monsou Lavandier?*" This Monsieur Lavandier was the village druggist, who had been called in to lend his aid. I did not know, in the midst of my pain, whether I should die from taking the man's nostrums or from bursting with laughter at his behaviour. The effects of this overdose of emetic were stopped in time, and I was set on my legs again.

The whole of our life is spent in wandering round our tomb: our illnesses are so many puffs of wind that send us more or less near to the haven. The first corpse I saw was that of a canon of Saint-Malo: he lay dead upon his bed, his features distorted with the final convulsions. Death is beautiful, he is our friend: and yet we do not recognise him, because he comes to us masked, and his mask frightens us.

I was sent back to school at the end of autumn.

I have been permitted to leave Dieppe, whither a police order had driven me, and to return to the Vallée-aux-Loups, where I continue my narrative. The soil trembles beneath the steps of the foreign soldier, who is invading my country at this very moment; I am writing, like the last of the Romans, to the sound of the Barbarian invasion. By day I compose pages as agitated as the events of the day;[1] at night, while the rolling of the distant cannon dies away in my woods, I return to the silence of years that sleep in the grave, to the peace of my youngest memories. How short and narrow is a man's past beside the vast present of the nations and their immeasurable future!

Mathematics, Greek, and Latin occupied all my winter at school. The time that was not devoted to study was given

---

[1] *De Buonaparte et des Bourbons.—Author's Note* (Geneva, 1831).

up to boyish sports, which are the same all over the world.
The little Englishman, the little German, the little Italian, the
little Spaniard, the little Iroquois, the little Bedouin, all trundle
the hoop and throw the ball. Brothers of one great family,
children do not lose their features of resemblance until they
lose their innocence, everywhere the same. Then the passions,
modified by climates, governments, and customs, make different
nations; the human race ceases to speak and understand the
same language: society is the real Tower of Babel.

One morning I was taking very energetic part in a game
of base in the playground, when I was told that I was wanted.
I followed the servant to the front gate. There I found a stout,
red-faced man, with abrupt and impatient manners and a
fierce voice; he carried a stick in his hand, wore a black and
ill-curled wig, a torn cassock with the ends tucked into his
pockets, dusty shoes, and stockings with holes at the heels.

"You little·scamp," said he, "are not you the Chevalier
de Chateaubriand de Combourg?"

"Yes, monsieur," I replied, quite bewildered at his manner
of addressing me.

"And I," he retorted, almost foaming at the mouth, "am
the last senior of your family; I am the Abbé de Chateaubriand de La Guerrande:[1] take a good look at me."

The proud ecclesiastic put his hand into the fob of a pair of
old plush breeches, took out a mouldy six-franc crown-piece
wrapped in a piece of dirty paper, flung it at my head, and
continued his journey on foot, muttering his matins as he went,
with a furious air. I have since learnt that the Prince de
Condé[2] had offered this rustic rector the post of tutor to the
Duc de Bourbon.[3] The overbearing priest replied that the
Prince, as the owner of the Barony of Chateaubriand, ought
to know that the heirs of that barony could have tutors, but
could not act as such. This haughtiness was the fault of
my family; in my father it was hateful; my brother pushed it

[1] Charles Hilaire de Chateaubriand (1708–1782), rector successively of a
number of country livings.—B.

[2] Louis Joseph (Louis V.) Prince de Condé (1736–1818), fourth in descent from
the Great Condé, and Commander-in-Chief of the Army of the Emigrants, 1789–
1800. At the Restoration, King Louis XVIII. made his kinsman Grand-Master
of the Household and Colonel-General of the Infantry.—T.

[3] Louis Henri Joseph (Louis VI.) Duc de Bourbon (1756–1830), son of Louis
V. Prince de Condé and of the Princesse Louise d'Orléans, and father of the
unhappy Duc d'Enghien. The Duc de Bourbon was found strangled—whether
by his own hands or those of his mistress, Madame de Feuchères, is uncertain—a
few days after the Revolution of 1830. He left the greater part of his large
fortune to the late Duc d'Aumale.—T.

to a ridiculous length; it has descended in a certain measure
to his eldest son. I am not sure that I myself, in spite of my
republican inclinations, have entirely shaken it off, although I
have been careful to conceal it.

The time approached for making my First Communion,
when the family used to decide upon the child's future condition. This religious ceremony took the place among young
Christians of the assumption of the *toga virilis* among the
Romans. Madame de Chateaubriand had come in order to be
present at the First Communion of her son, who, after being
united to his God, was about to part from his mother.

My piety seemed to be sincere; I edified the whole college;
there was ardour in my eyes; I was so persistent in my
fasting as to make my masters uneasy. They feared lest I
should drive devotion to excess; their religious enlightenment
sought to temper my fervour. My confessor was the superior
of the Eudist Seminary, a man of fifty, of stern appearance.
Each time that I presented myself at the confessional, he
anxiously questioned me. Surprised at the unimportance of my
sins, he did not know how to reconcile my distress with the
triviality of the secrets I confided to his bosom. The nearer
Easter approached, the more pressing did the priest's questions
become. "Are you keeping nothing back?" he would ask.
I replied, "No, father." "Have you not committed such and
such a sin?" "No, father." And it was always: "No,
father." He dismissed me doubtfully, sighing, gazing into my
very soul, while I left his presence pale and out of face, like a
criminal.

I was to receive absolution on the Wednesday in Holy
Week. I spent the night of Tuesday in praying and in reading with terror the *Confessions mal faites*. At three o'clock on
the Wednesday afternoon, we started for the seminary, accompanied by our parents. All the vain renown that has since
attached itself to my name would not have given Madame de
Chateaubriand one moment of the pride which she felt, as a
Christian and a mother, on beholding her son prepared to
participate in the great mystery of religion.

On reaching the church, I prostrated myself before the altar,
and lay as though annihilated. When I rose to go to the
sacristy, where the superior awaited me, my knees trembled
beneath me. I flung myself at the priest's feet; it was only
in the most broken accents that I was able to pronounce the
Confiteor. "Well, have you forgotten nothing?" asked the

messenger of Jesus Christ. I remained silent. He began to question me again, and the fatal "No, father," came from my lips. He lapsed into meditation, asked counsel of Him who conferred upon the Apostles the power of binding and loosing souls. Then, making an effort, he prepared to give me absolution.

Had the sky shot a bolt at me, it would have caused me less dread. I cried:

"I have not confessed everything!"

This formidable judge, this deputy of the Sovereign Arbiter, whose visage inspired me with so much fear, became the tenderest of shepherds; he took me in his arms and burst into tears:

"Come, my dear child," said he, "courage!"

I shall never experience such another moment in my life. Had the weight of mountains been lifted from me, I should not have been more relieved: I sobbed with happiness. I venture to say that it was from that day forward that I became an upright man; I felt that I should never outlive a remorse; how great must be the remorse for a crime, when I could suffer so terribly for concealing the little sins of a child! But also how divine is the religion which can thus take hold of our best instincts! What precepts of morality can ever take the place of these Christian institutions?

The first admission made, the rest cost me nothing. My suppressed childish offences, which would have made the world smile, were weighed in the balance of religion. The superior was very much perplexed; he would have liked to postpone my Communion; but I was about to leave Dol College, soon to enter the Navy. With great perspicacity, he discerned the nature of my proclivities from the very character of my juvenile faults, insignificant though they were; he was the first man to fathom the secret of the possibilities of my life. He divined my future passions; he did not conceal from me what he thought he saw good in me, but he also predicted the evils to come.

"After all," he added, "though time is short for your repentance, you are cleansed of your sins by your courageous, if tardy, confession."

Raising his hand, he pronounced the Absolution. On this second occasion, the fulminating hand showered upon my head only the heavenly dew; I bent my brow to receive it; my feelings partook of the joy of the angels. I rose and threw myself upon the bosom of my mother, who was awaiting me

at the foot of the altar. I no longer appeared the same being
to my masters and school-fellows; I walked with a light step
my head held high, a radiant air, in all the triumph of repentance.

On the next day, which was Holy Thursday, I was
admitted to the sublime and touching ceremony which I have
vainly endeavoured to describe in the *Génie du Christianisme*.[1]
I might here have felt again my usual little humiliations: my
nosegay and my clothes were less fine than those of my companions; but that day everything was of God and for God.
I know exactly what Faith means: the Real Presence of the
Victim in the Blessed Sacrament of the altar was as evident to
me as the presence of my mother by my side. When the
Host was laid upon my lips, I felt as though a light had been
kindled within me. I trembled with veneration, and the only
material thing that occupied my thoughts was the dread of
profaning the sacramental bread.

> Le pain que je vous propose
> Sert aux anges d'aliment,
> Dieu lui-même le compose
> De la fleur de son froment.[2]—RACINE.

I conceived besides the courage of the martyrs; at that
moment I could have confessed Christ on the rack or in the
midst of the lions.

I delight in recalling these joys which my soul felt but a
little while before it became filled with the tribulations of the
world. Those who compare these ardours with the transports
which I shall presently depict, who see the same heart
experiencing, within a space of three or four years, all that
is sweetest and most wholesome in innocence and in religion
and also all that is most seductive and most baneful in the
passions, will choose one of the two forms of joy; they will
see in which direction to seek happiness and, above all, peace.

Three weeks after my First Communion, I left Dol College.
I retain a pleasant remembrance of this house: our childhood leaves a trace of itself upon places it has beautified by
its presence, as a flower communicates a perfume to the
objects it has touched. To this day I am affected when I

[1] Part I. book i. chap. 7 : *De la communion.*—T.

[2] "The bread I offer for your taking
Is that which the angels eat;
It is bread of God's own baking
From the first fruits of his wheat."—T.

think of the scattering of my first friends and my first masters. The Abbé Leprince was appointed to a living near Rouen, but died soon after; the Abbé Égault received a cure in the Diocese of Rennes; and I saw the death of the good principal, the Abbé Porcher, at the commencement of the Revolution: he was a learned, gentle, and simple-hearted man. The memory of that obscure Rollin[1] will always be dear and venerable to me.

At Combourg I found a Mission on which to feed my piety; I followed its exercises. I received confirmation on the manor steps, with the peasant lads and lasses, from the hand of the Bishop of Saint-Malo. After that, a cross was erected; I helped to hold it, while it was being fixed upon its base. It still exists: it stands in front of the tower in which my father died. For thirty years, it has seen no one appear at the windows of that tower; it is no longer saluted by the castle children; every spring-time it waits for them in vain; it sees none return save the swallows, the companions of my childhood, more faithful to their nest than man to his house. How happy should I have been, had my life been spent at the foot of that mission cross, had my hair been whitened only by the years which have covered the arms of that cross with moss!

I did not long delay my departure for Rennes, where I was to continue my studies and complete my mathematical course, before submitting myself for examination as a Naval Guard[2] at Brest. M. de Fayolle was principal of Rennes College. The staff of that Breton Juilly[3] included three distinguished professors: the Abbé de Chateaugiron, master of the second form, the Abbé Germé, master of rhetoric, and the Abbé Marchand, of physics. There were a large number of boarders and day-scholars, and the classes were strong. Within living memory, Geoffroy[4] and Ginguené,[5] who were educated at the college, would have done honour to Sainte-Barbe[6] or the Plessis.

---

[1] Charles Rollin (1661–1741), a famous French professor and theologian.—T.

[2] The French Naval Guard (*Garde marine*) was a body of nobles from which the naval officers were appointed.—T.

[3] The name of a celebrated Oratorian college, near Meaux, suppressed by the Revolution of 1789.—T.

[4] Julien Louis Geoffroy (1743–1814), a distinguished dramatic critic. He originated the literary *feuilleton* in the *Journal des Débats.*—T.

[5] Pierre Louis Ginguené (1748–1815), Ambassador to Turin under the Directory, and author of the *Histoire littéraire d'Italie* and some poems, mostly imitated from the Italian.—T.

[6] The famous college on the Montagne Sainte-Géneviève in Paris, founded by Jean Hubert in 1430.—T.

The Chevalier de Parny[1] had also studied at Rennes; I succeeded to his bed in the room allotted to me.

Rennes seemed to me a Babylon, the college a world. The crowd of masters and school-boys, the size of the buildings, garden, and play-grounds appeared immense to my eyes.[2] I grew accustomed to it, however. On the saint's-day of the principal, we had a holiday; at the top of our voices we sang in his praise superb lines of our own composing, in which we said:

> O Terpsichore, ô Polymnie,
> Venez, venez remplir nos vœux ;
> La raison même vous convie.[3]

At the cost of a few buffets, I assumed over my new school-fellows the same ascendant that I had exercised over my old companions at Dol. The young Bretons are quarrelsome monkeys; on half-holidays we sent each other challenges to fight in the shrubbery of the garden of the Benedictines, called "the Thabor." Our arms consisted of compasses fastened to the end of a walking-stick, which gradually led to a hand-to-hand fight, more or less treacherous or courteous according to the gravity of the challenge. We had umpires who decided if battle was to be waged and how the champions should use their hands. The combat did not end until one of the two parties owned himself vanquished. I found my old friend Gesril presiding over these engagements, as at Saint-Malo. He offered to be my second in an affair in which I was engaged with Saint-Riveul,[4] a young noble who became the first victim of the Revolution. I fell under my adversary, refused to surrender, and paid dearly for my pride. I said, like Jean Desmarets[5] on his road to the scaffold, "I cry mercy to God alone!"

---

[1] Évariste Désiré Desforges, Chevalier de Parny (1753–1814), the author of a number of elegies and love-poems, which earned for him the name of "the French Tibullus."—T.

[2] Rennes College was one of the most important in France. It was founded by the Jesuits in 1607. When they left it, in 1762, a communal college was established in the same buildings. These are now occupied by the Lycée de Rennes, which, however, is greatly diminished in size.—B.

[3] "Listen to the vows we offer,
O Terpsichore, Polyhymnia !
Reason herself her prayers doth proffer."—T.

[4] André François Jean du Rocher de Saint-Riveul (1772–1789), son of Henri du Rocher, Comte de Saint-Riveul.—B. The Manuscript of 1826 mentions that he was killed in the street at Rennes, as he was going with his father to the Chamber of Nobles.—T.

[5] Jean Desmarets, advocate-general to the Parliament of Paris, beheaded in 1382 for his failure to suppress the revolt of the Maillotins.—T.

had a different incense for each divinity. But could the hymns which I sang while burning that incense be called " balsams," like the poems of the hierophant ?[1]

After Julie's marriage, I set out for Brest. On leaving the great College of Rennes, I did not feel the same regret that I had experienced on bidding farewell to the little College of Dol; perhaps I had lost the bud of innocence which turns everything into a charm for us; time was beginning to open it. My mentor in my new position was one of my maternal uncles, Vice-Admiral the Comte Ravenel de Boisteilleul,[2] one of whose sons,[3] a very distinguished artillery-officer in the armies of Bonaparte, married the only daughter[4] of my sister the Comtesse de Farcy.

On my arrival at Brest, I did not find my cadet's commission awaiting me; some accident had delayed it. I remained what was called an "aspirant," and, as such, was exempt from following the regular studies. My uncle put me to board in the Rue de Siam, at a cadets' ordinary, and introduced me to the naval commander, the Comte d'Hector.[5] Left for the first time to my own resources, instead of becoming intimate with my future messmates, I indulged in my instinct for solitude. My usual society was confined to my fencing-master, my drawing-master, and my mathematical tutor.

The sea which I was to behold upon so many coasts bathed, at Brest, the extremity of the Armorican Peninsula: beyond that prominent cape lay nothing but the boundless ocean and unknown worlds. My imagination revelled in all this space. Often, seated on some mast lying along the Quai de Recouvrance, I watched the movements of the crowd: shipwrights, sailors, soldiers, custom-house officers, convicts passed to and fro before my eyes. Passengers embarked and disembarked, pilots directed the steering, carpenters squared

[1] An allusion to the mystical hymns of Orpheus, which were called "perfumes" (θυμιάματα).—B.
[2] Jean Baptiste Joseph Eugène de Ravenel du Boisteilleul (1738–1815), first cousin of Chateaubriand's mother, and therefore uncle in the manner of Brittany of the great writer.—B.
[3] Hyacinthe Eugène Pierre de Ravenel du Boisteilleul (1784–1868), a captain of artillery, and decorated on the battle-field at Smolensk, 17 August 1812.—B.
[4] Pauline Zoé Marie de Farcy de Montavallon (1784–1850) married Hyacinthe de Ravenel du Boisteilleul, 16 November 1814.—B.
[5] Vice-Admiral Charles Jean Comte d'Hector (1722–1808), commander of the port of Brest from 1780 to 1791. He joined the Princes' Army at Coblentz, and was made colonel of a regiment consisting exclusively of naval officers. He died at Reading in Berkshire at the age of eighty-six.—B.

blocks of wood, cordwainers twisted hawsers, ship's boys lit
fires under coppers from which issued a thick smoke and the
healthy smell of tar. Bales of merchandise, sacks of victuals
were carried to and from the quay; trains of artillery were
rolled from the sea to the magazines, from the magazines to
the sea. Here, carts were pushed backwards into the water
to receive cargoes; there, loads were hoisted with tackle, while
cranes lowered stones and dredging-machines dug out the
alluvium. Forts fired signals, ships' boats came and went,
vessels set sail or returned to harbour.

My mind became filled with vague ideas on society, its
blessings and its evils. An indefinite sadness overtook me; I
left the mast on which I was sitting, walked up the Penfeld,
which runs into the port, and reached a turn where the port
disappeared from view. Here, with nothing before me except
a turfy valley, but with the confused murmur of the sea
and human voices still in my ears, I lay down upon the bank
of the little river. Watching by turns the rippling of the water
and the flight of the sea-mew, enjoying the silence around me
or listening to the strokes of the calker's hammer, I fell into the
deepest musing. In the midst of this reverie, if the wind
carried to me the sound of the gun of a ship leaving port, I
started, and tears moistened my eyes.

One day I had walked in the direction of the outer extremity
of the harbour, to the side of the sea: it was warm; I lay down
upon the beach and fell asleep. Suddenly I was awakened by
a grand noise; I opened my eyes like Augustus to see the
triremes in the anchorage of Sicily after the victory over
Sextus Pompey: reports of artillery followed one upon the
other; the roads were crowded with men-of-war; the great
French squadron was returning after the signing of peace.[1]
The ships manœuvred under full sail, bathed themselves in
flame, hoisted ensigns, turned their poops, bows, broadsides
towards the shore, stopped short by dropping anchor while
still under sail, or continued to skim over the billows. Nothing
ever gave me a higher idea of the human intelligence: man
seemed at that moment to borrow something from Him who
said to the sea, "Thus far shalt thou go and no further."

All Brest hastened to the port. Boats left the fleet and
landed at the mole. The officers with whom they were
crowded, their faces bronzed by the sun, had that foreign
look which is brought back from another atmosphere, and
the indescribable air of gaiety, of pride, of daring, worn by

[1] The Peace of Versailles, 1783.—T.

men who had restored the honour of the national ensign. These officers, so deserving, so illustrious, these companions of Suffren,[1] Lamotte-Piquet,[2] Couëdic, d'Estaing,[3] had escaped from the blows of the enemy only to fall beneath those of Frenchmen !

I was watching the gallant troop march by, when one of the officers disengaged himself from the others and fell upon my neck: it was Gesril. He seemed taller, but weak and ailing from a sword-thrust he had received in the chest. He left Brest the same evening to join his family. I only saw him once since, shortly before his heroic death: I will tell the occasion of the meeting later.

Gesril's sudden appearance and departure made me take a resolve which changed the course of my life: it was written that that young man should have an absolute empire over my destiny. One can see how my character was shaping, the turn my ideas were taking, the first attacks of my genius; for I can speak of that genius as a malady, whatever it may have been, rare or vulgar, worthy or unworthy of the name I give it for want of a word wherewith to express myself. Had I been more like the rest of mankind, I should have been happier: any one who could have succeeded, without depriving me of my intelligence, in killing what is called my talent would have treated me as a friend.

When the Comte de Boisteilleul took me to M. d'Hector, I heard old and young sailors discuss their campaigns and talk of the countries they had visited: one had returned from India, another from America; this one was to set sail to go round the world, the other was about to join the Mediterranean station, to visit the shores of Greece. My uncle pointed out La Pérouse[4] to me in the crowd, a new Cook, the manner of whose death has remained the secret of the tempests. I

[1] Pierre André de Suffren-Saint-Tropez (1726–1788), known as the Bailli de Suffren, had fought the English in India by sea and land in the war of 1782.—T.

[2] Comte de Lamotte-Piquet (1720–1791), lieutenant-general of the French Navy. Between 1737 and 1783 he took part in twenty-eight campaigns, and distinguished himself especially in America.—T.

[3] Charles Hector Comte d'Estaing (1720–1794), admiral in command of the combined fleets at Cadiz on the signature of the treaty of peace. He embraced the principles of the Revolution, and served in the Republican army and naval forces; but was guillotined in 1794.—T.

[4] Jean François Galaup, Comte de La Pérouse (1741–1788 [?]) set out on a voyage of discovery in 1785. He was known to have visited Japan and New Holland when, in 1788, all traces of him were lost. In 1827, Captain Dillon discovered the wrecks of his ships, the *Boussole* and the *Astrolabe*, off the coast of Vanikoro, since called the Pérouse, one of the Santa Cruz group, between the Solomon Islands and the New Hebrides.—T.

listened to everything, I looked at everything, without uttering
a word; but there was no sleep for me that night: I spent it,
in imagination, in delivering combats or discovering unknown
lands.

Be that as it may, on seeing Gesril return to his parents,
I thought that there was nothing to prevent me from going
home to my own. I should have much liked the naval service,
if my spirit of independence had not disinclined me to service
of any kind: I was born with an incapacity for obedience.
Voyages tempted me, but I felt that I should enjoy them only
in solitude, left free to follow my own will. At last, giving
my first proof of fickleness, without telling my uncle Ravenel,
without writing to my parents, without asking permission of
anybody, without waiting for my cadet's commission, I left
one morning for Combourg, where I dropped as though from
the clouds.

I am to this day astonished to think how, in view of the
terror with which my father inspired me, I could have dared to
take such a resolve; and what is quite as astonishing is the
manner in which I was welcomed. I had every reason to
expect transports of the most furious anger, and I was gently
received. My father was content to shake his head, as though
to say, "Here's a pretty trick!" My mother embraced me
with all her heart, grumbling the while, and my Lucile kissed
me in an ecstasy of joy.

BOOK III[1]

THREE years and six months have elapsed between the last date attached to these Memoirs, Vallée-aux-Loups, January 1814, and the date of to-day, Montboissier, July 1817. Did you hear the Empire fall? No: nothing has disturbed the repose of this spot. Nevertheless the Empire is lost; the immense ruin has crumbled in the course of my life like Roman remains overturned in the bed of some unknown stream. But events matter little to one who does not reckon them: a few years escaping from the hands of the Eternal Father will do justice to all these reports with an endless silence.

The previous chapter was written under the expiring tyranny of Bonaparte and by the light of the last flashes of his glory: I am commencing the present chapter under the reign of Louis XVIII. I have been in close proximity to kings, and my political illusions have vanished, as have the sweeter fancies of which I am continuing the tale. Let me first say what makes me resume my pen: the human heart is the toy of everything, nor can we foresee what trivial circumstance will cause its joys and sorrows. Montaigne remarked this: "There needeth no cause," he says, "to excite our minde. A doating humour without body, without substance, overswayeth and tosseth it up and down."[2]

I am now at Montboissier, on the borders of the Beauce and the Perche.[3] The castle situated upon this property,

---

[1] This book was written at the Château de Montboissier (July–August 1817) and at the Vallée-aux-Loups (November 1817), and revised in December 1846.—T.

[2] Florio's MONTAIGNE, Booke III. chap. 5: *Of Diverting and Diversions.*—T.

[3] In the Orléannais.—T. The castle stands in the commune of Montboissier, canton of Bonneval, Arrondissement of Châteaudun (Eure-et-Loire).—B.

belonging to Madame la Comtesse de Colbert-Montboissier,[1] was sold and demolished during the Revolution; only two pavilions remain, divided by a railing, and formerly inhabited by the lodge-keeper. The park, which is now laid out in the English style, retains some traces of its former French symmetry: straight walks, copses set within hedges give it a serious aspect; it has the attraction of a ruin.

Yesterday evening I was walking alone; the sky was like an autumn sky; a cold wind blew at intervals. I stopped at an opening in a thicket to look at the sun: it was sinking into the clouds above the tower of Alluye, from which Gabrielle,[2] occupying that tower, saw the sun set, as I did, two hundred years ago. What has become of Henry and Gabrielle? The same that shall have become of me when these Memoirs are published.

I was drawn from my reflections by the twittering of a thrush perched on the topmost branch of a birch-tree. At once that magic sound brought back before my eyes my father's domain: I forgot the catastrophes which I had lately witnessed, and suddenly carried back into the past, I saw once more the fields where I had so often heard the thrush's song. When I listened to it then, I was sad, as I am to-day; but that first sadness was of the kind which springs from a vague longing for happiness, at a time when we are without experience; the sadness which I now feel comes from the knowledge of things appreciated and judged. The song of the bird in the Combourg woods told me of a happiness which I hoped to achieve; the same song in the park at Montboissier reminded me of days wasted in the pursuit of that unattainable happiness. I have nothing more to learn; I have travelled faster than others, and have made the circuit of life. The hours fly and drag me with them; I have not even the certainty of being able to complete these Memoirs. In how many places have I already commenced to write them, and in what place shall I finish them? How long shall I wander on the edge of the wood? Let me make the most of the few moments left to me; let me hasten to depict my youth, while I am still in touch with it: the traveller quitting for ever an enchanted shore writes his journal in sight of the land which is withdrawing, soon to disappear from sight.

[1] The Comtesse de Colbert-Montboissier, grand-daughter of Malesherbes, and daughter of the Marquis de Montboissier. In 1803 she married Édouard Charles Victornien Comte de Colbert de Maulevrier, who was descended from the Comte de Maulevrier, brother to the great Colbert.—B.

[2] Gabrielle d'Estrées (circa 1565-1599), mistress to Henry IV., who created her Duchesse de Beaufort.—T.

I have described my return to Combourg and my reception by my father, my mother, and my sister Lucile. The reader will perhaps remember that my three other sisters were married and living on the estates of their new families in the neighbourhood of Fougères. My brother, whose ambition was beginning to display itself, was oftener in Paris than at Rennes. He first bought a post as *maître des requêtes*, which he sold in order to enter the military service. He entered the Royal Cavalry Regiment; he then joined the diplomatic service, and accompanied the Comte de La Luzerne to London, where he met André Chénier;[1] he was on the point of obtaining the Vienna Embassy, when our troubles broke out. He asked for Constantinople, but found a formidable competitor in Mirabeau, who had been promised this embassy as the price of his alliance with the Court party. My brother had therefore almost taken leave of Combourg at the time when I came to live there.

My father entrenched himself in his manor, which he never left, not even to attend the sittings of the States.[2] My mother went to Saint-Malo for six weeks in every year, at Eastertide; she looked forward to that time as the period of her deliverance, for she detested Combourg. A month before the journey, it was discussed as though it were a hazardous enterprise; preparations were made; the horses were rested. On the eve of departure, we went to bed at seven in the evening, in order to get up at two o'clock in the morning. My mother, to her great contentment, set out at three, and occupied the whole day in covering twelve leagues.

Lucile, who had been received as a canoness to the Chapter of the Argentière, was about to be transferred to that of Remiremont: while awaiting this change, she remained buried in the country. As for myself, after my escapade from Brest, I declared my wish to embrace the ecclesiastical state: the truth is that I was only seeking to gain time, for I did not know what I wished. I was sent to the college at Dinan to complete my humanities. I knew Latin better than my masters; but I began to learn Hebrew. The Abbé de Rouillac was the principal of the college, and the Abbé Duhamel my tutor.

[1] André de Chénier (1762-1794), son of the French Consul at Constantinople, and elder brother of the better-known Marie Joseph de Chénier. A poet of some merit, and a courageous antagonist of the Revolution.—T. He was a secretary at the London Embassy when M. de La Luzerne took it over in 1788.—B.

[2] The States of Brittany, which held their sittings at Rennes.—T.

Dinan, adorned with old trees, fortified with old towers, is built upon a picturesque site, on a high hill at the foot of which flows the tidal Rance, and overlooks sloping and pleasantly-wooded valleys. The mineral waters of Dinan have some renown. This historic city, which gave birth to Duclos,[1] displayed among its antiquities the heart of Du Guesclin: an heroic dust which, stolen during the Revolution, was on the point of being pounded by a glazier to be used for paint. Was it intended for pictures of victories won over the enemies of the country?

M. Broussais, my fellow-townsman, became my fellow-student at Dinan. The students were taken to bathe on Thursdays, like the clerks under Pope Adrian I., or on Sundays, like the prisoners under the Emperor Honorius. Once I was nearly drowned; on another occasion, M. Broussais was bitten by ungrateful leeches, which failed to foresee the future.[2] Dinan was at an equal distance from Combourg and Plancoët. I visited my uncle de Bedée at Monchoix and my own family at Combourg by turns.

M. de Chateaubriand, who found it cheaper to keep me at home, my mother, who wished me to persist in my religious vocation, but who would have scrupled to urge me, no longer insisted upon my residence at college, and I found myself imperceptibly settling down under the paternal roof.

I should take pleasure in recalling the habits of my parents even if they were no more to me than a touching remembrance; but I reproduce them the more readily in that the picture will appear as though traced from the vignettes in mediæval manuscripts: centuries separate the present days from those which I am about to depict.

On my return from Brest the gentry at Combourg Castle consisted of four: my father, my mother, my sister, and me. A woman-cook, a waiting-maid, two footmen and a coachman composed the whole household: two old mares and a sporting-dog were huddled in a corner of the stable. These twelve living beings were lost to sight in a manor-house where a hundred knights, their ladies, squires, and varlets, and King Dagobert's chargers and pack might almost have gone unnoticed.

All through the year, not a visitor presented himself at the

[1] Charles Pineau Duclos (1704–1772), historiographer of France (1745), member of the French Academy (1747), and perpetual secretary of that body (1755).—T. Mayor of his native city from 1744 to 1750.—B.

[2] Broussais belonged to the school which carried the use of dieting and leeches to excess.—T.

castle, save a few gentlemen, the Marquis de Montlouet,[1] the Comte de Goyon-Beaufort,[2] who begged a night's lodging on their way to plead their suits before the Parliament. They used to arrive in winter, on horseback, with pistols in their saddle-bows, hunting-knives at their sides, and followed by a servant, also on horseback, with a livery trunk behind him.

My father, always very ceremonious, received them bare-headed on the steps, in the midst of the wind and rain. Once inside the house, the country gentlemen would talk of their Hanoverian campaigns, their family affairs, their law-suits. At night they were conducted to the North Tower, to Queen Christina's bed-chamber, a state-room containing a bed seven feet by seven, hung with a double set of curtains in green muslin and crimson silk, and held up by four gilt Cupids. The next morning, when I came down to the great hall and looked out through the windows upon the country covered with floods or hoar-frost, I saw nothing except two or three travellers on the lonely embankment of the pond: it was our guests riding away to Rennes.

These visitors did not know much about the things of life; nevertheless our view was by their means extended a few miles beyond the horizon of our woods. When they were gone, we were reduced on week-days to our family circle, and on Sundays to the company of the village commoners and the neighbouring gentry.

On Sundays, in fine weather, my mother, Lucile, and I went to the parish church across the Little Mall and along a country road; when it rained, we went by the abominable Combourg High Street. We were not carried, like the Abbé de Marolles,[3] in a light chariot drawn by four white horses, captured from the Turks in Hungary. My father went but once a year to the parish church to perform his Easter duties; the rest of the year he heard Mass in the castle chapel. Seated in the pew of the lord of the manor, we received the incense and the prayers in front of the black marble sepulchre of Renée de Rohan: a symbol of mortal honours; a few grains of incense before a tomb!

Our Sunday diversions vanished with the day; they did

[1] François Jean Raphaël de Brunes, Comte (not Marquis) de Montlouet (1728-1787), Commissary of the States of Brittany.—B.
[2] Luc Jean Comte de Gouyon-Beaufort (1725-1794), Knight of St. Louis. Guillotined 15 February 1794.—B.
[3] The Abbé Michel de Marolles (1600-1681), an indifferent but indefatigable translator, and author of some historical works, including the Memoirs from which this reference is taken.—T.

not even recur regularly. During the bad weather, entire
months would pass and not a single human being knock at
the gate of our fortress. The sadness was great that hung
over the moors of Combourg, but greater still at the castle:
as one made his way beneath its vaultings, he experienced
the same feeling as on entering the Carthusian Monastery at
Grenoble.[1] When I visited the latter in 1805, I crossed a
wilderness which increased in desolation as I went; I thought
it would end at the monastery, but I was shown, within the
very convent walls, the gardens of the Carthusian Friars even
more neglected than the woods. And at length, in the centre
of the monument, I found, shrouded in the folds of all this
solitude, the former grave-yard of the community, a sanctuary
from which eternal silence, the genius of the place, spread
its dominion over the mountains and forests around.

The gloomy stillness of Combourg Castle was increased by
my father's taciturn and unsocial humour. Instead of drawing
his family and his retainers closer to him, he had dispersed
them to all the winds of the building. His bed-room was in
the small east tower, his study in the small west tower.
The furniture of this study consisted of three chairs in black
leather and a table covered with parchments and title-deeds.
A genealogical tree of the Chateaubriand family adorned the
chimney-mantel, and in the embrasure of a window hung arms
of all sorts, from a pistol to a blunderbuss. My mother's room
extended over the great hall, between the two small towers;
it had a parqueted flooring and was adorned with faceted
Venetian mirrors. My sister occupied a closet leading out of
my mother's room. The waiting-maid slept far away, on the
ground floor between the two great towers. Myself, I was
nestled in a sort of isolated cell at the top of the turret
containing the staircase which led from the inner yard to the
different parts of the castle. At the foot of this staircase, my
father's valet and the other man-servant lay in a vaulted
basement, and the cook kept garrison in the great west
tower.

My father rose at four o'clock in the morning, winter and
summer alike: he went to the inner yard to call and wake his
valet at the entrance to the turret staircase. A cup of coffee
was brought to him at five; he then worked in his study till
mid-day. My mother and sister each breakfasted in her own
chamber at eight o'clock. I had no fixed time for rising or

---

[1] The Grande-Chartreuse is the waste-land near Grenoble which gives its name
to the Carthusian Order.—T.

breakfasting; I was supposed to study till noon: the greater part of the time I did nothing.

At half-past eleven, the bell rang for dinner, which was served at twelve. The great hall did duty as both dining-room and drawing-room : we dined and supped at one end, on the east side; when the meal was over, we went and sat at the other end, the west side, before a huge chimney. The hall was wainscoted, painted whity-grey, and adorned with old portraits ranging from the reign of Francis I. to that of Louis XIV. Among these portraits one recognized those of Condé and Turenne: a picture representing Achilles slaying Hector beneath the walls of Troy hung over the chimney-piece.

After dinner we remained together until two o'clock. Then, if it was summer, my father went fishing, visited his kitchen-gardens, walked within the limits of the home park; in the autumn and winter he went shooting. My mother withdrew to the chapel, where she spent some hours in prayer. This chapel was a gloomy oratory, adorned with fine pictures by the greatest masters, such as one would scarcely expect to find in a feudal castle in the heart of Brittany. I still have in my possession a Holy Family by Albani, painted on copper, which was taken from this chapel: it is all that remains to me of Combourg. When my father had left the house and my mother gone to her prayers, Lucile withdrew to her room and I either returned to my cell or went out to roam about the country.

At eight o'clock the bell rang for supper. After supper, in fine weather, we sat out on the steps. My father, armed with his gun, shot at the brown owls which issued from the battlements at nightfall. My mother, Lucile and I watched the sky, the woods, the dying rays of the sun, the rising stars. At ten o'clock we went in and retired to bed.

The autumn and winter evenings were different. Supper over, the four of us would leave the table and gather round the chimney. My mother flung herself, with a sigh, upon an old couch covered in imitation Siam; a stand was put before her with a candle. I sat down with Lucile by the fire; the servants cleared the table and withdrew. My father then began a tramp which lasted till he went to bed. He was dressed in a white ratteen gown, or rather a kind of cloak, which I have seen no one wear except him. His half-bald head was covered with a big white cap that stood straight up on end. When he walked away to a distance from the fire-place, the huge hall was so badly lighted by its solitary candle that he was no longer visible; we could only hear him still walking in the darkness: then he would slowly return towards the light and gradually emerge from the dusk, like a ghost, with his white gown, his white cap, his long pale face. Lucile and I exchanged a few words in a low voice when he was at the other end of the hall; we hushed when he drew nearer to us. He asked, as he passed, "What were you talking about?" Terror-stricken, we made no reply; he continued his walk. For the rest of the evening, the ear heard nothing save the measured sound of his steps, my mother's sighs, and the murmuring of the wind.[1]

The hour of ten struck on the castle clock: my father stopped; the same spring which had raised the hammer of the clock seemed to have arrested his steps. He drew out his watch, wound it, took a great silver candle-stick holding a tall candle, went for a moment to the small west tower, then returned, candle in hand, and went towards his bed-room, which formed part of the small east tower. Lucile and I placed ourselves on his way; we kissed him and wished him good-night. He turned his dry, hollow cheek to us without replying, continued his road, and withdrew inside the tower, the doors of which we heard closing behind him.

The spell was broken: my mother, my sister and myself, who had been changed into statues by my father's presence, recovered the functions of life. The first effect of our disenchantment took the form of an overflow of words: silence was made to pay us dear for having so long oppressed us. When torrent of words had sped, I called the waiting-woman and escorted my mother and sister to their rooms. Before I went, they made me look under the beds, up the chimneys, behind the doors, and inspect the surrounding stairs, passages

[1] "A solitary incident would vary these evenings, which might figure in a romance of the eleventh century. Sometimes my father would interrupt his walk and come and sit down by the hearth to tell us the story of his youthful distress and the crosses of his life. He described storms and dangers, a journey in Italy, a shipwreck on the Spanish coast.

"He had seen Paris; he spoke of it as he might speak of a haunt of abomination and of a foreign country. The Bretons looked upon China as being in their neighbourhood, but Paris seemed to them the end of the world. I eagerly listened to my father. When I heard this man who was so hard to himself regret that he had not done enough for his family and complain in short but bitter words of his fate, when I saw him at the conclusion of his recital rise brusquely, wrap himself in his cloak, and renew his tramp, first hastening his steps and then slowing them to correspond with the movements of his heart, filial love would fill my eyes with tears; I revolved my father's troubles in my mind, and it seemed to me that the sufferings undergone by the author of my days should have fallen upon me and me alone."—*Manuscript of* 1826.

and corridors. All the traditions of the castle concerning robbers and ghosts returned to their memory. The servants were persuaded that a certain Comte de Combourg, with a wooden leg, who had been dead three centuries, appeared at certain intervals, and that he had been seen in the great staircase of the turret; sometimes also his wooden leg walked alone, accompanied by a black cat.

These stories took up the whole of the time occupied by my mother and sister in preparing for the night: they got into bed dying of fright; I climbed to the top of my turret; the cook returned to the main tower, and the men went down to their basement.

The window of my donjon opened upon the inner courtyard; by day I had a view of the battlements of the curtain opposite, where hart's-tongues grew and a wild plum-tree. Some martins, which in summer buried themselves, screeching, in the holes in the walls, were my sole companions. At night I could see only a small strip of sky and a few stars. When the moon shone and sank in the east, I knew it by the beams which struck my bed across the lozenged window-panes. Owls, flitting from one tower to the other, passed and passed again between the moon and me, outlining the mobile shadow of their wings upon my curtains. Banished to the loneliest part, at the opening of the galleries, I lost not a murmur of the darkness. Sometimes the wind seemed to trip with light steps; sometimes it uttered wailings; suddenly my door was violently shaken, groans issued from the basement, and then these sounds would die away, only to commence anew. At four o'clock in the morning, the voice of the master of the castle, calling the footman at the entrance to the venerable vaults, made itself heard like the voice of the last phantom of the night. This voice supplied for me the place of the sweet harmony with the sound of which Montaigne's father was wont to awaken his son.[1]

The Comte de Chateaubriand's stubbornness in making a child sleep alone at the top of a tower might have had its inconvenience, but it turned out to my advantage. This violent manner of treatment left me with the courage of a man, without taking from me that vivid imagination of which it is nowadays the tendency to deprive the young. Instead of seeking to persuade me that ghosts did not exist, they obliged me to set them at defiance. When my father asked me, with an

---

[1] *Cf.* Florio's MONTAIGNE, Booke I. chap. 25 : *Of the Institution and Education of Children.*—T.

ironical smile, "Is monsieur le chevalier afraid?" he could have made me sleep with a corpse. When my excellent mother said, "My child, nothing happens without God's leave; you have nothing to fear from evil spirits so long as you remain a good Christian," I was more reassured than by all the arguments of philosophy. So complete was my success, that the night winds, in my uninhabited tower, served but as playthings for my fancies and wings for my dreams. My imagination, thus kindled, spread over every object, found nowhere sufficient nourishment, and could have devoured heaven and earth. It is this moral condition which it is now my task to describe. Immersed once more in the days of my youth, I will try to grasp myself in the past, to depict myself such as I was, such as perhaps I regret that I no longer am, despite the torments which I then endured.

Scarcely had I returned from Brest to Combourg when a revolution took place in my existence; the child vanished and there appeared the man, with his joys which pass and his troubles which remain. At first all became passion with me, pending the arrival of the passions themselves. When, after a silent dinner, at which I had dared neither to eat nor speak, I succeeded in escaping, my delight was incredible. I could not descend the steps then and there: I should have flung myself headlong. I was obliged to sit upon one of the steps to allow my excitement to subside; but so soon as I had reached the Cour Verte and the woods, I began to run, to leap, to bound, to skip, to rejoice until I fell down exhausted, panting, drunk with frolic and liberty.

My father took me with him shooting. I was seized with the taste for sport, and carried it to excess; I still see the field where I killed my first hare. Often, in autumn, I have stood for four or five hours to my waist in water, waiting at the edge of a pond for wild-duck; to this very day I lose my composure when I see a dog point. Nevertheless, my first ardour for sport was built upon a basis of independence; to leap ditches, to tramp over fields, marshes, moors, to find myself with a gun in an unfrequented spot, alone and powerful, all this was my natural manner of being. When out shooting, I would go so far that I had not the strength to walk back, and the keepers were obliged to carry me on twisted branches.

However, the pleasures of the chase no longer satisfied me; I was fretted with a longing for happiness which I could neither control nor understand; my mind and my heart ended by forming as it were two empty temples, without altars or sacrifices; it was not yet known which god would be worshipped there.   I grew up by the side of my sister Lucile: our friendship was all our life.

Lucile was tall and endowed with remarkable, but serious, beauty. Her pale features were shaded with long black tresses; she often fixed her eyes on heaven or cast looks around her full of sadness or fire.   Her gait, her voice, her smile, her expression showed something pensive and suffering.

Lucile and I were mutually useless.   When we spoke of the world, it was of that which we carried within ourselves, a world very unlike the true world.   She saw in me her protector, I in her my friend.   She was seized with gloomy fits of thought which I had difficulty in dispelling: at the age of seventeen she bewailed the loss of her youth; she wished to bury herself in a convent.   Everything to her was a care, a sorrow, a hurt: an expression she sought for, an illusion she entertained would torment her for months on end.   I have often seen her, with one arm thrown over her head, dream without life or movement; the life that was in her ebbed to her heart, and ceased to show itself without; her very bosom no longer heaved.   Her attitude, her melancholy, her beauty gave her the air of a funeral Genius.   I then endeavoured to console her, and the next moment was myself plunged in inexplicable despair.

Lucile liked to read some pious book, in the evening, alone : her favourite oratory was the junction of two country-roads, marked by a stone cross and a poplar-tree, whose long stylus rose into the sky like a pencil.   My mother, devout and quite charmed, said that her daughter reminded her of a Christian of the primitive Church, praying at the stations called *Lauræ*.

My sister's concentration of mind gave birth to extraordinary intellectual effects : in her sleep, she dreamt prophetic dreams; waking, she seemed to read the future.   A clock ticked upon a landing of the staircase in the main tower, and struck the hours amid the silence. Lucile, when unable to sleep, would go to sit upon a stair opposite the clock and watch its face by the light of her lamp placed upon the ground. When the two hands met at midnight and in their formidable conjunction engendered the hour of disorder and crime, Lucile heard sounds which revealed distant deaths to her.   She was in Paris a few days before the 10th of August, staying with my other sisters near the Carmelite Convent, and casting her eyes upon a mirror, she gave a cry, and said, " I have just seen Death come in." On the moors of Scotland, Lucile would have been one of the celestial women of Walter Scott, gifted with second sight; on the moors of Brittany, she was no more than a lonely creature favoured with beauty, genius and misfortune.

The life which my sister and I led at Combourg heightened the exaltation natural to our age and character. Our chief pastime was to walk side by side in the Great Mall, in spring on a carpet of primroses, in autumn on a bed of dead leaves, in winter on a sheet of snow edged by the footprints of birds, squirrels, and weazels. We were young as the primroses, sad as the dead leaves, pure as the newly-fallen snow : our recreations were in harmony with ourselves.

It was during one of these walks that Lucile, hearing me speak rapturously of solitude, said, "You ought to write all that down." These words revealed the muse to me; a divine inspiration passed over me. I began to lisp verses, as though it were my natural language; day and night I sang my pleasures, in other words my valleys and my woods; I wrote a multitude of little idylls or pictures of nature.[1] I wrote in verse long before writing in prose: M. de Fontanes used to maintain that I had received both instruments.

Did this talent which friendship foresaw for me ever really come to me ? How many things have I awaited in vain ! In the *Agamemnon* of Æschylus, a slave is placed as sentry on the roof of the palace of Argos; his eyes seek to discern the concerted signal for the return of the ships; he sings to while away his vigils, but the hours speed by and the stars set, and the torch does not shine forth. When, after many years, its tardy light appears upon the billows, the slave is bent beneath the weight of time; there is naught left for him but to reap misfortunes, and the chorus says to him that "an old man is a shadow that wanders by day."

Οναρ ἡμερόφαντον ἀλαίνει

Under the first spell of my inspiration, I engaged Lucile to do as I did. We spent days in mutual consultation, in communicating to each other what we had done and what we proposed to do. We undertook works in common; guided by our instincts, we translated the finest and saddest passages in Job

[1] See my Complete Works.—*Author's Note.*

and Lucretius upon life: the *Tædet animam meam vitæ meæ,*[1] the *Homo natus de muliere,*[2] the *Tum porro puer, ut sævis projectus ab undis navita,*[3] and so forth. Lucile's thoughts were sheer feeling; they issued with difficulty from her soul; but when she succeeded in expressing them, there was nothing higher. She has left some thirty pages in manuscript; it is impossible to read them without profound emotion. The elegance, the suavity, the dreaminess, the passionate tenderness of these pages present a combination of the Greek and German genius.[4]

My brother sometimes vouchsafed to spend a few moments with the hermits of Combourg. He was in the habit of bringing with him a young counsellor of the Parliament of Brittany, M. de Malfilatre,[5] cousin to the unfortunate poet of the same name.[6] I believe that, unknown to herself, Lucile felt a secret passion for this friend of my brother's, and that this stifled passion lay at the root of my sister's melancholy. She possessed, moreover, Rousseau's folly without his pride: she thought that everybody was in a conspiracy against her. She came to Paris in 1789, accompanied by her sister Julie, whose loss she deplored with an affection tinged with the sublime. All who knew her admired her, from M. de Malesherbes to Chamfort.[7] Thrown into the revolutionary crypts at Rennes,[8] she was on the point of being imprisoned at Combourg Castle, which had been turned into a gaol during the Terror. After her release from prison, she married M. de Caud,[9] who

---

[1] JOB, x. 1.—T.   [2] JOB, xiv. 1.—T.   [3] LUCR., v. 223.—T.

[4] I omit three short prose poems by Lucile de Chateaubriand. The curious will find them in a volume entitled, *Lucile de Chateaubriand, ses contes, ses poèmes, ses lettres, précédés d'une Étude sur sa vie,* edited by M. Anatole France (Paris: 1879).—T.

[5] Alexandre Henri de Malfilatre (1757-1803). He took orders during the Emigration, and died at Somers Town, London.—B.

[6] Jacques Charles Louis de Clinchamp de Malfilatre (1733-1767), a minor poet and translator, who died of hunger and the results of his excesses at the early age of thirty-four.—T.

[7] Sébastien Roch Nicolas (1741-1794) adopted the name of Chamfort on commencing his career as a poet and man of letters. He was private secretary to the Prince de Condé, and later reader to the Princesse Élisabeth. On the outbreak of the Revolution he joined Mirabeau's party. In 1794 he was arrested and tried to commit suicide; he was subsequently released, but died in a few weeks of his self-inflicted wounds.—T.

[8] She was arrested in December 1793, imprisoned in the Convent of the Good Shepherd, and released in November 1794.—B.

[9] Lieutenant-Colonel Jacques Louis René Chevalier de Caud (1727-1797), Knight of St. Louis. He was sixty-nine years of age when he married Lucile, then thirty-one, in August 1796; and he died seven months later, 16 March 1797.—B.

left her a widow within a year.   I met the friend of my childhood on my return from my emigration: I will tell how she
disappeared, when it pleased God to afflict me.

I have returned from Montboissier, and these are the last
lines that I shall trace in my hermitage; I have to leave it, filled
with the tall striplings which already hide and crown their
father in their close ranks.   I shall not see again the magnolia
which promised its blossom to the tomb of my fair Floridan,
the Jerusalem pine-tree and the cedar of Lebanon consecrated
to the memory of Jerome, the laurel of Granada, the Greek
plane-tree, the Armorican oak, at whose feet I drew Blanca,
sang Cymodocée, invented Velléda.   These trees were born
and grew with my dreams, of which they were the hamadryads.
They are about to pass under another's sway: will their new
master love them as I have loved them?   He will allow them
to wither, he will cut them down perhaps: I am doomed to
keep nothing upon this earth.   While bidding farewell to the
woods of Aulnay I shall recall the farewell which long ago I
bade to the woods of Combourg: my days are all farewells.

The taste for poetry with which Lucile had inspired me
was as fuel added to the flames.   My sensations gathered new
strength; vain thoughts of fame passed through my mind; for
a moment I believed in my "talent," but soon recovered a
proper mistrust of my own powers, and began to entertain
doubts of that talent, as I have always done.   I looked upon
my work as a temptation of the Evil One; I was angry with
Lucile for arousing an unfortunate propensity within me: I
ceased writing and began to mourn my future glory as one
might mourn his glory that is past.
Returning to my former state of idleness, I felt more
strongly what was lacking to my youth: I was a mystery to
myself.   I could not see a woman without feeling confused; I
blushed if she spoke to me.   My shyness, already excessive
with people in general, became so great in the presence of a
woman that I would have preferred any torture to that of
being left alone with her: no sooner was she gone than I
recalled her with all my wishes.   The descriptions of Virgil,
Tibullus and Massillon, it is true, presented themselves to
my memory; but the image of my mother and sister covered
all with its purity and made thicker the veils which nature
sought to raise: my filial and brotherly affection deceived
me with respect to an affection less disinterested.   Had the

loveliest slaves of the seraglio been handed over to me, I should not have known what to ask of them. Chance enlightened me.

A neighbour of the Combourg domain came to spend a few days at the castle with his wife, a very pretty woman. Something, I know not what, happened in the village; we ran to one of the windows of the hall to look. I reached the window first, the fair visitor followed close upon my heels, I turned to give her my place. Involuntarily she obstructed my way, and I felt myself pressed between her and the window. I was no longer conscious of what was happening around me.

From that moment I was aware that to love and be loved in a manner unknown to me must be the supreme happiness. Had I done what other men do, I should soon have become acquainted with the pains and pleasures of the passion whose germs I bore within me; but everything in me assumed an extraordinary character. The ardour of my imagination, my shyness, the solitude in which I lived caused me, rather than rush out of doors, to fall back upon myself; for want of a real object, I evoked, by the strength of my vague longings, a phantom which never left my side. I do not know whether the history of the human heart offers another instance of this nature.

And so I built up a woman out of all the women whom I had seen: she had the figure, the hair, the smile of the stranger who had pressed me to her bosom; I gave her the eyes of one of the young girls of the village, the complexion of another. The portraits of the fine ladies of the time of Francis I., Henry IV. and Louis XIV. which adorned the drawing-room supplied me with other features, and I even borrowed graces from the pictures of the Virgins that hung upon the church walls.

This invisible charmer accompanied me wherever I went; I communed with her as with a real being; she varied in the measure of my folly: Aphrodite unveiled; Diana clad in the dew and the blue of heaven; Thalia with her laughing mask; Hebe bearing the cup of youth; sometimes she became a fairy who laid nature at my feet. I touched and retouched my canvas; I took one attraction from my beauty to replace it with another. I also changed her finery; I borrowed it from every country, every century, every art, every religion. Then, when I had completed a masterpiece, I dispersed my drawings and paints again; my one woman turned into a crowd of women in whom I idolized separately the charms I had adored when united.

Pygmalion was less enamoured of his statue : my difficulty was how to please mine. Recognizing in myself none of the qualities calculated to awaken love, I lavished upon myself all that I lacked. I rode like Castor and Pollux ; I played the lyre like Apollo ; Mars wielded his arms with less power and skill : a hero of romance or history, I heaped fictitious adventures on fiction itself! The shades of Morven's daughters, the sultanas of Bagdad and Granada, the ladies of the castles of olden time ; baths, perfumes, dances, Asiatic delights were all borne to me by a magic wand.

See this young queen coming, decked in diamonds and flowers (it was still my sylph): she fetches me at midnight, across gardens of orange-trees, in the galleries of a palace bathed by the waves of the sea, on the balmy shore of Naples or Messina, beneath a sky of love pierced by the light of Endymion's star; she advances, an animated statue by Praxi-teles, amidst motionless statues, pale pictures and frescoes white and silent in the moonlight: the soft sound of her progress over the marble mosaic mingles with the imperceptible murmurs of the deep. The royal jealousy encompasses us. I fall at the knees of the sovereign of Enna's plains ; the silk waves from her loosened diadem fall caressingly upon my brow as she bends her girlish head over my face, and her hands rest upon my breast, throbbing with respect and with desire.

On emerging from these dreams, when I found myself once more a poor little obscure Breton lad, without fame, beauty, or talents, who would attract the looks of none, who would pass unknown, whom no woman would ever love, I was seized with despair: I no longer dared lift my eyes to the dazzling image I had attached to my steps.

This delirium lasted two whole years, during which the faculties of my soul attained the loftiest pitch of exaltation. I used to speak little, I now spoke not at all; I used still to study, I flung my books aside; my taste for solitude redoubled. I had all the symptoms of a violent passion : my eyes grew hollow; I fell away; I could not sleep; I was absent, melancholy, ardent, fierce. My days slipped by in a manner that was wild, odd, insensate, and yet full of delights.

To the north of the castle stretched a waste land strewn with druidical stones ; I would go and sit upon one of these stones at sunset. The gilded summit of the woods, the splen-dour of the earth, the evening star twinkling through the rosy clouds brought me back to my dreams: I longed to enjoy this sight with the ideal object of my desires. I followed in thought the luminary of the day; I gave him my beauty to escort, so that he might present her all radiant with himself to the homage of the universe. The evening breeze shattering the web woven by insects upon the tips of the blades of grass, the field-lark alighting upon a pebble recalled me to reality: I turned my steps back to the castle, with heart oppressed and downcast face.

On stormy days in summer, I climbed to the top of the great west tower. The thunder roaring beneath the castle lofts, the torrents of rain which fell dashing upon the cone-shaped roof of the towers, the lightning which furrowed the clouds and marked the brass weathercocks with its electric flame aroused my enthusiasm: like Ismen on the ramparts of Jerusalem, I invoked the thunder, I hoped that it would bring Armida to me.

If the sky was clear, I crossed the Great Mall, around which lay meadows divided by hedges of willow-trees. In one of these willows, I had contrived a seat, like a nest: here, isolated between heaven and earth, I spent hours with the singing birds; my nymph was by my side. I also associated her image with the beauty of those spring nights filled with the freshness of the dew, the sighs of the nightingale and the murmuring of the breeze.

At other times I followed a deserted path, a stream adorned with its river-side plants; I listened to the sounds that issued from unfrequented parts; I lent an ear to every tree; I thought I heard the moonlight singing in the woods: I tried to tell these pleasures, and the words died upon my lips. I know not how I found my goddess again in the accents of a voice, the vibration of a harp, the velvety or liquid sounds of a horn or an harmonica. It would take too long to describe the fine journeys I took with my flower of love; how, hand in hand, we visited famous ruins, Venice, Rome, Athens, Jerusalem, Memphis, Carthage; how we crossed the seas; how we asked happiness of the palm-trees of Otaheite, of the scented groves of Timor and Amboyna; how, on the summit of the Himalayas, we went to wake the dawn; how we descended the sacred rivers whose spreading waves encircle gilt-domed pagodas; how we slept on the banks of the Ganges, while the Bengali, perched on the mast of a bamboo wherry, sang his Hindoo boat-song. Earth and Heaven no longer existed for me; above all, I forgot the latter; but though it no longer received my prayers, it heard the voice of my secret misery: for I suffered, and sufferings pray.

The sadder the season, the greater its harmony with myself; the time of hoar-frost makes communication less easy and isolates those who dwell in country-places: one feels more beyond the reach of men.

A moral character clings to autumn scenery: those leaves which fall like our years, those flowers which fade like our days, those clouds which fleet like our illusions, that light which fails like our intelligence, that sun which cools like our love, those streams which freeze like our life bear a secret relation to our destinies.

I beheld with ineffable pleasure the return of the season of storms, the passing of the swans and the ring-doves, the muster of the crows on the pond field, and their perching at nightfall on the tallest oaks in the Great Mall. When the evening raised a bluish vapour in the cross-roads of the forest, and the plaintive lays of the wind moaned in the withered moss, I entered into full possession of the sympathies of my nature. If I met some ploughman at the end of a field, I stopped to look at that man who had shot up in the shadow of the wheat with which he was to be reaped, and who, turning over the earth of his tomb with the plough-share, mingled his burning sweat with the icy rains of autumn: the furrow which he dug was the monument intended to outlive him. What did my elegant dæmon then do? By means of her magic, she wafted me to the banks of the Nile, and showed me the Egyptian pyramid sunk beneath the dust, as one day the Armorican furrow would lie hidden beneath the heather: I congratulated myself on having placed the fables of my felicity beyond the circle of human realities.

In the evening I embarked upon the pond, and, alone in my boat, rowed amidst the rushes and the broad floating leaves of the water-lilies. Overhead was the meeting-place of the swallows preparing to quit our climes. Not one of their twitterings did I lose; the child Tavernier [1] followed less closely the traveller's tale. They played on the water at sundown, chased the flies, darted together into the air, as though to test their wings, dropped down upon the surface of the lake, and then perched upon the reeds, which scarcely bent beneath their weight, and which were filled with their warbling turmoil.

[1] Jean Baptiste Tavernier (1605-1686), a great traveller and linguist, and author of a famous book of Voyages in Turkey, Persia, and India.—T.

Night fell; the reeds shook their fields of swords and distaves, among which the feathered caravan of moor-fowl, teal, kingfishers, snipe lay silent; the lake washed against its shores; the loud voices of autumn issued from the woods and marshes; I ran my boat aground and returned to the castle. Ten o'clock struck. I went to my room, and at once opened the windows, fixed my eyes upon the sky, and commenced an incantation. In company with my witch I mounted the clouds: enveloped in her tresses and her veil, I was swept along by the tempest, shaking the forest-tops, hustling the mountain-summits, whirling upon the seas. I plunged into space, I dropped from the Throne of God to the gates of the abyss, and the worlds were surrendered to the power of my love. Amid the disorder of the elements, I frenzically wedded the idea of danger to that of pleasure. The breath of the north wind brought to me but the sighs of voluptuousness; the murmur of the rain summoned me to sleep upon a woman's breast. The words which I addressed to that woman would have revived the senses of old age and warmed the marble of the tombs. Nothing-knowing and all-knowing, at once maid and lover, Eve before and after the fall, the enchantress from whom I derived my madness was a commixture of mystery and passion: I placed her on an altar and worshipped her. The pride of being loved by her yet further increased my love. When she walked, I prostrated myself to be trod beneath her feet or kiss their traces. I grew confused at her smile; I trembled at the sound of her voice; I thrilled with desire if I touched what she had touched. The air exhaled from her moist mouth penetrated into the marrow of my bones, coursed through my veins instead of blood. At a look from her I would have flown to the ends of the earth: a desert would have sufficed me with her! With her at my side, the lions' den would have changed into a palace, and millions of centuries would have been too short to exhaust the fires with which I felt myself consumed.

To this madness was added a moral idolatry: by a further play of my imagination, the Phryne that clasped me in her arms also represented glory to me and, above all, honour; virtue performing its noblest sacrifices, genius conceiving the rarest thoughts would scarcely give an idea of this other kind of happiness. I found at one and the same time in my marvellous creation all the blandishments of the senses and all the joys of the soul. Overwhelmed and as it were submerged beneath these dual delights, I no longer knew which was my true existence: I was a man and was not a man; I became cloud, wind, sound; I was a pure spirit, a creature of the air, singing the sovereign felicity. I divested myself of my nature to become one with the maiden of my desires, to be transmuted into her, to touch beauty more closely, to be at once passion given and received, love and the object of love. Suddenly, struck with my madness, I flung myself upon my couch; I rolled myself in my grief; I watered my pillow with scalding tears which none saw, piteous tears which flowed for a non-existent thing.

Soon, no longer able to remain in my tower, I climbed down through the darkness, furtively opened the door leading to the steps, like a murderer, and went to wander in the great wood. After walking at random, waving my hands, embracing the winds which escaped me like the shadow, the object of my pursuit, I leant against the trunk of a beech-tree; I watched the crows which I made fly from one tree to settle on another, or the moon lingering over the unclothed summits of the forest: I would have liked to inhabit this dead world, which reflected the pallor of the tomb. I felt neither the cold nor the dampness of the night; not even the icy breath of dawn would have drawn me from the depth of my thoughts, if at that hour the village bell had not made itself heard.

In most of the villages of Brittany, it is the custom at daybreak to toll the bell for the dead. The peal consists of three repeated notes, which give a monotonous, melancholy, rustic little tune. Nothing suited my sick and wounded soul better than to be recalled to the tribulations of existence by the bell which announced its end. I pictured to myself the herdsman expiring in his unknown hut, and laid in a grave-yard no less unknown. What had he come to do in the world? And I, what was I doing in this world? Since I should have to go at last, was it not better to depart in the cool of morning, to arrive early, than to complete the journey beneath the weight and in the heat of day? The blush of longing mantled on my face; the idea of ceasing to exist took possession of my heart in the manner of a sudden joy. At the period of the errors of my youth, I often hoped not to outlive happiness: there lay in the first success a measure of felicity that led me to aspire to destruction.

Bound ever more closely to my phantom, unable to enjoy what did not exist, I was like those mutilated men who contemplate a state of bliss to them unattainable and conjure up dreams whose pleasures rival the tortures of hell. I had, moreover, a presentiment of the misery of my future lot; ingenious in the fabrication of sufferings, I had placed myself between two forms of despair: sometimes I thought myself a mere nullity, incapable of rising above the vulgar herd; sometimes I seemed to feel within myself qualities which would never be appreciated. A secret instinct warned me that, as I moved onward through the world, I should find no part of that which I sought.

Everything furnished food for the bitterness of my disgust: Lucile was unhappy; my mother did not console me; my father made me feel the terrors of life, His moroseness increased with years; old age stiffened his soul as it did his body; he constantly spied upon me to chide me. When I returned from my wild rounds and saw him sitting on the steps, one might have killed me rather than make me enter the castle. Yet this but postponed my torture: obliged as I was to appear at supper, I sat down sheepishly upon the edge of my chair, my cheeks wet with the rain, my hair entangled. I sat motionless beneath my father's glances, and the perspiration stood upon my brow: the last glimmer of reason escaped me.

I now come to a moment when I shall need some strength to confess my weakness. The man who attempts to take his own life displays less the vigour of his soul than the exhaustion of his nature. I owned a fowling-piece whose worn trigger often went off when uncocked. I loaded this gun with three bullets, and went to a remote part of the Great Mall. I cocked the gun, placed the muzzle of the barrel in my mouth, and struck the butt-end against the ground; I several times repeated the ordeal; the charge did not go off; the appearance of a keeper stopped my resolve. Involuntary and unconscious fatalist that I was, I presumed that my hour had not come, and I deferred the execution of my project to another day. Had I killed myself, all that I have been would have been buried with me; none would have known of the history that led to my catastrophe; I should have swelled the crowd of nameless unfortunates, I should not have let myself be followed by the traces of my sorrows as a wounded man is followed by the traces of his blood.

Those who might be troubled by these descriptions and tempted to imitate these follies, those who might attach themselves to my memory through my illusions, must remember that they are listening only to a dead man's voice. Reader, whom

I shall never know, nothing remains: nought is left of me save that I am in the hands of the living God who has judged me.

An illness, the fruits of this unruly life, put an end to the torments which brought me the first inspirations of the Muse and the first attacks of the passions. These passions with which my soul was overwrought, these yet vague passions resembled the storms at sea which rush from every point of the horizon: inexperienced pilot that I was, I knew not in which direction to spread my sail to the uncertain winds. My chest swelled, a fever laid hold of me; they sent to Bazouges, a small town some five or six leagues from Combourg, for an excellent doctor called Cheftel, whose son[1] played a part in the affair of the Marquis de La Rouërie. He examined me attentively, ordered remedies, and declared that it was essential that I should be removed from my present mode of life. I lay six weeks in danger. One morning my mother came and sat on my bed, and said:

"It is time for you to take a decision; your brother is in a position to obtain a benefice for you; but before going to the seminary, you must take good counsel with yourself, for although I wish you to adopt the ecclesiastical state, I would rather see you a man of the world than a scandalous priest."

Those who have read the foregoing pages will be able to judge if the proposal of my pious mother came at a good moment. I have always, in the more important events of my life, at once known what to avoid: I am prompted by a movement of honour. As a priest, I struck myself as ridiculous. As a bishop, the majesty of the sacerdotal office overawed me, and I respectfully recoiled before the altar. Should I, as a bishop, make efforts to acquire virtues, or content myself with hiding my vices? I felt myself too weak to take the first course, too candid to adopt the second. They who treat me as a hypocrite and an ambitious man know me but little; I

---

[1] As I advance in years, I continue to meet persons mentioned in my Memoirs: the widow of Dr. Cheftel's son has just been admitted to the Marie-Thérèse Infirmary; this is a further proof of my veracity.—*Author's Note* (Paris, 1834).

Doubtless from pity and from gratitude to the doctor who tended him, Chateaubriand does not describe the part played by Cheftel the Younger. He was not content with selling the Marquis de La Rouërie's secrets: he betrayed the very corpse of him who had been his friend. His perfidious operations led to the revolutionary tribunal those whose plans he had pretended to serve; and he was the cause through which three heroic women mounted the scaffold: Thérèse de Moëlien, Madame de La Motte de la Guyomarais, and Madame de La Fonchais, sister to André Desilles.—B.

shall never succeed in the world, precisely because I lack one passion and one vice: ambition and hypocrisy. The first of these would with me be at the most a form of injured self-love; I might sometimes wish to be a minister or king in order to laugh at my enemies; but in twenty-four hours I should throw my portfolio or my crown out of window.

I therefore told my mother that my religious vocation was not sufficiently strong. For the second time I changed my plans: I had refused to become a sailor, and now I was no longer willing to be a priest. There remained the military career, which I loved: but how to suffer the loss of my independence and the restraint of European discipline? I took an absurd idea into my head: I declared that I would go to Canada and clear forests, or to India and take service in the armies of the princes of that country. By one of those contrasts which we perceive in all men, my father, so reasonable in other respects, was never greatly shocked by an adventurous project. He chided my mother for my fickleness, but decided to ship me to India. I was dispatched to Saint-Malo, where an expedition was being fitted out for Pondicherry.

Two months elapsed: I found myself back and alone in my maternal island. Villeneuve had just died there. I went to weep for her beside the poor, empty bed on which she had breathed her last, and saw the little wicker go-cart in which I had learnt to stand upright upon this world of sorrows. I pictured my old nurse lying on her pillow and fixing her feeble gaze upon that basket on wheels: this first memorial of my life opposite the last memorial of the life of my second mother, the thought of the wishes for the happiness of her nursling which the kind Villeneuve addressed to Heaven on leaving this world, this proof of an attachment so constant, disinterested and pure broke my heart with tenderness, gratitude and regret.

I found nothing else to remind me of my past at Saint-Malo: in the harbour I sought in vain for the ships in whose rigging I had played; they were gone or broken up; in the town, the house where I was born had been turned into an inn. I was scarce out of my cradle, and already a whole world had fallen into decay. I was a stranger in the parts of my childhood; people who met me asked who I was, for the sole reason that my head rose a few inches higher above the ground towards which it will sink again in a few years. How rapidly and how often we change our manner of existence and

our illusions! Friends leave us, others take their place; our ties alter: there is always a time at which we possessed nothing of what we now possess, at which we have nothing of what we once had. Man has not one self-same life: he has several on end, and that is his calamity.

Henceforward friendless and alone, I explored the beach which had borne my sand-castles: *campos ubi Troja fuit.* I walked on the shore deserted by the sea. The strand abandoned by the rising tide offered me the picture of those desolate places which our illusions leave around us when they go. Abailard, my fellow-Breton,[1] like myself watched these rollers eight hundred years ago, thinking of his Héloïse; like me, he saw some vessel speed (*ad horizontis undas*), and his ear, like mine, was lulled with the monotone of the waves. I exposed myself to the breakers while indulging in the baleful imaginings which I had brought with me from the woods at Combourg. A head called Cap Lavarde was the limit of my walks: seated at the extremity of this head, I remembered with the bitterest reflections that these same rocks had served to hide me as a child during the fairs; I had there gulped down my tears, while my playmates elated themselves with joy. I felt neither better loved nor happier than at that time. Soon I was to leave the country of my birth to crumble away my days in various climes. These reflections wounded me to death, and I was tempted to let myself fall into the waves.

A letter called me back to Combourg: I arrived, I supped with my family, monsieur my father did not speak a word, my mother sighed, Lucile appeared dismayed. At ten o'clock we retired. I questioned my sister; she knew nothing. At eight o'clock the next morning I was sent for. I went downstairs: my father was waiting for me in his study.

"Monsieur le chevalier," he said, "you must renounce your follies. Your brother has procured you a sub-lieutenant's commission in the Navarre Regiment. You will go first to Rennes, and thence to Cambrai. Here are a hundred louis: be sparing with them. I am old and ill; I have not long to live. Conduct yourself as a good man and never disgrace your name."

He kissed me. I felt that severe, wrinkled face press with emotion against mine: it was the last paternal embrace I was to receive.

[1] Pierre Abailard, or Abélard (1079–1142), the hero of the Héloïse idyll, was a native of Pallet, near Nantes, in Brittany.—T.

At that moment the Comte de Chateaubriand, a man so formidable in my eyes, appeared to me only as a father most worthy of my affection. I flung myself upon his emaciated hand and wept. He was threatened with an approaching attack of paralysis, which brought him to the grave; his left arm had a convulsive movement which he was obliged to check with his right hand. He was thus holding his arm when, after giving me his old sword, without leaving me time to recover myself, he led me to the cabriolet which was waiting for me in the Cour Verte. He made me get in before him. The post-boy drove off, while I with my eyes bade farewell to my mother and sister, who dissolved into tears on the steps.

I drove along the road by the pond; I saw the reeds of my swallows, the mill-stream and the meadow; I cast a look at the castle. Then, like Adam after his sin, I proceeded towards unknown ground, and " the world was all before me."[1]

From that day I saw Combourg but three times: after my father's death we met, in mourning, to share our inheritance and take leave of each other. On another occasion I accompanied my mother to Combourg: she was engaged in furnishing the castle, in expectation of the arrival of my brother, who was to bring my sister-in-law to Brittany. My brother did not come; he was soon, with his young wife, to receive at the hands of the executioner a different pillow from that prepared by my mother's hands. Lastly, I passed through Combourg a third time on my road to Saint-Malo to embark for America. The castle was abandoned, I had to put up at the steward's lodge. Wandering through the Great Mall, from the bottom of a dark avenue I caught sight of the deserted steps, the closed door and windows, and fainted away. I had difficulty in making my way back to the village: I sent for my horses and left in the middle of the night.

After an absence of fifteen years, and before again leaving France on my visit to the Holy Land, I went to Fougères to embrace what remained of my family. I had not the courage to undertake the pilgrimage to the fields to which the most vivid portion of my existence was attached. It is in the woods of Combourg that I became what I am, that I began to feel the first

---

[1] Cf. MILTON, *Paradise Lost*, XII., 646–647:

> " The world was all before them, where to choose
> Their place of rest, and Providence their guide."—T.

attacks of the weariness which I have dragged with me through life, of the sadness which has been my torment and my felicity. There I sought for a heart that could beat in touch with mine; there I saw my family united only to disperse. My father there dreamt of his name restored, of the fortunes of his house revived: another illusion which time and the revolutions have dispelled. Of six children that we were, we remain but three: my brother, Julie and Lucile are no more, my mother died of grief, my father's ashes were snatched from his grave.

If my works survive me, if I am to leave a name behind me, perhaps one day, prompted by these Memoirs, some traveller will come to visit the spots I have depicted. He will be able to recognize the castle; but he will look in vain for the great wood: the cradle of my dreams has vanished like those dreams. Left standing alone upon its rock, the ancient keep mourns the oaks, the old friends that surrounded it and protected it against the storm. Isolated also, I too have seen falling around me the family which beautified my days and lent me its shelter: fortunately my life is not built upon the earth so solidly as the towers in which I spent my youth, nor does man offer to the tempests a resistance so great as that of the monuments raised by his hands.

BOOK IV[1]

IT is a far cry from Combourg to Berlin, from a young dreamer to an old ambassador. In the foregoing pages I find these words: "In how many places have I already commenced to write these Memoirs, and in what place shall I finish them?" Nearly four years have passed between the date at which I wrote down the facts I have just related and that at which I resume these Memoirs. A thousand things have happened; a second man has shown himself in me, the politician: I care very little for him. I have defended the liberties of France, which alone can secure the duration of the lawful Throne. With the aid of the *Conservateur,*[2] I have set M. de Villèle in power; I have seen the Duc de Berry die, and done honour to his memory.[3] In order to reconcile everybody, I have gone away; I have accepted the Berlin Embassy.[4]

Yesterday I was at Potsdam, an ornate barrack, now void of soldiers: I studied the mock Julian in his mock Athens. At Sans-Souci, I was shown the table on which a great German monarch turned the maxims of the Encyclopædists into little French verses; the room occupied by Voltaire, decorated with carved monkeys and parrots; the mill which he who laid

---

[1] This book was written in Berlin in March and April 1821 and revised in July 1846.—T.

[2] The *Conservateur* was founded by Chateaubriand in October 1818, with the motto, *Le Roi, la Charte et les Honnêtes Gens.* Some of Chateaubriand's most perfect work is to be found in this collection, and the other writers included the Abbé de Lamennais, the Vicomte de Bonald, Fiévée, Berryer the Younger, Eugène Genoude, the Vicomte de Castelbajac, the Marquis d'Herbouville, M. Agier, the Cardinal de La Luzerne, the Duc de FitzJames, &c. The *Conservateur* ceased to appear in March 1820 in consequence of the revival of the censorship.—B.

[3] *Cf.* the *Mémoires sur la vie et la mort de Monseigneur le Duc de Berry* (April 1820).—T.

[4] Chateaubriand was appointed, by an Order in Council of 28 November 1820, Envoy Extraordinary and Minister Plenipotentiary to the Court of Prussia.—B.

provinces waste made light of respecting; the tomb of the horse César and of the greyhounds Diane, Amourette, Biche, Superbe, and Pax. The royal infidel took pleasure in profaning even the religion of the tomb by raising mausoleums to his dogs; he had marked out a burying-place near them for himself, less from contempt of mankind than an ostentation of annihilation.

They showed me the New Palace, already falling to pieces. In the old palace of Potsdam, they preserve the tobacco-stains, the worn and soiled chairs, in a word, all the traces of the renegade Prince's uncleanliness. This place immortalizes at once the dirt of the cynic, the impudence of the atheist, the tyranny of the despot, and the glory of the soldier. One thing alone attracted my attention: the hands of a clock fixed at the moment of Frederic's death; I was deceived by the immobility of the picture: hours never stay their flight; it is not man that stops the career of time, it is time that stops the career of man. Besides, it matters little what part we have played in life; the brilliancy or obscurity of our doctrines, our riches or poverty, our joys or sorrows in no way influence the length of our days. Whether the hands of the clock move over a golden or wooden face, whether the face be large or small, and fill the bezel of a ring or the rose-window of a cathedral, the hour has but one duration.

In a vault of the Protestant church, immediately below the pulpit of the unfrocked schismatic, I saw the coffin of the crowned sophist. The coffin is of bronze; when you strike it, it resounds. The dragoon who slumbers in this brassy bed would not even be roused from sleep by the noise of his fame; he will awake only to the sound of the trumpet which shall summon him to his last battle-field, face to face with the Lord of Hosts.

I had so great a need of a change of impressions that I found relief in visiting the Marble House. The king who built it once spoke some flattering words to me when, a poor officer, I passed through his army. This king at least shared the ordinary failings of mankind: vulgar like other men, he took refuge in pleasures. Do the two skeletons trouble themselves to-day about the difference that once existed between them, when one was Frederic the Great and the other Frederic William?[1] Sans-Souci and the Marble House are both ruins without masters.

Upon the whole, though the immensity of the events of

---

[1] Frederic William II. (1744-1797), the nephew and successor of Frederic the Great.—T.

our own time has lessened past events, though Rosbach, Lissa, Liegnitz, Torgau are mere skirmishes beside the battles of Marengo, Austerlitz, Jena, the Moskowa, Frederic suffers less than other personages by comparison with the giant enchained at St. Helena. The King of Prussia and Voltaire are two strangely-grouped figures who will live : the second destroyed a society with a philosophy which assisted the first in founding a kingdom.

The Berlin evenings are long. I occupy a house belonging to the Duchesse de Dino.[1] My secretaries[2] leave me so soon as night sets in. When there is no entertainment at Court for the wedding of the Grand-Duke and Grand-Duchess Nicholas,[3] I stay at home. Seated all alone by a cheerless stove, I hear nothing save the call of the sentry at the Brandenburg Gate and the steps on the snow of the man who whistles the hours. How shall I spend my time ? With books ? I have scarcely any. If I were to continue my Memoirs ?

You last saw me on the road from Combourg to Rennes : I alighted in the latter place at the house of one of my kinsmen. He informed me with delight that a lady of his acquaintance, who was going to Paris, had a seat to give away in her carriage, and that he undertook to persuade this lady to take me with her. I accepted, cursing my kinsman's civility as I did so. He settled the matter, and quickly presented me to my travelling-companion, a sprightly, free-and-easy milliner, who began to laugh when she saw me. The horses arrived at midnight and we set out.

Behold me in a post-chaise, alone with a woman, in the middle of the night. How was I, who had never in my life looked at a woman without blushing, to descend from the height of my dreams to this terrifying reality ? I did not know where I was ; I clung to my corner of the carriage for fear of touching Madame Rose's gown. When she spoke to me, I stammered without being able to reply. She had to pay the postilion, to take everything upon herself, for I was capable

---

[1] Dorothea Princess of Courlande (1795-1862) married in 1810 the Comte Edmond de Périgord, nephew to Talleyrand, who abandoned to him his title of Duc de Dino. The duke subsequently came into the title of Duc de Talleyrand-Périgord, by which the duchess was known at the time of her death.—B.

[2] The Comte Roger de Caux and the Chevalier de Cussy.—B.

[3] Now Emperor and Empress of Russia.—*Author's Note* (Paris, 1832).

Nicholas I. (1796-1855) married Charlotte, daughter of King Frederick William III. of Prussia. He ascended the Russian throne in 1825, on the death of his eldest brother, the Tsar Alexander I., and by virtue of the renunciation, for himself and his heirs, of the Grand-Duke Constantine.—T.

of nothing. When day broke, she looked with fresh amazement at this booby with whom she regretted having saddled herself.

When the aspect of the landscape began to change and I ceased to recognize the dress and accent of the Breton peasants, I fell into a profound despondency, which increased the contempt in which Madame Rose held me. I noticed the feeling I inspired, and I received from this first trial of the world an impression which time has not wholly effaced. I was born shy but not shamefaced; I had the modesty but not the embarrassment of my years. When I suspected that I was ridiculous because of my good side, my shyness changed into insurmountable timidity. I was unable to speak a word: I felt that I had something to conceal, and that this something was a virtue; I made up my mind to self-concealment in order to wear my innocence in peace.

We sped towards Paris. As we came down from Saint-Cyr, I was struck by the width of the roads and the evenness of the plantations. Soon we reached Versailles: the orangery with its marble stairs amazed me. The success of the American War had brought triumphs to Louis XIV.'s palace; the Queen reigned there in all the splendour of youth and beauty; the Throne, so near its fall, seemed never to have been more solidly established. And I, an obscure passer-by, was destined to outlive this pomp, to survive to see the woods of Trianon as deserted as those which I was then leaving.

At last we drove into Paris. I saw a bantering look in every face: like the Périgord squire, I thought people looked at me to make fun of me. Madame Rose made them drive to the Hôtel de l'Europe in the Rue du Mail, and hastened to rid herself of her simpleton. Scarce had I stepped from the carriage when she said to the porter:

"Give this gentleman a room. Your servant," she added, with a bob courtesy.

I never saw Madame Rose again in my life.

A woman preceded me up a dark and steep staircase, holding a labelled key in her hand; a Savoyard followed with my little trunk. When we reached the third floor, the chambermaid opened a room; the Savoyard put the trunk across the arms of a chair.

The chamber-maid asked: "Does monsieur require anything?"

I answered, "No."

Three whistles sounded; the chamber-maid cried, "Coming!"

rushed out, closed the door, and tumbled downstairs with the Savoyard. When I found myself alone in my room, my heart became so strangely full that I was nearly taking the road back to Brittany. All that I had heard tell of Paris returned to my mind; I was embarrassed in a hundred ways. I should have liked to go to bed, and the bed was not made; I was hungry, and did not know how to set about dining. I was afraid of committing a solecism: ought I to call the people of the hotel? Ought I to go downstairs? To whom should I apply? I ventured to put my head out of the window: I saw only a small inner yard, deep as a well, through which people came and went who would never dream of giving a thought to the prisoner on the third floor. I went and sat down beside the dirty recess in which I was to sleep, reduced to examining the figures on the paper with which its walls were hung. A distant sound of voices reached my ears, increased, drew nigh; my door opened: in came my brother and one of my cousins, the son of a sister of my mother's who had made none too good a marriage. Madame Rose had after all taken pity on the numskull, and had sent word to my brother, whose address she learnt at Rennes, that I had arrived in Paris. My brother clasped me in his arms. My Cousin Moreau was a big fat man, daubed all over with snuff, who ate like an ogre, talked a great deal, was always trotting about, puffing, choking, with his mouth half open, his tongue half out, who knew everybody, and was equally at home in gaming-houses, antechambers, and drawing-rooms.

"Come, chevalier," he cried, "so here you are in Paris; I am going to take you to Madame de Chastenay's!"

Who was this woman whose name I heard uttered for the first time? This proposal set me against my Cousin Moreau.

"The chevalier is no doubt in need of rest," said my brother; "we will go and see Madame de Farcy, and then he shall come back to dine and sleep."

A feeling of gladness entered my heart: the thought of my family amid an indifferent world was as balm to me. We went out. Cousin Moreau raised a storm about the badness of the room, and charged my host to put me at least one floor lower. We stepped into my brother's carriage and drove to the convent where Madame de Farcy lived.

Julie had been some time in Paris to consult the physicians. Her charming appearance, her elegance and her wit had soon caused her to be sought after. I have already said that she was born with a real talent for poetry. She became a saint, after having been one of the most attractive women of her age: the Abbé Carron wrote her life.[1] The apostles who go everywhere in search of souls feel for her the love which one of the Fathers of the Church attributes to the Creator: "When a soul reaches Heaven," says this Father, with the simplicity of heart of a Primitive Christian and the directness of Greek genius, "God takes it upon His knees and calls it His daughter."

Lucile has left a striking lament: *À la sœur que je n'ai plus.* The Abbé Carron's admiration for Julie explains and justifies Lucile's words. The narrative of the saintly priest also shows that I said true in the preface to the *Génie du Christianisme,* and serves as a proof for some portions of my Memoirs.

The innocent Julie gave herself up to repentance; she consecrated the treasures of her austerities to the redemption of her brothers; and following the example of the illustrious African her patron saint,[2] she became a willing martyr.

The Abbé Carron, author of the *Vie des justes,* is the ecclesiastic from my part of the country,[3] the Francis of Paula of exile, whose fame, revealed by the afflicted, pierced even through the fame of Bonaparte. The voice of a poor proscribed priest was not stifled by the noise of a revolution which overthrew society; he seems to have returned expressly from foreign shores to write of my sister's virtues: he sought among our ruins and found a forgotten victim and tomb.

When the new hagiographer describes Julie's pious cruelties, it is as though one heard Bossuet preach his sermon on the profession of faith of Mademoiselle de la Vallière:[4]

"Will she dare to touch that body so tender, so dear, so gently treated? Will she not take pity on that delicate complexion? On the contrary, it is that principally which the soul

---

[1] I have inserted the life of my sister Julie in the supplement to these Memoirs.—*Author's Note.* This life, extracted from the Abbé Carron's *Vie des justes,* I omit. It will be found in the last series of the *Vie des justes,* entitled, *Dans les plus hauts rangs de la société.* The Abbé Guy Toussaint Julien Carron (1760-1820) was the founder of the Institut Royal de Marie-Thérèse, established under the patronage of the Duchesse d'Anjoulême for the daughters of families which had lost their fortune in the Revolution, in addition to a number of charitable institutions founded during the Emigration at Somers Town, to which Chateaubriand refers *infra.*—T.

[2] St. Julia, Virgin and Martyr (22 May), was born at Carthage, and died for the Faith in Corsica, *circa* 439.—T.

[3] The Abbé Carron was born at Rennes.—T.

[4] Louise Françoise de La Baume Le Blanc de La Vallière (1644-1710), the unselfish mistress of Louis XIV. After twice seeking refuge in a convent, she definitely withdrew to the Carmelites in the Faubourg Saint-Jacques in 1674, and took the veil in 1675, from which date to that of her death she submitted herself to exercises of the most austere piety.—T.

arraigns as its most dangerous seducer; she hems herself round with safeguards; fenced in in every direction, she can no longer breathe except heavenwards!"

I cannot suppress a certain confusion at reading my name in the last lines traced by the hand of Julie's venerable biographer. What have I, with my weaknesses, to do with such lofty perfections? Have I kept all that my sister's letter made me promise, when I received it during my emigration in London? Is a book sufficient for God? Is it not my life that I ought to offer Him? And is that life, pray, true to the *Génie du Christianisme?* What matter that I have drawn more or less brilliant pictures of religion, if my passions cast a shade over my faith! I have not gone on to the end; I have not donned the hair-shirt: that tunic of my viaticum would have drunk up and dried my sweat. Instead, a weary traveller, I sat down by the roadside: tired or not, I shall have to get up again in order to arrive where my sister has arrived.

There is nothing wanting to Julie's glory: the Abbé Carron has written her life; Lucile has mourned her death.

When I saw Julie again in Paris, she was in all the pomp of worldliness; she appeared covered with those flowers, adorned with those necklaces, veiled in those scented fabrics which St. Clement forbids the early Christian women. St. Basil wishes the middle of the night to be for the solitary what the morning is for the others, so that he may profit by the silence of nature. The middle of the night was the hour at which Julie went to parties at which her verses, recited with marvellous euphony by herself, formed the principal attraction.

Julie was infinitely handsomer than Lucile: she had soft blue eyes and dark hair, which she wore plaited or in large waves. Her hands and arms, models of whiteness and shape, added, by their graceful movements, something yet more charming to her already charming figure. She was brilliant, lively, laughed much, but without affectation, and, when she laughed, showed teeth like pearls. A crowd of portraits of women of the time of Louis XIV. resembled Julie, among others those of the three Mortemarts; but she had more elegance than Madame de Montespan.[1]

---

[1] The Marquise de Montespan (1641-1707), mistress to Louis XIV. and successor to Mademoiselle de La Vallière, was one of the three daughters of Gabriel de Rochechouart, Duc de Mortemart; her sisters were the Marquise de Thianges and the Abbesse de Fontevrault.—T.

Julie received me with the affection which one finds only in a sister. I had a sense of protection when pressed in her arms, her ribbons, her bouquet of roses, and her laces. Nothing replaces the attachment, delicacy and devotion of a woman; a man is forgotten by his brothers and friends, denied by his companions: but never by his mother, his sister, or his wife. When Harold was slain at the Battle of Hastings, none could point him out in the crowd of the dead; they had to seek the assistance of a young girl whom he loved. She came, and the unfortunate Prince was recognized by Edith the swan-necked:

Editha swaneshales, quod sonat collum cycni.

My brother took me back to my hotel; he ordered my dinner and left me. I dined alone, and went sadly to bed. I passed my first night in Paris regretting my moors and trembling before the dimness of my future.

At eight o'clock the next morning, my fat cousin arrived; he had already done five or six errands:

"Well, chevalier, we are going to breakfast; we shall dine with Pommereul, and this evening I shall take you to Madame de Chastenay's."

This seemed to me a fate, and I resigned myself. Everything happened as my cousin had proposed. After breakfast he pretended to show me Paris, and dragged me through the dirtiest streets in the neighbourhood of the Palais Royal, telling me of the dangers to which a young man was exposed. We were punctual in keeping our appointment for dinner, at an eating-house. Everything put before us seemed bad to me. The conversation and the dinner-guests revealed a new world to me. The talk turned upon the Court, the financial projects, the Academy sittings, the women and intrigues of the day, the latest piece, the success of the actors, actresses and authors.

Several Bretons were among the guests, including the Chevalier de Guer[1] and Pommereul.[2] The latter was a good talker, who has since described some of Bonaparte's campaigns,

---

[1] Julien Hyacinthe de Marnière, Chevalier de Guer (1748–1816), born at Rennes, an active member of the Royalist party.—B.

[2] François René Jean, Baron de Pommereul (1745–1823), born at Fougères, became a general of division in 1796 and director-general of the State press and publishing department in 1811. The work to which Chateaubriand alludes is Pommereul's *Campagnes du général Bonaparte en Italie pendant les années IV. et V. de la République Française.*—B.

and who, when I met him again, was at the head of the Publishing Department.

Under the Empire, Pommereul achieved a sort of renown by his hatred for the nobility.[1] And nevertheless Pommereul claimed, and with just cause, to be of gentle birth himself. He signed his name "Pommereux," and spoke of his descent from the Pommereux family mentioned in the letters of Madame de Sévigné.[2]

After dinner my brother wanted to take me to the play, but my cousin claimed me for Madame de Chastenay, and I went with him to meet my destiny. I saw a handsome woman, no longer in her first youth, but still capable of inspiring an attachment. She received me kindly, tried to put me at my ease, asked me about my part of the country and my regiment. I was awkward and embarrassed; I made signs to my cousin to cut short the visit. But he, without looking at me, was inexhaustible on the subject of my merits, declaring that I had written verses at my mother's breast, and calling upon me to sing Madame de Chastenay. She relieved me from this painful situation, begged me to forgive her for being obliged to go out, and invited me to come back and see her the next morning, in so gentle a voice that I involuntarily promised to obey.

The next day I returned alone: I found her in bed in an elegantly fitted room. She told me that she was not very well, and that she had the bad habit of rising late. For the first time I found myself by the bedside of a woman who was neither my mother nor my sister. She had observed my shyness on the evening before, and so far conquered it that I ventured to express myself with some sort of ease. She stretched towards me a half-bared arm and the most beautiful hand in the world, and said with a smile:

"We shall become friends."

I did not even kiss that beautiful hand; I withdrew quite confused. The next day I left for Cambrai. Who was this Dame de Chastenay? I have no idea: she passed like a charming shade across my life.

The mail-coach brought me to my quarters. One of my brothers-in-law, the Vicomte de Chateaubourg (he had married

---

[1] I omit a remark of Pommereul's, applied to the nobles who accepted the post of Chamberlain at the Imperial Court, which is too indelicate for translation.—T.

[2] Of 4, 11, and 18 December 1675.—B.

my sister Bénigne, widow of the Comte de Québriac[1]) had
given me letters of recommendation to some of the officers
of my regiment. The Chevalier de Guénan, a man of very
good company, introduced me to a mess at which dined officers
distinguished for their talents, Messieurs Achard, des Mahis,
La Martinière. The Marquis de Mortemart[2] was colonel of
the regiment; the Comte d'Andrezel[3] major: I was placed
under the special protection of the latter. I met both of them
in after years: one of them became my colleague in the House
of Peers; the other applied to me for some services which I
was happy to show him. There is a melancholy pleasure in
meeting persons whom we have known at different periods of
our life, and in contemplating the changes that have taken
place in their mode of existence and our own. Like land-
marks left behind us, they trace for us the road which we have
followed in the desert of the past.

I joined my regiment in mufti; within twenty-four hours I
had assumed the military dress, and I felt as though I had
worn it always. My uniform was blue and white, like my
vowing-clothes of years before: I marched under the same
colours as a young man and as a child. I was submitted to
none of the trials which the sub-lieutenants were in the habit
of inflicting upon a newcomer; for some reason not known
to me, they did not venture to indulge in this military child's-
play with me. Before I had been a fortnight with the regiment, I was treated like an "ancient." I learnt the manual
exercise and theory with ease; I passed my steps of corporal
and sergeant to the applause of my instructors. My room
became the meeting-place of the old captains as well as of
the young sub-lieutenants; the former went over their campaigns with me, the latter confided to me their love-affairs.

La Martinière would come to fetch me to hang about the
door of a belle of Cambrai whom he adored; this happened five
or six times a day. He was very ugly, and his face was pitted
with the small-pox. He told me of his passion while quaffing
large glasses of gooseberry-syrup, which I sometimes paid for.

[1] Bénigne Jeanne de Chateaubriand, Comtesse de Québriac, married as her
second husband, in 1786, Paul François de la Celle, Vicomte de Chateaubourg, a
captain in the Condé Regiment, and a knight of St. Louis.—B.
[2] Victurnien Bonaventure Victor de Rochechouart, Marquis de Mortemart
(1753–1823), served in the army of Condé under the Emigration, and was created
a peer of France and lieutenant-general at the Restoration.—B.
[3] Christophe François Thérèse Picon, Comte d'Andrezel (1746–1821), also emigrated and fought in the Princes' Army. On the return of the Bourbons he
exercised the functions of sub-prefect of Saint-Dié from 1815 till the year of his
death.—B.

All would have gone wonderfully well, but for my insane rage for dress. At that time they affected the stiffness of the Prussian uniform: a small hat, small curls pressed tight to the head, a pig-tail tied very fast, a closely-buttoned coat. I disliked this greatly; I submitted to these shackles during the day, but in the evening, when I hoped to escape the eyes of my superior officers, I put on a larger hat; the barber lowered the curls of my hair and loosened my pig-tail; I unbuttoned and turned back the facings of my coat. In this fond undress, I would go a-wooing on La Martinière's behalf under the cruel Fleming's windows. But one fine day brought me face to face with M. d'Andrezel.

"What is this, sir?" said the terrible major. "Consider yourself under arrest for three days."

I felt somewhat humiliated, but recognized the truth of the proverb that it is an ill wind that blows nobody good: I was delivered from my messmate's love-affairs.

I read *Télémaque* beside Fénelon's tomb:[1] I was not much in the humour for the philanthropic tale of the cow and the bishop. It amuses me to recall the beginning of my career. When passing through Cambrai with the King, after the Hundred Days, I looked for the house I had lived in and the coffee-house I used to frequent, but could not find them: all had vanished, men and monuments.

In the same year in which I was undergoing my military apprenticeship at Cambrai, we heard of the death of Frederic II.;[2] I am now ambassador to that great King's nephew,[3] and am writing this portion of my Memoirs in Berlin. Upon that piece of important public news followed sorrowful news for me: Lucile wrote to me that my father had been carried off by a fit of apoplexy two days after the Angevin Fair, one of the delights of my childhood.

Among the authentic documents which I keep for consultation I find the death-certificates of my parents. As these documents also in a special manner mark the death of a century, I place them on record here as constituting a page of history.

[1] François de Salignac de La Mothe-Fénelon (1651-1715), author of the *Aventures de Télémaque*, was Archbishop of Cambrai and is buried in the cathedral.—T.

[2] Frederic II., or the Great (1712-1786), King of Prussia, died on the 17th of August, twenty days before the Comte de Chateaubriand, as mentioned above. —T.

[3] Frederic William III. (1770-1840), son of Frederick William II., and grand-nephew of Frederick the Great, succeeded his father in 1797.—T.

" Extract from the death-register of the parish of Combourg, for 1786, upon which is written as follows, page 8, *verso:*

" The body of the high and mighty Messire René de Chateaubriand, knight, Count of Combourg, Lord of Gaugres, the Plessis-l'Épine, Boulet, Malestroit in Dol, and other places, husband of the high and mighty Dame Appoline Jeanne Suzanne de Bedée de La Bouëtardais, Lady Countess of Combourg, aged about sixty-nine years, who died in his castle of Combourg, on the sixth of September, about eight o'clock of the evening, was interred on the eighth, in the vault of the said lordship, situated in the crypt of our church of Combourg, in presence of messieurs the undersigned noblemen, officers of the jurisdiction, and other notable burgesses. Signed in the register: Comte de Petitbois, de Monlouët, de Chateaudassy, Delaunay, Morault, Noury de Mauny, advocate; Hermer, procurator; Petit, advocate and procurator-fiscal; Robion, Portal, le Donarin, de Trevelec, Rector and Dean of Dingé; Sévin, rector."

In the "collated copy" delivered in 1812 by M. Lodin, Mayor of Combourg, the nineteen words giving the titles "high and mighty Messire" &c., are struck out.

"Extract from the death-register of the town of Saint-Servan, first arrondissement of the Department of Ille-et-Vilaine, for the Year VI. of the Republic, page 35, *recto*, upon which is written as follows:

" On the twelfth of Prairial Year Six of the French Republic, before me, Jacques Bourdasse, municipal officer of the commune of Saint-Servan, elected to public office on the fourth of Floréal last, have appeared Jean Baslé, gardener, and Joseph Boulin, day-labourer, who have declared to me that Appoline Jeanne Suzanne de Bedée, widow of René Auguste de Chateaubriand, died this day, at one o'clock after noon, at the house of Citizeness Gouyon, situated at the Ballue, in this commune. After which declaration, of the truth of which I have made sure, I have drawn up the present deed, which Jean Baslé alone has signed with me, Joseph Boulin declaring that he did not know how, after question put.

" Done at the communal house on the said day and year. Signed: Jean Baslé and Bourdasse."

In the first extract, the old society exists: M. de Chateaubriand is a "high and mighty lord," &c., &c.; the witnesses

are "noblemen" and "notable burgesses"; among the signa-
tories I find the Marquis de Monlouët, who used to stop at
Combourg Castle in the winter, the Curé Sévin, who had so
much difficulty in believing me to be the author of the *Génie
du Christianisme:* faithful guests of my father even at his last
abode. But my father did not sleep long in his shroud:
he was cast out of it when Old France was cast into the
common sewer.

In the mortuary extract of my mother, the earth revolves
upon another axis: a new world, a new era; even the com-
putation of the years and the names of the months are changed.
Madame de Chateaubriand is nothing more than a poor woman
who departs this life at the residence of "Citizeness" Gouyon;
a gardener and a day-labourer, who does not know how to sign
his name, alone testify to my mother's death: of friends and
relations there are none; no funeral state; sole by-stander, the
Revolution.[1]

I mourned the death of M. de Chateaubriand: it showed
him to me better than he was; I remembered neither his harshness nor his failings. I seemed to see him as he walked in the
evenings in the hall at Combourg; I was moved by the thought
of these family scenes. If my father's affection for me was
affected by his natural severity, it was none the less deep at
heart. The ferocious Maréchal de Montluc,[2] who, disfigured
by a terrible cut in the nose, was obliged to conceal the horrible
nature of his glory beneath a strip of rag, this man of blood
reproaches himself for his harshness towards a son whom he
has lost:

"This poor lad," he said, "has seen nothing of me save
a frowning face and full of scorn; he has died in this belief,
that I neither knew how to love him nor to esteem him to his
deserts. For whom did I keep it to discover the singular
affection which I bore him in my soul? Was it not he who
should have had all the pleasure of it and all the obligation?
I have constrained and tortured myself to keep on this vain
mask, and in thus doing have lost the pleasure of his converse,

---

[1] My nephew, Breton fashion, Frédéric de Chateaubriand, son of my cousin
Armand, has purchased the Ballue, where my mother died.—*Author's Note.*

[2] Marshal Blaise de Montluc (*circa* 1502–1577), a valiant captain of Francis I.,
Henry II. and Francis II. Under Charles IX. he defeated the Huguenots in
several encounters, and set himself to extirpate heresy by means of wholesale
executions, which earned for him the nickname of the Royalist Butcher. He
received his marshal's baton at the hands of Henry III.—T.

and his will in all things, which he cannot have borne to me other than very coldly, having never received from me aught save rudeness, nor been treated save in tyrannous fashion."

My "will was not borne very coldly" towards my father, and I do not doubt that, in spite of his "tyrannous fashion," he loved me tenderly: he would, I am sure, have regretted me had Providence called me before him. But would he, had we remained on earth together, have set store by the fame that has sprung from my life? A literary reputation would have wounded his nobility; he would have seen nothing but degeneration in his son's gifts; even the Berlin Embassy, conquered by the pen, not the sword, would have indifferently satisfied him. His Breton blood, besides, made him a political malcontent, a great opponent of taxation and a violent enemy of the Court. He read the *Gazette de Leyde*, the *Journal de Francfort*, the *Mercure de France*, and the *Histoire philosophique des deux Indes*, the declamatory style of which delighted him. He called the Abbé Raynal[1] "a master man." In diplomacy, he was an anti-Mussulman; he declared that forty thousand "Russian rascals" would march over the Janissaries' stomachs and take Constantinople. Hater of the Turks though he were, my father nevertheless bore a grudge in his heart against the "Russian rascals," because of his encounter at Dantzic.

I share M. de Chateaubriand's opinions as regards literary and other reputations, but for different reasons. I do not know of a fame in history that tempts me: had I to stoop to pick up at my feet and to my advantage the greatest glory in the world, I would not take the trouble. If I had formed my own clay, perhaps I would have created myself a woman, for love of them; or if I had made myself a man, I would in the first place have granted myself beauty; next, as a safeguard against weariness, my stubborn enemy, it would have suited me fairly well to be a consummate but unknown artist, using my talent only for the benefit of my solitude. In life, weighed by its light weight, measured by its short measure, relieved of all its cheating, there are but two things true: religion with intelligence, love with youth; that is to say, the future and the present: the rest is not worth while.

---

[1] Guillaume Thomas François Raynal (1713–1796), editor of the *Mercure* and author of, among other works, the *Histoire philosophique des établissements et du commerce des Européens dans les Deux-Indes* (1770). This work is full of political and anti-religious declamations, and was placed upon the Index in consequence. He published in 1780 a new and still bolder edition, which was condemned in 1781.—T.

With my father's death ended the first act of my life; the paternal home became empty; I pitied it, as though it were capable of feeling desertion and solitude. Thenceforth I was independent and master of my fortune: this liberty frightened me. What should I do with it? To whom give it? I mistrusted my strength: I retreated before myself.

I obtained a furlough. M. d'Andrezel, promoted to Lieutenant-colonel of the Picardy Regiment, was leaving Paris: I served as his courier. I passed through Paris, where I refused to stop for a quarter of an hour; I set eyes upon the moors of my Brittany with more joy than that with which a Neapolitan, banished to our climes, would gaze again upon the shores of Portici, the champaign of Sorrento. My family came together; we settled the division of the property; when that was done, we dispersed, as birds fly away from the paternal nest. My brother, who had come from Paris, returned there; my mother established herself at Saint-Malo; Lucile accompanied Julie; I spent a part of my time with Mesdames de Marigny, de Chateaubourg and de Farcy. Marigny,[1] my eldest sister's country-seat, is pleasantly situated, three leagues from Fougères, between two lakes, and amidst woods, rocks and meadows. I stayed there peacefully for some months; a letter from Paris came to disturb my repose.

At the moment of entering the service and marrying Mademoiselle de Rosanbo, my brother had not yet quitted the long robe; for this reason he was unable to obtain the privilege of riding in the King's coaches. His eager ambition suggested to him to make me enjoy Court honours in order to prepare the way for his own rise. Our proofs of nobility had been made out for Lucile when she was received into the Chapter of the Argentière, so that everything was ready; the Maréchal de Duras was to be my sponsor. My brother wrote to me that I was on the high-road to fortune; that already I was to obtain the rank of a cavalry captain, an honorary and courtesy rank; that it would be easy to secure my admission to the Order of Malta, by means of which I should enjoy fat benefices. This letter came upon me like a thunder-bolt: to return to

[1] The Château de Marigny exists in the commune of Saint-Germain-en-Coglès, canton of Saint-Brice-en-Coglès, Arrondissement of Fougères (Ille-et-Vilaine). Balzac laid the scene of his *Chouans* in the neighbourhood of Fougères, and wrote his novel at Marigny, where he was staying as the guest of General the Baron de Pommereul. The Comtesse de Marigny died 18 July 1860, in her one hundred and first year.—B.

Paris, to be presented at Court, I who almost swooned away when I met three or four strangers in a drawing-room! To imbue me with ambition, who only dreamt of living forgotten! My first impulse was to reply to my brother that it was his duty, as the eldest, to keep up his name; that, as for me, a plain Breton younger son, I would not give up the service, as there was a chance of war; but that, though the King might have need of a soldier in his army, he had no need of a poor gentleman at his Court.

I hastened to read this romantic reply to Madame de Marigny, who uttered loud cries; she sent for Madame de Farcy, who laughed at me; Lucile would have supported me, but she dared not contend with her sisters. They tore my letter from me, and, weak as always where I myself am concerned, I informed my brother that I was ready to go.

I did go; I went to be presented at the first Court in Europe, to make the most brilliant start in life; and I looked like a man who is being dragged to the galleys or expecting a sentence of death.

I entered Paris by the same road which I had taken the first time; I went to the same hotel, in the Rue du Mail: I knew no other. I was taken to a room next door to my old one, but a little larger and overlooking the street.

My brother, whether because he felt embarrassed by my manners, or because he took pity upon my shyness, did not take me with him into the world, and introduced me to nobody. He lived in the Rue des Fossés-Montmartre; I went to him at three o'clock every day for dinner; we then parted and did not see one another till the next day. My fat Cousin Moreau was no longer in Paris. I walked twice or thrice past Madame de Chastenay's house, without venturing to ask the porter if she was still there.

Autumn set in. I rose at six; went to the riding-school; breakfasted. Luckily at that time I had a passion for Greek; I translated the *Odyssey* and the *Cyropædia* until two o'clock, interspersing my labours with the study of history. At two o'clock I dressed and went to my brother; he asked me what I had done, what I had seen; I replied, "Nothing." He shrugged his shoulders and turned his back upon me. One day there was a noise outside; my brother ran to the window and called to me: I refused to leave the arm-chair in which I lay stretched at the back of the room. My poor brother prophesied to me that I should die unknown, useless to myself or my family. At four o'clock I went home and sat down at my window. Two young girls of fifteen or sixteen used to come at that hour to sketch at the window of a house opposite, on the other side of the street. They had noticed my punctuality, as I had theirs. From time to time they raised their heads to look at their neighbour; I was infinitely grateful to them for this mark of attention: they formed my only society in Paris.

When night drew near, I went to the play. I took pleasure in the desert of the crowd, though it always cost me a little effort to take my ticket at the door and mix with other men. I corrected the ideas which I had formed at the Saint-Malo theatre. I saw Madame Saint-Huberti[1] as Armida; I felt that there had been something lacking in the sorceress of my creating. When I did not imprison myself in the Opera-house or at the Français, I wandered from street to street or along the quays until ten or eleven in the evening. To this day I cannot see the row of street-lamps from the Place Louis XV. to the Barrière des Bons-Hommes, without remembering the agonies which I endured when I followed that road to go to Versailles for my presentation.

On returning home, I spent a portion of the night with my head bowed over my fire, which told me nothing: I had not, like the Persians, an imagination rich enough to persuade me that the flame resembled the anemone, the cinders the pomegranate. I listened to the carriages coming, going, crossing each other; their distant rolling imitated the murmur of the sea upon the shores of my Brittany or of the wind in the Combourg woods. These worldly sounds which reminded me of those of solitude aroused my regrets; I conjured up my old trouble, or else my imagination would invent the story of the persons whom those chariots were bearing away: I saw radiant drawing-rooms, balls, loves, conquests. Soon, relapsing into myself, I saw myself as I was, alone in an inn, seeing the world through the window and hearing it by the echoes of my fireside.

Rousseau considers that he owes it to his sincerity, and to the instruction of mankind, to confess the covert pleasures of his life; he even supposes that he is being seriously questioned and asked for an account of his sins with the

---

[1] Antoinette Cécile Clavel (*circa* 1756–1812), first singer at the Opera. Her features were not beautiful but exceedingly expressive; she excelled in Gluck's operas. She was first married to an adventurer called Saint-Huberti, and later to the Comte d'Entragues, whom she had followed into the Emigration. They were both assassinated at their cottage on the Terrace, Barnes, by an Italian servant who had been dismissed the day before.—T.

donne pericolante of Venice. Had I prostituted myself to the
courtesans of Paris, I should not have thought myself obliged
to inform posterity of the fact; but I was too shy on the one
hand, too much exalted on the other, to allow myself to be
seduced by women of the town. When I passed through
groups of these unfortunates falling upon the passers-by in
order to drag them up to their rooms, like the Saint-Cloud
cabmen trying to induce travellers to enter their flies, I was
seized with horror and disgust. The pleasures of adventure
would have suited me only in the days of old.

In the fourteenth, fifteenth, sixteenth, and seventeenth
centuries, our imperfect civilization, our superstitious beliefs,
our strange and half-barbarous customs mingled romance with
everything: characters were strongly marked, imagination
was powerful, existence mysterious and concealed. At
night, around the high walls of the graveyards and convents,
beneath the deserted ramparts of the town, along the chains
and ditches of the market-places, on the skirts of enclosures
in narrow, lampless streets, where robbers and murderers lay
in ambush, where meetings took place sometimes by torchlight,
sometimes in the thick of darkness, it was at the risk of his
head that one sought the trysting-place granted by some
Héloïse. To abandon himself to disorder, one had really
to love; to violate public morals, one had to make great
sacrifices. Not only was it a matter of confronting fortuitous
dangers and defying the sword of the law, but one was obliged
to overcome the empire of regular habits, the authority of
the family, the tyranny of domestic customs, the opposition
of conscience, the terrors and duties of the Christian. All
these obstacles doubled the energy of the passions.

In 1788, I would not have followed a starving wretch who
would have dragged me to the den where she lived under
police supervision; but it is probable that, in 1606, I should
have seen the end of an adventure of the kind which Bassompierre[1] has told so well.

"Five or six months ago," says the marshal, "each time
that I passed over the Petit Pont"—for in those days the Pont
Neuf was not built—"a pretty woman, a sempstress at the

---

[1] François Maréchal Baron de Bassompierre (1579–1646), figured at the
Court of Henry IV., and in the wars of Henry IV. and Louis XIII. The latter
monarch created him a marshal, and employed him upon various embassies. He
succeeded, however, in incurring the displeasure of Richelieu, who imprisoned
him in the Bastille in 1631, where he remained until the Cardinal's death in 1643.
It was there that he wrote his famous Memoirs.—T.

sign of the Two Angels, made me deep courtesies and followed me with her eyes as far as she could; and as I had heeded her action, I also looked at her and greeted her with greater care.

"It happened that when I arrived from Fontainebleau in Paris, passing over the Petit Pont, so soon as she saw me coming, she put herself at the door of her shop, and said, as I passed:

"'Sir, I am your servant.'

"I returned her greeting, and turning round from time to time, I saw that she followed me with her eyes as far as she could."

Bassompierre obtained an assignation.

"I found," he says, "a very beautiful woman, twenty years of age, who had her head dressed for the night, wearing naught but a very fine shift and a short petticoat of green stuff, and slippers on her feet, with a wrapper around her. She pleased me mightily. I asked her if I could not see her once again.

"'If you wish to see me again,' she replied, 'it shall be at the house of one of my aunts, who lives in the Rue Bourg-l'Abbé, near the Markets, next to the Rue aux Ours, the third door on the side of the Rue Saint-Martin; I will await you there from ten o'clock till midnight, and later yet; I will leave the door open. At the entrance, there is a little passage through which you will go quickly, for the door of my aunt's room opens on it, and you will find a stair which will bring you to the second floor.'

"I came at ten o'clock and found the door she had indicated, and a great light, not only on the second floor, but on the third and the first too; but the door was closed. I knocked to show that I had come; but I heard a man's voice ask who I was. I returned to the Rue aux Ours, and having returned for the second time, finding the door opened, I climbed to the second floor, where I found that the light was the straw of the bed which they were burning, and two naked bodies lying upon the table in the room. Thereupon I retired greatly amazed, and in going out I met some crows"—buriers of the dead— "who asked me what I sought; and I, to make them turn aside, took sword in hand and passed out, returning to my lodging, somewhat moved by this unlooked-for sight."[1]

I in my turn went on a voyage of discovery, with the address given, two hundred and forty years before, by Bassompierre. I crossed the Petit Pont, passed the Markets, and

---

[1] *Mémoires du maréchal de Bassompierre, contenant l'histoire de sa vie et ce qui s'est fait de plus remarquable à la cour de France jusqu'en* 1640, I. 305.—B.

followed the Rue Saint-Denis as far as the Rue aux Ours, on the right; the first street on the left, ending in the Rue aux Ours, is the Rue Bourg-l'Abbé. Its inscription, smoky as though through time and a fire, gave me good hope. I found the "third little door on the side of the Rue Saint-Martin," so faithful are the historian's directions. There, unfortunately, the two centuries and a half, which at first I thought had lingered in the street, disappear. The frontage of the house is modern; no light issued from the first, nor from the second, nor from the third floor. From the attic-windows, beneath the roof, hung a garland of nasturtiums and sweet peas; on the ground-floor, a hairdresser's shop displayed a variety of towers of hair behind the window-panes.

In great discomfiture, I entered this museum of the Eponines: since the Roman Conquest, the Gallic women have always sold their yellow tresses to foreheads less richly decked; my Breton countrywomen still let themselves be shorn on certain fair-days, and barter the natural veil of their heads for an Indian kerchief. Addressing a barber, who was drawing a wig over an iron comb:

"Sir," said I, "do you happen to have purchased the hair of a young sempstress who used to live at the sign of the Two Angels, near the Petit Pont?"

He stood dumfoundered, unable to say either yes or no. I asked a thousand pardons, and made my way out through a labyrinth of toupees.

I wandered next from door to door: no sempstress, twenty years of age, making me "deep courtesies;" no frank, disinterested, passionate young woman, "her head dressed for the night, wearing naught but a very fine shift, a short petticoat of green stuff, and slippers on her feet, with a wrapper around her." A grumbling old crone, ready to join her teeth in the tomb, was near to beating me with her crutch: perhaps it was the aunt of the assignation!

What a fine story, that story of Bassompierre's! One of the reasons for which he was so resolutely loved has to be understood. At that time, the French were divided into two classes, one dominant, the other semi-servile. The sempstress clasped Bassompierre in her arms like a demi-god who had descended to the bosom of a slave: he gave her the illusion of glory, and Frenchwomen alone among women are capable of intoxicating themselves with that illusion. But who will reveal to us the unknown causes of the catastrophe? Was the body which lay upon the table by the side of another body that of the pretty wench of the Two Angels? Whose was the other body? Was it the husband, or the man whose voice Bassompierre had heard? Had the plague (for the plague was raging in Paris) or jealousy reached the Rue Bourg-l'Abbé before love? The imagination can easily find matter for its exercises in such a subject as this. Mingle with the poet's inventions the chorus of the populace, the approaching grave-diggers, the "crows," and Bassompierre's sword, and a magnificent melodrama springs from the adventure.

You will also admire the chastity and reserve of my youthful life in Paris: in that capital I was free to give way to all my whims, as in the Abbey of Thélème, where each acted according to his wish. Nevertheless, I did not abuse my independence: I had no commerce except with a courtesan two hundred and sixty years of age, who had formerly been smitten with a marshal of France, the rival of the Bearnese [1] for the affections of Mademoiselle de Montmorency, and the lover of Mademoiselle d'Entragues, sister to the Marquise de Verneuil, [2] who speaks so ill of Henry IV. Louis XVI., whom I was about to see, had no suspicion of my secret relations with his family.

The fatal day arrived; I had to set out for Versailles, more dead than alive. My brother took me there the day before my presentation, and carried me to the Maréchal de Duras, a worthy man with a mind so commonplace that it reflected a certain homeliness over his fine manners; nevertheless, the good marshal frightened me terribly.

The next morning I went alone to the palace. He has seen nothing who has not seen the pomp of Versailles, even after the disbanding of the old Royal Household: Louis XIV. still lingered there. All went well so long as I had only to pass through the guard-room: military display has always pleased and never awed me. But when I entered the Œil-de-bœuf and found myself among the courtiers, my distress commenced. I was scrutinized; I heard them ask who I was. One must remember the former prestige of royalty to realize the importance of a presentation in those days. A mysterious destiny clung to the *débutant;* he was spared the contemptuous air

---

[1] Henry IV. (1553–1610), King of France and Navarre, born at Pau in the Province of Béarn.—T.

[2] Catherine Henriette de Balzac d'Entragues, Marquise de Verneuil (1583–1633), daughter of François d'Entragues, Governor of Orleans, and of Marie Touchet, mistress of Charles IX. She became Henry IV.'s mistress after the death of Gabrielle d'Estrées, and bitterly resented his marriage to Marie de Médicis, the more so as the King had given her a written promise of marriage, which was torn up by the Duc de Sully.—T.

of protection which, coupled with extreme politeness, composed the inimitable manners of the grandee. Who was to tell that that *débutant* would not become the master's favourite? In him was respected the future familiarity with which he might be honoured. Nowadays we rush to the palace with even greater eagerness than before, and, strangely enough, with no illusions: a courtier reduced to living on truths is very near to dying of hunger.

When the King's levee was announced, the persons not presented withdrew; I felt an impulse of vanity: I was not proud of remaining, but I should have felt humiliated at leaving. The door of the King's bed-chamber opened; I saw the King, according to custom, complete his toilet, in other words take his hat from the hand of the first lord-in-waiting. The King came towards me on his way to Mass; I bowed; the Maréchal de Duras mentioned my name:

"Sire, the Chevalier de Chateaubriand."

The King looked at me, returned my bow, hesitated, appeared to wish to address me. I should have replied boldly: my shyness had vanished. To speak to the general of the army, to the head of the State, seemed quite simple to me, though I could not account for what I felt. The King's embarrassment was greater than mine; he could think of nothing to say to me, and passed on. The vanity of human destinies: this sovereign whom I saw for the first time, this powerful monarch was Louis XVI., but six years removed from the scaffold! And the new courtier at whom he scarcely looked, charged with separating dead bones from dead bones, after having been presented, upon proof of nobility, to the majesty of the son of St. Louis, was one day to be presented to his dust upon proof of fidelity! A two-fold tribute of respect to the two-fold royalty of the sceptre and the palm. Louis XVI. might have answered his judges as Christ answered the Jews: "Many good works I have showed you . . . for which of those works do you stone me?"[1]

We hurried to the gallery to find ourselves in the way of the Queen on her return from the chapel. She soon appeared in sight, environed with a glittering and numerous retinue; she made us a stately courtesy; she seemed enraptured with life. And those beautiful hands, which at that time carried with such great grace the sceptre of so many kings, were destined, before being bound by the executioner, to mend the rags of the widow, a prisoner at the Conciergerie!

[1] JOHN, x. 33.—T.

My brother had obtained a sacrifice of me, but it was beyond his power to make me go through with it. He vainly entreated me to stay at Versailles in order to assist at the Queen's cards at night :

"You will be presented to the Queen," he said, "and the King will speak to you."

He could have given me no stronger reason for taking to flight. I hastened to go and hide my glory in my hotel, happy to escape from Court, but seeing still before me the terrible day of the coaches, of the 19th of February 1787.

The Duc de Coigny[1] sent to inform me that I was to hunt with the King in the forest of Saint-Germain. I set out in the early morning towards my punishment, in the uniform of a *débutant*, a grey coat, red waistcoat and breeches, lace tops, Hessian boots, a hunting-knife in my belt, a small, gold-laced French hat. There were four of us *débutants* at the Palace of Versailles, myself, the two Messieurs de Saint-Marsault, and the Comte d'Hautefeuille.[2] The Duc de Coigny gave us our instructions : he warned us not to interrupt the hunt, as the King flew into a passion if any one passed between him and the quarry. The Duc de Coigny bore a name fatal to the Queen.[3] The meet was at Val, in the forest of Saint-Germain, a domain leased by the Crown from the Maréchal de Beauvau.[4] The custom was for the horses of the first hunt in which the newly-presented men took part to be supplied from the royal stables.[5]

[1] Marie Henry François Franquetot, Duc de Coigny (1737-1821), the King's First Equerry. Under the Restoration, he was created a peer of France in 1814, appointed Governor of the Invalides in 1816, and a marshal of France in the same year.—B.

[2] I have met M. le Comte d'Hautefeuille again ; he is engaged in translating selections from Byron ; Madame la Comtesse d'Hautefeuille is the gifted author of the *Ame exilée*, &c.—*Author's Note.*

Charles Louis Félicité Texier, Comte d'Hautefeuille (1770-1865), after fighting in the Princes' Army, took service in Sweden, in the Royal Guards, and did not return to France till 1811. He married, in 1823, Mademoiselle de Beaurepaire, daughter of one of the bravest officers in the Vendean Army. The Comtesse d'Hautefeuille published a number of noteworthy works under the pseudonym of "Anna-Marie."—B.

[3] The Duc de Coigny was accused by the detractors of Marie Antoinette of having been in her good graces in the early years of the reign of Louis XVI.—T.

[4] Charles Juste Maréchal Duc de Beauvau (1720-1793), member of the French and Della Cruscan Academies.—T.

[5] The following appears in the *Gazette de France* of Tuesday 27 February 1787 :

"The Comte Charles d'Hautefeuille, the Baron de Saint-Marsault, the Baron de Saint-Marsault Chatelaillon and the Chevalier de Chateaubriand, who had previously had the honour of being presented to the King, had, on the 19th, that of riding in His Majesty's carriages and following him in the hunt."—*Author's Note.*

The drums beat the salute: a voice gave the order to present arms. They cried, "The King!" The King left the house and entered his coach: we rode in the coaches following. It was a long cry from this hunting expedition with the King of France to my hunting expeditions on the moors of Brittany; and further still to my hunting expeditions with the savages of America: my life was to be filled with these contrasts.

We reached the rallying-point, where a number of saddle-horses, held in hand under the trees, showed signs of impatience. The coaches drawn up in the forest with the keepers; the groups of men and women; the packs held back with difficulty by the huntsmen; the baying of the hounds, the neighing of the horses, the sound of the horns composed a very animated scene. The hunting-parties of our kings recalled both the old and the new customs of the monarchy, the rude pastimes of Clodion, Chilperic, and Dagobert and the gallantries of Francis I., Henry IV., and Louis XIV.

I was too full of my reading not to behold on every hand Comtesses de Chateaubriand,[1] Duchesses d'Étampes,[2] Gabrielles d'Estrées, La Vallières, and Montespans. My imagination seized upon the historic aspect of this hunting-party, and I felt at my ease: besides, I was in a forest, and therefore at home.

On alighting from the coaches, I handed my ticket to the huntsmen. A mare called *L'Heureuse* had been provided for me, a fast animal, but hard-mouthed, skittish, and full of tricks; a tolerable likeness of my fortune, which has constantly set back its ears. The King mounted and rode off; the members of the hunt followed, taking different roads. I stayed behind, struggling with *L'Heureuse*, who refused to let her new master get astride of her; I ended, however, in leaping upon her back: the hunt was already far ahead.

At first I mastered *L'Heureuse* fairly well; compelled to

---

[1] Françoise Comtesse de Chateaubriand (1475-1537), daughter of Jean de Foix, Vicomte de Narbonne, and sister of the Vicomte de Lautrec and the Maréchal de Foix. She inspired a passion in Francis I., but after a year was supplanted by the Duchesse d'Étampes (*vide infra*), and remained the victim of the jealousy of her husband, who has been accused of hastening her death.—T.

[2] Anne de Pisseleu, Duchesse d'Étampes (*circa* 1508–*circa* 1576), first known as Mademoiselle d'Heilly, maid-of-honour to the Comtesse d'Angoulême, mother of Francis I. She became the King's mistress at the age of eighteen; he married her to a certain Jean de Brosse, and gave her the county of Étampes, first raising it to a duchy. She practically governed France for two-and-twenty years, until the King's death in 1547, when she retired into obscurity and solaced her solitude by embracing the Reformation.—T.

LOUIS XVI

shorten her stride, she put down her neck, shook her bit, which was white with foam, and bounded along sideways; but when she drew near the scene of action, it became impossible to hold her. She bore down her head, drove my hand down upon the saddlebow, dashed at full gallop into a group of hunters, clearing everything in her course, and only stopped when she struck against the horse of a woman whom she nearly knocked over, amid the roars of laughter of some and the screams of terror of others. I have made useless efforts to-day to remember the name of the woman who received my excuses so politely. There was nothing else talked of than the *débutant's* "adventure."

I had not come to the end of my trials. About half-an-hour after my discomfiture, I was riding through a long opening in a deserted part of the wood; at the end stood a summer-house: I at once began to think of the palaces scattered through the Crown forests, in memory of the origin of the long-haired kings and their mysterious pleasures. A shot was heard; *L'Heureuse* turned short, scoured the thicket with lowered head, and carried me to the exact spot where the roe-buck had just been killed: the King appeared.

I then remembered, but too late, the Duc de Coigny's injunctions: the accursed *Heureuse* had done all. I leapt to the ground, pushing my mare back with one hand, holding my hat low in the other. The King looked and saw only a *débutant* who had come in at the death before himself; he felt a need to speak; instead of flying into a passion, he said, in a good-natured voice and with a broad laugh:

"He did not hold out long."

That is the only word I ever had from Louis XVI. People came up from every side; they were astonished to find me "talking" with the King. The *débutant* Chateaubriand created a sensation with his two "adventures;" but, as has ever happened to him since, he did not know how to turn either his good or his bad fortune to account.

The King hunted three other buck. As the *débutants* were only allowed to hunt the first animal, I returned to Val with my companions to await the return of the hunt. The King came back to Val; he was in spirits and discussed the accidents of the chase. We drove back to Versailles. A fresh disappointment for my brother: instead of going to dress in order to be present at the unbooting, the moment of triumph and favour, I flung myself into my carriage and drove home to Paris, rejoicing at being delivered of my honours and my troubles. I told my brother that I was determined to return to Brittany. Satisfied with having made his name known, and hoping one day to bring to maturity, by means of his own presentation, what had proved abortive in mine, he placed no obstacle in the way of the departure of so eccentric a spirit.[1]

Such was my first experience of the Town and the Court. Society appeared even more hateful in my eyes than I had imagined it; but, though it frightened, it did not discourage me; I felt, in a confused fashion, that I was superior to what I had seen. I took an invincible dislike to the Court; this dislike, or rather this contempt, which I have been unable to conceal, will either prevent me from succeeding or will cause me to fall from the summit of my career.

For the rest, if I judged the world without knowing it, the world, in its turn, knew nothing of me. None, at my first entrance, guessed what I might be good for, and when I came back to Paris, they guessed it no more. Since attaining my sad celebrity, I have been told by numbers of people, "How we should have noticed you, if we had met you in your youth!" This obliging contention is only the illusion attaching to an established reputation. Outwardly men resemble each other; it is in vain for Rousseau to tell us that he had a pair of small, quite charming eyes; it is none the less certain, witness his portraits, that he had the appearance of a schoolmaster or a cross-grained shoemaker.

To have done with the Court, I will add that after re-visiting Brittany and coming back to Paris to live with my younger sisters, Lucile and Julie, I plunged more deeply than ever into my habits of solitude. You ask what became of the story of my presentation. It remained where it was.

"Then you did not hunt with the King again?"

"No more than with the Emperor of China."

"And you never went back to Versailles?"

"I twice went as far as Sèvres; my heart failed me, and I returned to Paris."

"So you made nothing of your position?"

"Nothing at all."

"What did you do then?"

"I was bored."

[1] The *Mémorial historique de la Noblesse* has printed a hitherto unpublished document, annotated in the King's hand, taken from the Archives of the Kingdom, register M 813 and portfolio M 814; it contains the "Entrances." My own name and my brother's appear in it : this shows that my memory has not been at fault as regards dates.—*Author's Note* (Paris, 1840).

" So you felt no ambition ? "

" Yes, indeed : by means of intrigue and trouble, I attained the glory of printing in the *Almanach des Muses* an idyll the appearance of which almost killed me with hope and fear.[1]   I would have given all the King's coaches to have written the ballad, *O ma tendre musette !* or, *De mon berger volage.*"

Good for everything where others, good for nothing where I myself am concerned : there you have me.

[1] This idyll appears in the *Almanach des Muses* for 1790, p. 205, under the title : *L'Amour de la campagne* and the signature : " By the Chevalier de C * * *." Chateaubriand included it in his Complete Works.—B.

BOOK V[1]

ALL that has been read in the previous chapter was written in Berlin. I have returned to Paris for the christening of the Duc de Bordeaux,[2] and have resigned my embassy through political fidelity to M. de Villèle,[3] who has left the Cabinet. Restored to leisure, let me write. The more these Memoirs become filled with my years that have passed, the more do they remind me of the lower bulb of an hour-glass which marks what has fallen from my life: when all the sand shall have passed through, I would not turn over my glass clock, if God gave me power to do so.

The new solitude into which I entered in Brittany, after my presentation, was no longer that of Combourg; it was

---

[1] This book was written in Paris between June and December 1821, and revised in December 1846.—T.

[2] The *Moniteur* of Sunday 29 April 1821 contains the following, under the heading, *Paris, 28 April:* "M. le Vicomte de Chateaubriand, French Minister Plenipotentiary in Berlin, arrived in Paris on the day before yesterday." The Duc de Bordeaux was christened at Notre-Dame on the 1st of May 1821.—B.

[3] Villèle left the Cabinet on the 27th of July 1821; Chateaubriand resigned his ambassadorship on the 31st of July.—B.

not so entire, nor so serious, nor, to tell the truth, so forced: I was free to leave it; it lost its value. An old armorial lady of the castle, an old escutcheoned baron, watching over their last son and their last daughter in a feudal manor, presented what the English call "characters:" there was nothing provincial, nothing narrow in that life, because it was not the common life.

With my sisters, provincial life went on as usual amid the fields: neighbours danced at each other's houses or acted plays, in which I performed occasionally and very badly. In the winter one had, at Fougères, to submit to the society of a small town, with its balls, assemblies, and dinners, and I could not live forgotten, as in Paris.

On the other hand, I had not seen the army, the Court, without undergoing a certain change in my ideas. In spite of my natural inclinations, an indefinite something struggled within me against obscurity, and besought me to emerge from the shadow. Julie detested country life, and the instinct of genius and beauty impelled Lucile towards a wider stage.

I thus felt a discomfort in my existence which warned me that that existence was not my destiny.

Nevertheless, I continued to love the country, and round about Marigny it was charming.[1] My regiment had moved its quarters: the first battalion was garrisoned at the Havre, the second at Dieppe. I joined the latter; my presentation at Court made a personage of me. I acquired a taste for my profession; I worked hard at my training; I was placed in charge of recruits, whom I drilled on the pebbly beach: the sea has been the background of almost all the scenes of my life.

La Martinière did not concern himself at Dieppe with his homonym of Lamartinière,[2] nor with the Père Simon,[3] who wrote against Bossuet, Port-Royal, and the Benedictines, nor with Pecquet[4] the anatomist, whom Madame de Sévigné[5] calls "little Pecquet;" but La Martinière was in love at Dieppe as at

[1] Marigny has greatly changed since my sister occupied it. It has been sold and now belongs to Messieurs de Pommereul, who have rebuilt it and much improved it.—*Author's Note.*

[2] Antoine Auguste Bruzen de Lamartinière (1662-1746), compiler of the *Dictionnaire géographique, historique et critique.* He was born and spent his youth at Dieppe, and was the nephew of Richard Simon (*vide infra*).—T.

[3] Richard Simon (1638-1712), an early Rationalist, author of a number of works on the Old and New Testaments, which were promptly condemned by the Holy See.—T.

[4] Jean Pecquet (1610-1674), discoverer of the chyle reservoir or *réservoir de Pecquet.*—T.

[5] See Madame de Sévigné's letters of 22 December 1664, January 1665, 19 November 1670, and 11 July 1672.—B.

Cambrai: he pined away at the feet of a lusty woman of Caux,[1] whose cap and head-dress were half a fathom high. She was not young: by an odd chance, her name was Cauchie, and she was apparently the grand-daughter of that other native of Dieppe, Anne Cauchie, who, in 1645, was one hundred and fifty years old.

In 1647, Anne of Austria, like myself watching the sea from the windows of her chamber, amused herself by seeing the fire-ships burn for her diversion. She allowed the nations which had been faithful to Henry IV. to guard young Louis XIV., and gave endless benisons to those nations "in spite of their villainous Norman speech."

At Dieppe there still prevailed some of the feudal fines which I had seen paid at Combourg: there were due to the burgess Vauquelin three pigs' heads, each with an orange between its teeth, and three marked sous of the oldest known coinage.

I went to spend a week at Fougères. There reigned a noble spinster, called Mademoiselle de La Belinaye,[2] aunt to the Comtesse de Tronjoli of whom I have spoken. An agreeable, but ugly, sister of an officer in the Condé Regiment attracted my admiration: I was not bold enough to raise my eyes to beauty; I dared to risk a respectful tribute only by favour of a woman's imperfections.

Madame de Farcy, continuing in ill-health, at last resolved to leave Brittany. She persuaded Lucile to accompany her; Lucile, in her turn, overcame my repugnance: we set out for Paris; it was the sweet partnership of the three youngest birds of the brood. My brother was married; he lived with his father-in-law, the Président de Rosanbo, in the Rue de Bondy. We agreed to settle in his neighbourhood: through the good offices of M. Delisle de Sales,[3] who lived in the Pavillons de Saint-Lazare, at the top of the Faubourg Saint-Denis, we secured an apartment in these same "pavilions."[4]

Madame de Farcy had become acquainted, I know not how, with Delisle de Sales, who had formerly been sent to Vincennes

---

[1] The district of Caux, in Upper Normandy, which includes Dieppe, is noted for the beauty of its women and the singularity of their head-dresses.—T.

[2] Renée Élisabeth de La Belinaye (1728–1816), eldest daughter of Armand Magdelon Comte de La Belinaye, and sister of Thérèse de La Belinaye who married Anne Joseph Jacques Tuffin de La Rouërie, and was the mother of the Marquis Armand de La Rouërie, the famous conspirator.—B.

[3] Jean Baptiste Isoard (1743–1816), known as Delisle de Sales, and nicknamed Diderot's Ape. Nevertheless, and although certain of his philosophical treatises were indicted and burned, he fought against Atheism and Materialism. His works ran into scores of volumes and made no mark whatever.—T.

[4] Or "villas," as we should say nowadays.—T.

for some philosophical nonsense or other. At that time, one became a celebrity if he had scribbled a few lines of prose or published a quatrain in the *Almanach des Muses*. Delisle de Sales, a very worthy man, most decidedly under the average, suffered from a serious relaxation of the intellect, and allowed his years to slip from under him. The old man had got together a handsome library consisting of his own works, which he dealt in abroad, and which nobody read in Paris. Every year, in spring, he went to Germany to renew his stock of ideas. He wore a greasy, unbuttoned coat, and carried a roll of dirty paper which one saw protruding from his pocket: on this he would jot down his thoughts of the moment at the street-corners. On the pedestal of his own bust in marble he had himself placed the following inscription, borrowed from the bust of Buffon: "God, man and nature: he explained them all." Delisle de Sales explaining everything! These boasts are very pleasant, but very discouraging. Who is in a position to flatter himself that he possesses real talent? May we not all, such as we are, be under the sway of an illusion similar to that of Delisle de Sales? I would wager that some author will read this phrase who believes himself a genius and is none the less a blockhead.

If I have expatiated at too great length on the subject of the worthy man of the Pavillons de Saint-Lazare, the reason is that he was the first man of letters I met. He introduced me to the company of others. The presence of my two sisters made life in Paris less unbearable to me; my love of study still further overcame my distaste. Delisle de Sales I considered an eagle. I met at his rooms Carbon Flins des Oliviers,[1] who fell in love with Madame de Farcy. She laughed at him; he put a good face upon it, for he prided himself upon being a man of breeding. Flins introduced me to his friend Fontanes, who became mine.

Flins was the son of an administrator of woods and forests at Rheims, and had received a neglected education; he was for all that a man of sense, and sometimes of talent. It was impossible to imagine anything uglier than he: short and bloated, with large, prominent eyes, bristling hair, dirty teeth, and yet a not over-vulgar air. His manner of life, which was that of nearly all the men of letters in Paris at that time, deserves to be told. Flins occupied a lodging in the Rue Mazarine, pretty near La Harpe, who lived in the Rue

[1] Claude Marie Louis Emmanuel Carbon de Flins des Oliviers (1757–1806) edited the *Journal de la Ville et des Provinces, ou le Modérateur* with Fontanes, and produced, not without success, a number of comedies in verse.—B.

Guénégaud. He was waited upon by two Savoyards, disguised as flunkeys by means of livery cloaks; they followed him at night, and opened the door to his visitors in the daytime. Flins went regularly to the Théâtre Français, which at that time was situate in the Odéon and excelled particularly in comedy. Brizard[1] had only just retired; Talma[2] was commencing; Larive,[3] Saint-Phal, Fleury,[4] Molé,[5] Dazincourt, Dugazon,[6] Grandmesnil,[7] Mesdames Contat,[8] Saint-Val,[9] Desgarcins, Olivier[10] were in the full vigour of their talent, pending the arrival of Mademoiselle Mars,[11] daughter of Monvel,[12] who

[1] Jean Baptiste Britard (1721-1791), known as Brizard, a well-known player of heavy fathers and kings. He retired on the 1st of April 1786.—B.

[2] François Joseph Talma (1763-1826) made his first appearance in 1787, and is regarded as the greatest actor of his day. Napoleon Bonaparte admitted him to his intimacy, and twice paid his debts. He had been educated in England, knew English perfectly, and played in London on more than one occasion.—T.

[3] Jean Mauduit de Larive (1749-1827) held the stage at the Français until eclipsed by Talma, when he retired and opened a school of declamation. He accompanied Joseph Bonaparte to Naples as reader in 1806, and built the hamlet of Larive on his property at Montlignon, near Montmorency.—T.

[4] Joseph Abraham Bénard (1750-1822), known as Fleury, a very popular light-comedy actor.—T.

[5] François René Molet (1734-1802), known as Molé, another player of light-comedy parts, principally those then known as *fats* and *petits-maîtres*: fops and dandies. He was an active member of the Comédie Française for forty-two years, from 1760 to the day of his death.—T.

[6] Henri Gourgaud (1714-1809), known as Dugazon, played comic men-servants' parts. He was the brother of Madame Vestris, the tragic actress.—T.

[7] Jean Baptiste Fouchard de Grandménil (1737-1816) gave up the bar for the stage. He excelled in *rôles à manteaux* or mysterious strangers' parts. He was a member of the Academy of Fine Arts, and professor at the Conservatoire.—T.

[8] Mademoiselle Contat (1760-1813), a very perfect and versatile actress, who created the part of Suzanne in Beaumarchais' *Mariage de Figaro* in 1784. She married M. de Parny, nephew to the poet.—T.

[9] Mademoiselle Saint-Val the younger. Her elder sister had left the Comédie Française in 1779.—B.

[10] Jeanne Adélaïde Gérardine Olivier (1765-1787), a native of London. A very charming actress; she was scarcely nineteen when she created the part of Chérubin in the *Mariage de Figaro*, achieving a success almost equal to that of Mademoiselle Contat as Suzanne.—B.

[11] Anne Françoise Hippolyte Boutet (1779-1847), known as Mademoiselle Mars, one of the most famous of French comic actresses. She made her first appearance at the Théâtre Montansier when thirteen years of age, in 1792, and did not definitely leave the stage until 1841, when she was sixty-two. She created over one hundred parts at the Théâtre Français alone, which she joined in 1798.—T.

[12] Jacques Marie Boutet (1745-1811), known as Monvel, an exceedingly intelligent actor. He commenced by playing Molé's parts at the Comédie Française, and in later life made a successful heavy father at the Théâtre de la République. He also wrote a number of successful comedies and comic operas, and under the Empire became a professor at the Conservatoire and a Member of the Institute.—T.

Monvel was the father of Mademoiselle Mars by a provincial actress called Marguérite Salvetat, who acted under the name of Madame Mars, whence the daughter took her stage-name.—B.

was preparing to make her first appearance at the Théâtre Montansier.[1] The actresses protected the authors, and sometimes became the occasion of their fortune.

Flins, who had only a small allowance from his family, lived on credit. When Parliament was not sitting, he pawned his Savoyards' liveries, his two watches, his rings and underclothing, paid his debts with the amount thus raised, went to Rheims, spent three months there, returned to Paris, redeemed, with the money his father had given him, the articles which he had pledged at the pawnshops, and resumed his round of life, ever gay and popular.

In the course of the two years that elapsed between my settling in Paris and the opening of the States-General, the circle in which I moved increased. I knew the elegies of the Chevalier de Parny by heart, as I know them still. I wrote to him to ask leave to set eyes upon a poet whose works delighted me; I received a civil reply, and called upon him in the Rue de Cléry. I found a man still fairly young in years, of very pleasant manners, tall, spare, with a face pitted with the small-pox. He returned my visit; I introduced him to my sisters. He cared little for society, and was soon driven from it on account of his politics: at that time he belonged to the old party. I have never known a writer who more closely resembled his works: poet and Creole[2] as he was, all he needed was the Indian sky, a fountain, a palm-tree, and a woman by his side. He dreaded noise, tried to glide unnoticed through life, sacrificed everything to his idleness, and, amid the obscurity in which he dwelt, was betrayed only by his pleasures, which played upon his lyre as they passed.[3]

It was this inability to escape from his indolence which turned the Chevalier de Parny from the furious aristocrat that he was into a wretched revolutionary, insulting persecuted religion and priests on the scaffold, purchasing repose at all costs, and foisting upon the muse that had sung Éléonore the language of the houses where Camille Desmoulins went to haggle for the pleasures of love.

The author of the *Histoire de la littérature italienne*, who crept into the Revolution in Chamfort's wake, came to visit us, thanks to the cousinship that exists among all Bretons. Ginguené lived in society upon a reputation acquired through

[1] Now the Théâtre du Palais-Royal.—B.
[2] Parny was born in the Île Bourbon.—T.
[3] I here omit some lines quoted from Parny.—T.

a rather graceful set of verses, the *Confession de Zulmé*, which obtained for him a paltry place in M. de Necker's[1] offices: hence his article upon his admission to the office of the Controller-General. Somebody disputed Ginguené's claim to the authorship of the *Confession de Zulmé*, upon which his fame was based; but it was, as a matter of fact, his own.

The Rennes poet was a good musician and wrote ballads. Humble as he began by being, we saw his pride grow as he succeeded in hanging upon the skirts of some well-known man. About the time of the summoning of the States-General, Chamfort employed him to scribble articles for the newspapers and speeches for the clubs: he then became arrogant. At the first Federation he said: "There's a fine entertainment! In order to light it better, we ought to burn an aristocrat at each of the four corners of the altar!" There was nothing original in this aspiration; long before him, Louis Dorléans, the Leaguer, had written in his *Banquet du Comte d'Arète* that "one ought to fasten the Protestant ministers by way of faggots to the stake of the Midsummer's Night bonfires, and put King Henry IV. into the barrel where one put the cats."

Ginguené knew of the revolutionary murders before they took place. Madame Ginguené warned my sisters and my wife of the massacre planned at the Carmelites, and gave them shelter: she lived in the Cul-de-sac Férou, near the place where throats were to be cut.

After the Terror, Ginguené became a sort of head of the department of Public Instruction; it was then that he sang the *Arbre de la liberté* at the Cadran-Bleu, to the air of *Je l'ai planté, je l'ai vu naître*. He was considered sufficiently pious, philosophically, for an embassy to the Court of one of the kings who were being discrowned. He wrote from Turin to M. de Talleyrand that he had "overcome a prejudice:" he had caused his wife to be received at Court in a *pet-en-l'air*.[2] After falling from mediocrity to importance, from importance to silliness, and from silliness to absurdity, he ended his days as a distinguished

---

[1] Jacques Necker (1732-1804), Controller-General from 1776 to 1781, 1788 to 1789, and 1789 to 1790.—T.

[2] Ginguené was accredited as Ambassador of the French Republic at Turin in the early part of 1798. By affectation of simplicity, and also doubtless from economy, he caused his wife to be dispensed from appearing at the audiences in Court dress. He did not lose an hour before despatching a special courier to carry the great piece of news to the Foreign Minister: the Citizeness Ambassadress had appeared in a *pet-en-l'air!* Within a very few days, Talleyrand had signed Ginguené's recall.—B.

A *pet-en-l'air* is a very vulgar term for a short morning gown.—T.

critic, and what is better, as an independent writer in the *Décade*:[1] nature had restored him to the place whence Society had to such ill purpose taken him. His information is second-hand, his prose dull, his verse correct and sometimes agreeable.

Ginguené had a friend, the poet Le Brun.[2] Ginguené protected Le Brun, in the way in which a man of talent, who knows the world, protects the simplicity of a man of genius; Le Brun in his turn cast his radiancy over Ginguené's eminence. Nothing more comical was seen than the part played by these two cronies who, by a gentle commerce, did each other all the services which two men excelling in different spheres are able to render one to the other.

Le Brun was simply a mock gentleman of the Empyrean; his poetic spirit was as cold as his transports were icy. His Parnassus was a top room in the Rue Montmartre, furnished with a pile of books heaped pell-mell on the floor, a trestle-bed, the curtains of which consisted of two dirty towels dangling from a rusty iron rod, and the half of an ewer propped up against a bottomless chair. It was not that Le Brun was in needy circumstances; but he was a miser and addicted to loose women.

At M. de Vaudreuil's "classical supper,"[3] he impersonated Pindar. Among his lyrical poems are to be found energetic or elegant stanzas, as in the ode on the ship *Vengeur* or the ode on the *Environs de Paris*. His elegies issued from his head, rarely from his soul; his was a laboured, not a natural, originality; he created only by sheer force of art: he toiled to distort the meanings of words and to unite them in monstrous alliances. Le Brun had only one real talent, that of satire; his epistle on *La bonne et la mauvaise plaisanterie* enjoyed a well-deserved renown. Some of his epigrams are worthy of mention with J. B. Rousseau's; La Harpe above all inspired him. One more justice should be done him: he retained

---

[1] The *Décade philosophique*, founded 10 Floréal Year II. (29 April 1794). Ginguené was its editor-in-chief. In 1804, after the Empire had been established, it changed its title to that of *Revue philosophique, littéraire et politique*. It ceased to appear in 1807.—B.

[2] Ponce Denis Escouchard Le Brun (1729-1807), nicknamed the French Pindar, a versatile poet and epigrammatist, who sang by turns, and with equal fervour, the Monarchy, the Republic, and the Empire. Ginguené edited and published his Collected Works in 1811.—T.

[3] For an account of this "classical supper," see the Recollections of Madame Vigée-Lebrun. Le Brun recited imitations of Anacreon, crowned with Pindar's laurels.—B.

his independence under Bonaparte, and has left trenchant verses directed against the oppressor of our liberties.[1]

But unquestionably the most atrabiliary of the men of letters whom I knew in Paris at that time was Chamfort. Attacked with the disorder that produced the Jacobins, he was unable to forgive mankind for the accident of his birth.[2] He betrayed the houses to which he was admitted; he took the cynicism of his language for a picture of the manners of the Court. It would not be possible to deny that he had wit and talent, but wit and talent of the kind which does not reach posterity. When he saw that he was unable to attain to any position under the Revolution, he turned against himself the hands which he had raised against society. No longer to his vanity did the Phrygian cap appear as but another kind of crown, sans-culottism as a sort of nobility, of which Marat and Robespierre were the grandees. Furious at finding inequality of rank in the very world of sorrow and of tears, condemned to remain no more than a "villein" in the feudality of executioners, he tried to kill himself in order to escape from superiority in crime; he failed in his attempt: death laughs at those who summon it and who mistake it for annihilation.

I did not meet the Abbé Delille[3] until 1798, in London, and I never saw Rulhière,[4] who lives through Madame d'Egmont[5] and makes her live, nor Palissot,[6] nor Beaumarchais,[7] nor

---

[1] It is true that Le Brun wrote trenchant verses against Bonaparte, but he kept them to himself, and took care to publish those in which he extolled him. Bonaparte awarded him a pension of 6000 francs.—B.

[2] Chamfort was his adopted name. He never knew his real name nor that of his father.—T.

[3] Jacques Delille (1738–1813) translated the *Georgics*, the *Æneid*, and *Paradise Lost* into French verse. He had a facile talent for versification, and was admitted to the French Academy in 1774. He appears to have been in orders, and undoubtedly for some time held the abbey of Saint-Séverin, but he never followed an ecclesiastical career, and he married after the Revolution.—T.

[4] Claude Carloman de Rulhière (1735–1791) was elected to the Academy in 1787. He commenced life as aide-de-camp to the Maréchal de Richelieu in Guyenne. He then became secretary to the Baron de Breteuil, whom he accompanied on his embassy to Russia in 1760. In 1765, having meantime enjoyed a pension of 6000 francs for that purpose, he completed his *Histoire de la révolution de Russie en 1762*. This work, however, could not be published during the lifetime of Catherine II., and it eventually saw the light in 1797, six years after the death of the author. He published some poetry, in addition to the above and other historical works.—T.

[5] The Comtesse d'Egmont was the daughter of the Maréchal de Richelieu, and it was she who urged Rulhière to adopt a literary career.—B.

[6] Charles Palissot de Montenoy (1730–1814), author of a number of more or less polemical comedies, poems, and historical works.—T.

[7] Pierre Augustin Caron de Beaumarchais (1732–1799), author of the *Barbier de Séville*, the *Folle Journée, ou le Mariage de Figaro*, *Tarare*, &c.—T.

Marmontel.[1] The same with Chénier,[2] whom I never met, who
has often attacked me, to whom I never replied, and whose
place at the Institute was to be the cause of one of the crises
of my life.

When I read over again the majority of the writers of the
eighteenth century, I am amazed to think of the renown which
they achieved and of my former admiration for them. Whether
it be that the language has made progress, or that it has gone
backward, or that we have advanced in civilization or retreated
towards barbarism, it is certain that I find something threadbare, antiquated, grizzled, cold, and lifeless in the authors who
were the delight of my youth. I find even in the greatest
writers of the Voltairean age things that are poor in sentiment,
thought, and style.

Whom am I to blame for my disappointment? I fear
the chief guilt lies with myself; born innovator that I am, I
may perhaps have communicated to younger generations the
malady with which I was seized. Terror-stricken, in vain I
cry to my children, "Do not forget your French!" They
reply in the words of the Limosin to Pantagruel, that they
come "from alme, inclyte and celebrate academy, which is
vocitated Lutetia."[3]

This habit of latinizing and hellenizing our language
is not new, as we see: Rabelais cured it, it reappeared in
Ronsard;[4] Boileau attacked it. In our time it has been
revived by science; our revolutionaries, great Greeks by nature,
have compelled our merchants and farmers to calculate in
hectares, hectolitres, kilometers, millimeters, decagrams:
politics have "ronsardized" everything.

I might have spoken here of M. de La Harpe, whom I knew
at that time, and to whom I will return; I might have added
M. de Fontanes' portrait to my gallery; but although my
acquaintance with that excellent man began in 1789, it was
not until we met in England that I became united to him
in a friendship which ever increased with bad, and never

---

[1] Jean François Marmontel (1723-1799), author of the *Contes moraux* and a
large number of miscellaneous and voluminous works.—T.
[2] Marie Joseph de Chénier (1764-1811), the poet, brother of André de Chénier.
Chateaubriand succeeded to his chair at the Institute.—T.
[3] Urquhart and Motteux' RABELAIS, Book II. chap. 6: *How Pantagruel
met with a Limosin, who affected to speak in learned phrase.*—T.
[4] Pierre de Ronsard (1524-1585), the leading French poet of his day, but also
noted for a pedantic affectation of erudition and a barbarous neologism which
made Boileau say of him:
Que sa muse en français parla grec et latin.
("That his muse, speaking French, talked in Latin and Greek").—T.

diminished with good fortune: I will tell you of him later in all the effusion of my heart. I shall have no talents to depict but those which no longer console the earth. The death of my friend has occurred at the moment when my recollections were leading me to trace the commencement of his life.[1] So great a flight is our existence that, if we do not write down in the evening what has happened in the morning, our work obstructs us, and we no longer have the time to keep it posted up. This does not prevent us from wasting our years, from flinging to the winds the hours which are for men the seeds of eternity.

While my inclination and that of my two sisters threw me into this literary society, our position obliged us to frequent another set; the family of my brother's wife was naturally the centre for us of this second circle.

The Président Le Peletier de Rosanbo, who since died with such great courage,[2] was at the time of my arrival in Paris a model of frivolity. At that period, men's minds and manners were in every way unsettled, a symptom of a coming revolution. Magistrates were ashamed to wear the robe, and mocked at the gravity of their fathers. The Lamoignons, the Molés, the Séguiers, the d'Aguesseaus[3] wished to fight

[1] Chateaubriand wrote this page in June 1821; Fontanes had died on the 17th of March previous.—B.

[2] Rosanbo was guillotined on 1 Floréal Year II. (20 April 1794).—B.

[3] These are the four leading magisterial or parliamentary families of France under the Old Order. The Lamoignons produced Guillaume de Lamoignon (1617-1677), First President of the Parliament of Paris (1658-1677), himself the son of a chief justice; his sons Chrétien François de Lamoignon, a chief justice (1690) and Nicolas Lamoignon de Baville (1648-1724), Counsellor to the Parliament (1670), Master of Requests (1675), and lastly, Intendant of Languedoc; Guillaume de Lamoignon, Seigneur de Malesherbes, Chancellor of France (1750-1768), son of Chrétien François; his son, Chrétien Guillaume de Malesherbes (1721-1794), the famous minister and counsel for Louis XVI. at the King's trial; and Chrétien François Lamoignon (d. 1789), Chief Justice of the Parliament of Paris (1758) and Chancellor in 1787, great-grandson of the first Guillaume de Lamoignon. His son, Christian de Lamoignon, was created a peer of France, and died in 1827; in him the family of Lamoignon became extinct. The Molés held chief-justiceships from 1602 to the Revolution. The more remarkable members of the family were Édouard Molé (1558-1641), its founder, son of a counsellor to the Parliament, himself successively a counsellor, Procurator-General, and Chief Justice of the Parliament of Paris (1602); Matthieu Molé (1584-1656), his son, counsellor (1606), Procurator-General (1614), Chief Justice (1641) and Keeper of the Seals (1650); and more recently Matthieu Louis Molé (1781-1855), son of the Président Molé de Champlatreux, Minister of Justice under Bonaparte (1813), who created him a count of the Empire, Minister of Marine (1815-1818) under the Restoration, when he became a peer of France, Foreign Minister (1830-1836), and Premier (1836-1839) under Louis Philippe. In 1840 he was elected a member of the French Academy. Of the Séguiers, Pierre Séguier (1504-1580) was an

instead of judging. The Presidents' wives ceased to be respectable mothers of families and left their gloomy mansions in order to seek brilliant adventures.[1] The priest in the pulpit avoided pronouncing the name of Jesus Christ and spoke only of the " Law-giver of the Christians ; " the ministers were falling pell-mell; power slipped through each one's fingers. The height of fashion was to be American in town, English at Court, Prussian in the army; to be anything except French. All that was said, all that was done, was one long series of inconsistencies. They wished to keep up the commendatory clergy, and would have none of religion; none could be an officer who was not of gentle birth, whereas the nobility was railed at; equality was introduced into the drawing-rooms together with flogging into the camps.

M. de Malesherbes had three daughters,[2] Mesdames de Rosanbo, d'Aulnay, and de Montboissier; he loved Madame de Rosanbo the best, because her opinions resembled his own. The Président de Rosanbo[3] also had three daughters, Mesdames de Chateaubriand, d'Aulnay,[4] and de Tocqueville, and one son, whose brilliant mind clothed itself in Christian perfection. M. de Malesherbes was happy in the midst of his children, grandchildren, and great-grandchildren. Time after time I have seen him, in the early days of the Revolution, arrive at Madame de Rosanbo's, all heated with politics, fling off his

advocate, Advocate-General, and Chief Justice; his son, Antoine Séguier (1552–1626), was a counsellor to the Parliament, Advocate-General, and Ambassador of Henry IV. at Venice; Pierre Séguier (1588–1672), grandson of the first Pierre, was Intendant of Guyenne, Keeper of the Seals (1633), and Chancellor (1635); Antoine Louis Séguier (1726–1791) was Advocate-General to the Grand Council and subsequently to the Parliament (1755–1790) and a member of the French Academy (1757); and his son, Matthieu Séguier (d. 1848), was for many years a chief justice. Henri François d'Aguesseau (1688–1751) was the son of an intendant of Limousin, and was Chancellor of France from 1717 to 1718, 1720 to 1722, and 1737 to 1750.—T.

[1] Cf., inter alia, the character of the Présidente de Tourvel in Choderdos de Laclos' Liaisons dangereuses.—T.

[2] This must be a slip of the pen. Malesherbes had only two daughters: Marie Thérèse, born 1756, who married, in 1769, Louis Le Peletier, Seigneur de Rosanbo, and Françoise Pauline, born 1758, who married, in 1775, Charles Philippe Simon de Montboissier-Beaufort-Canillac, commanding the Orleans Regiment of Dragoons.—B.

[3] The Président de Rosanbo's three daughters married the Comte de Chateaubriand, the author's brother, the Comte Lepelletier d'Aulnay, and the Comte de Tocqueville. The last was made a lord of the Bed-chamber and a peer of France by Charles X., and was the father of Alexis de Tocqueville, author of the Démocratie en Amérique.—B.

[4] Louis Le Peletier, Vicomte de Rosanbo (1777–1858) was created a peer of France on the same day as Chateaubriand, 17 August 1815, and together with the latter, retired from the Upper House in August 1830, refusing to take the oath to the usurper.—B.

wig, lie down upon the carpet of my sister's room, and submit to the uproarious teasing of the rebellious children. His manners would have been considered almost vulgar, if he had not possessed a certain brusqueness which saved him from being commonplace: at the first words he uttered, one recognized the bearer of an old name and the superior magistrate. His natural virtues were somewhat tainted with affectation, thanks to the philosophy which he mingled with them. He was full of knowledge, honesty, and courage, but impetuous and passionate to such an extent that he once said to me, speaking of Condorcet:

"That man was once my friend; to-day I would not scruple to kill him like a dog."

The tide of the Revolution overwhelmed him, and his death established his glory. This great man would have remained hidden beneath his merits, if misfortune had not revealed him to the world. A noble Venetian lost his life at the moment when he discovered his title-deeds amid the falling ruins of an old palace.

M. de Malesherbes' free ways removed all my constraint. He found that I was not without information; this first point gave us something in common: we spoke of botany and geography, two of his favourite subjects. It was in the course of my conversations with him that I first conceived the idea of making a journey in North America, with the object of discovering the ocean seen by Hearne and later by Mackenzie.[1] We also held views in common on politics: the generous sentiments which were at the root of our earlier troubles appealed to the independence of my character; my natural antipathy to the Court gave strength to this inclination. I was on the side of M. de Malesherbes and of Madame de Rosanbo as against M. de Rosanbo and my brother, who was nicknamed "the raving Chateaubriand." The Revolution would have carried me away, had it not started in crime: I saw the first head carried on the end of a pike, and I drew back. Murder will never to my eyes be an object of admiration or an argument in favour of liberty; I know nothing more servile, more contemptible, more cowardly, more shallow than a Terrorist. Have I not in France seen the whole of this race of Brutus take service with Cæsar and his police? The levellers, regenerators, cut-throats had been transformed into

[1] Navigated in recent years by Captain Franklin and Captain Parry.—*Author's Note* Geneva, 1831).

C. G. LAMOIGNON DE MALESHERBES

· lackeys, spies, sycophants, and even less naturally into dukes, counts, and barons: such a mediævalism!

Lastly, what attached me still more to the illustrious old man was his predilection for my sister: in spite of the Comtesse Lucile's shyness, we succeeded, with the aid of a glass of champagne, in inducing her to take a part in a little play on the occasion of M. de Malesherbes' birthday; her performance was so touching that it turned that good and great man's head. He was even more eager than my brother in urging her translation from the Chapter of the Argentière to that of Remiremont, which insisted upon the rigorous and difficult proofs of the "sixteen quarterings." For all his philosophy, M. de Malesherbes possessed principles of birth in an eminent degree.

This picture of men and society at the time of my entrance into the world must be spread over a space of about two years, from 25 May 1787, the date of the closing of the first Assembly of Notables, to 5 May 1789, that of the opening of the States-General. During these two years, my sisters and I did not continually live in Paris, nor in the same part of Paris. I will now go back and carry my readers to Brittany.

I must add that I was still infatuated with my illusions; now that I no longer had my woods, I had discovered a new solitude in remote times instead of places. In old Paris, in the enclosures of Saint-Germain-des-Près, in the cloisters of the convents, in the vaults of Saint-Denis, in the Sainte Chapelle, in Notre Dame, in the little streets of the Cité, at the modest door of Héloïse, I again met my enchantress; but beneath the Gothic arches and among the tombs she had assumed a deathlike aspect: she was pale, she looked at me with sad eyes; she was but the shadow or the manes of the dream which I had loved.

My political education commenced with my different visits to Brittany in 1787 and 1788. The Provincial States furnished the model of the States-General; also the local troubles which heralded those of the nation broke out in two districts possessing States, Brittany and Dauphiné.

The transformation that had been developing for two centuries was nearing its termination. France had passed from feudal monarchy to the monarchy of States-General, from the monarchy of States-General to the monarchy of parliaments, from the monarchy of parliaments to absolute monarchy, and was now tending towards representative monarchy, across the struggle between the magistracy and the royal power.

The Maupeou Parliament,[1] the establishment of provincial assemblies, coupled with individual voting-power, the first and second Assemblies of Notables, the Plenary Court, the formation of grand bailiwicks, the reinstatement of the Protestants in their civil rights, the partial abolition of torture and of forced labour, the equal division of taxation were so many successive proofs of the revolution which was at work. But at that time these facts were not seen as a whole : each event appeared in the light of an isolated accident. At every period of history, there exists a guiding thought. Looking only at one point, one fails to see the rays converging at the centre of all the other points ; one does not go back as far as the secret agency which gives life and movement to the whole, like water and fire in machinery : that is why, at the outset of revolutions, so many people believe that it is enough to break this wheel or that to prevent the torrent from rushing or the steam from exploding.

The eighteenth century, a century of intellectual action, not of material action, would not have succeeded in so promptly altering the laws, had it not found its vehicle : the parliaments, and notably the Parliament of Paris, became the instruments of the philosophical system. Every opinion dies an impotent or distracted death, if it be not lodged in an assembly which turns it into a power, supplies it with a will, furnishes it with a tongue and a pair of arms. Revolutions succeed, and always will succeed, only by means of corporate assemblies, lawful or unlawful.

The parliaments had their cause to avenge : absolute monarchy had stolen from them the authority which they had usurped from the States-General. Enforced registrations,[2] beds of justice, sentences of exile, while making the magistrates popular, drove them to demand liberties of which, in their hearts, they were not the sincere upholders. They called for the restoration of the States-General, not daring to admit that they wished to secure the legislative and political power for themselves; and thus they hastened on the resurrection of a body of which they had gathered the inheritance, a body which, on returning to life, would at once reduce them to their own department. Men are almost invariably deceived as to their true interests, whether moved by wisdom or passion : Louis XVI. restored the

---

[1] René Nicolas Maupeou (1714–1792) succeeded his father in 1768 as Chancellor of France. In 1771 he banished the Parliament of Paris and installed in its stead the King's Privy Council, which was derisively nicknamed the "Maupeou Parliament" by the public, and which continued in power until the death of Louis XV. in 1774, when the Parliament was restored and Maupeou banished in his turn.—T.

[2] Of the royal edicts.—T.

parliaments which forced him to summon the States-General; the States-General, converted into a National Assembly and soon into a Convention, destroyed the throne and the parliaments, and sent to their deaths both the judges and the monarch from whom justice emanated. But Louis XVI. and the parliaments acted in this manner because they were the unconscious instruments of a social revolution.

The idea of the States-General was, therefore, in all men's heads; only they did not see whither it would lead them. It was the question, for the crowd, how to make up a deficit which the smallest banker of to-day would undertake to remove. The application of so violent a remedy to so small an evil proves that the public was being carried towards unknown political regions. For the year 1786, the only year of which the financial state has been affirmed, the revenue amounted to 412,924,000, the expenditure to 593,542,000 livres, leaving a deficit of 180,618,000 livres, which was reduced to 140 millions through economies amounting to 40,618,000 livres. In this budget, the Royal Household figures for the immense sum of 37,200,000 livres: the Princes' debts, the purchase of country-seats, and the Court malversations were the cause of this additional burden.

It was desired to have the States-General in the form they assumed in 1614. The historians always quote this form as though one had never heard speak of States-General or of a demand for their convocation since 1614. And yet in 1651 the orders of the nobility and the clergy, meeting in Paris, demanded States-General. A bulky collection of acts passed and speeches delivered on that occasion exists. The Parliament of Paris, which was then all-powerful, far from seconding the wishes of the two upper orders, quashed their meetings as illegal: as indeed they were.

And since I am treating of this subject, I wish to note another serious fact which has escaped those who have concerned, and are still concerning, themselves with writing the history of France, without knowing it. People talk of "the three orders" as being essential to the constitution of the States known as States-General. Well, it often happened that bailiwicks appointed deputies for only one or two orders. In 1614, the bailiwick of Amboise appointed none for either the clergy or the nobility; the bailiwick of Châteauneuf-en-Thimerais sent none for the clergy nor for the third estate; the Puy, the Rochelle, the Lauraguais, Calais, the Haute-Marche, Châtellerault sent none for the clergy, and Montdidier and Roye none for the nobility. Nevertheless, the States of 1614 were called States-General. Thus the ancient chronicles express themselves more correctly when they say, in speaking of our national assemblies, "the three estates," or "the burgess notables," or "the barons and bishops" as the case may be, and they attribute the same legislative power to the assemblies thus composed. In the different provinces, the third estate, even though convoked, often refrained from deputing representatives, and this for an unheeded but very natural reason. The third estate had taken possession of the magistracy, from which it had driven out the men-at-arms; it held absolute sway, except in a few parliaments, in the offices of judge, advocate, procurator, registrar, clerk, and so forth; it made civil and criminal laws, and, thanks to its parliamentary usurpation, it exercised even the political power. The fortune, honour, and lives of the citizens depended upon the third estate: all obeyed its decrees, every head fell beneath the sword of its justices. Seeing, therefore, that it enjoyed unlimited power, to the exclusion of the other estates, what need had it to go begging for a portion of that power in assemblies in which it appeared upon its knees?

The people, metamorphosed into monks, had resorted to the cloisters, and governed society through the power of religious opinion; the people, metamorphosed into tax-gatherers and bankers, had resorted to finance, and governed society through the power of money; the people, metamorphosed into magistrates, had resorted to the tribunals, and governed society through the power of the law. This great Realm of France, so aristocratic in its parties and in its provinces, was democratic when taken as a whole, under the direction of its King, with whom it acted in admirable concert and nearly always went hand in hand. This is the explanation of its long existence. There is an entirely new history of France to be written, or rather, the history of France has not yet been written.

All the above-mentioned important questions were especially vexed in the years 1786, 1787, and 1788. The heads of my fellow-Bretons found abundant cause for excitement in their natural vivacity, in the privileges of the province, the clergy, and the nobles, in the collisions between the Parliament and the States. M. de Calonne,[1] for a short while Intendant of Brittany, had increased the internal strife by favouring the cause of the third estate. M. de Montmorin [2] and M. de Thiard were not

---

[1] Charles Alexandre de Calonne (1734–1802), Controller-General of Finance (1783–1787).—T.
[2] Armand Marc Comte de Montmorin-Saint-Hérem (1746–1792), Minister of Foreign Affairs under Necker, and killed in the massacres of September.—T.

sufficiently strong leaders to ensure the ascendency of the Court party. The nobility entered into a coalition with the Parliament, which was itself noble; now it opposed M. Necker, M. de Calonne, the Archbishop of Sens;[1] now it thrust back the popular movement, which its own early resistance had favoured. It assembled, deliberated, and protested; the communes or municipalities assembled, deliberated and protested in opposition. The private question of hearth-money was mixed up with the general questions and increased the reigning ill-will. To understand this, it is necessary to explain the constitution of the Duchy of Brittany.

The States of Brittany varied more or less in their formation, in common with all the States of Feudal Europe, which they resembled. The Kings of France were established into the rights of the Dukes of Brittany. The marriage-contract of the Duchess Anne,[2] in 1491, not only brought Brittany by way of dower to the crown of Charles VIII. and Louis XII., but contained a covenant by virtue of which an end was put to a contention which traced its origin to Charles of Blois[3] and the Count of Montfort.[4] Brittany contended that daughters were entitled to inherit the Duchy; France maintained that the succession could take place only in the main line, and that when this line came to be extinguished, Brittany, as a great feod, returned to the Crown. Charles VIII. and Anne, and subsequently Anne and Louis XII., mutually surrendered their rights or claims to each other. Claudia, daughter of Anne and Louis XII., who became the wife of Francis I., on her death left the Duchy of Brittany to Francis I., her husband, upon the petition of the States assembled at Vannes, and by an edict published at Nantes in 1532 united the Duchy to the Crown of France, guaranteeing the Duchy's rights and privileges.

[1] Étienne Charles de Loménie, Comte de Brienne (1727–1794), successively Bishop of Condom, Archbishop of Toulouse, Archbishop of Sens, and a cardinal. In 1787 he was appointed Controller-General, and soon after became Prime Minister. He was arrested in 1793 and died in prison in 1794.—T.

[2] Anne of Brittany (1476–1514), daughter and heiress of Duke Francis II., was first married by proxy to the Emperor Maximilian I. The marriage was not consummated, and in 1491 Anne married King Charles VIII. of France. Charles died in 1498, and in 1499 his widow married his cousin and successor, Louis XII.—T.

[3] Charles of Blois, son of Margaret, sister of Philip VI., married in 1337 Joan of Penthièvre, daughter of Guy, and niece of John III., Duke of Brittany, on the understanding that he was to succeed to the latter's estates. Upon the death of John in 1341, a war broke out between Charles and the Count of Montfort (*vide infra*) which lasted until 1364, when Charles was slain at the Battle of Auray.—T.

[4] John Count of Montfort, brother of John III. Duke of Brittany, assumed the title of John IV. He died in 1345, and was succeeded by his son John V., who eventually entered into possession of the Duchy.—T.

At that time the States of Brittany were summoned every year; but in 1630 the sittings became biennial. The Governor proclaimed the opening of the States. The three orders sat, according to the place, in a church or in the halls of a convent. Each order deliberated apart: they formed three separate assemblies with their various tempests, which turned into a general hurricane when the clergy, the nobles, and the third estate came to meet together. The Court breathed discord, and talents, vanities and ambitions came into play in this restricted field as in any more extended arena.

The Père Grégoire de Rostrenen, a Capuchin friar, in the dedication to his *Dictionnaire françois-breton*, addresses Their Lordships the States of Brittany as follows:

"If it was meet for none save the Roman orator worthily to praise the august assembly of the Roman Senate, was it meet for me to venture upon the praise of your august assembly, which so worthily recalls to us the image of all that ancient and modern Rome possessed that was majestic and venerable?"

Rostrenen proves that Celtic is one of those primitive languages which Gomer, the eldest son of Japhet, brought to Europe, and that the Lower Bretons, despite their short stature, descend from the giants. Unfortunately, Gomer's Breton children, long separated from France, allowed part of their old title-deeds to perish: their charters, to which they did not attach sufficient importance as linking them to general history, too often lack the authenticity to which the decipherers of diplomas, on their side, attach too high a price.

The time of the holding of the States in Brittany was a time of balls and festivals: one dined with M. le Commandant, dined with M. le Président de la Noblesse, dined with M. le Président du Clergé, dined with M. le Trésorier des États, dined with M. l'Intendant de la Province, dined with M. le Président du Parlement; one dined everywhere: and drank! At long refectory tables sat Du Guesclins who were husbandmen, Duguay-Trouins who were seamen, wearing at their side their iron swords with old-fashioned guards or their short cutlasses. All the gentlemen assisting at the States in person bore no slight resemblance to a Diet of Poland, of Poland on foot, not on horseback, a diet of Scythians, not of Sarmatians.

Unfortunately, they played too much. The balls never ended. The Bretons are noted for their dances and dance-tunes. Madame de Sévigné has described our political festivals in the midst of the waste-lands, like the revels of fairies and goblins which were held at night on the moors:

"You shall now," she writes,[1] "have news about our States for your pains of being a Breton. M. de Chaulnes made his entry on Sunday evening, with all the noise that Vitré could afford: on Monday morning he sent me a letter, which I answered by going to dine with him. They dine at two tables in the same room; there are fourteen covers at each table; Monsieur presides at one, and Madame at the other. The good cheer is excessive, whole dishes of roast meat are carried away uncut; and the pyramids of fruit are so tall, that the doorways have to be made higher. Our forefathers did not foresee this kind of machines, seeing that they did not even understand that a door ought to be higher than themselves. . . . After dinner, Messieurs de Lomaria and Coëtlogon danced some marvellous jigs with two Breton ladies, and minuets with an air which our courtiers cannot approach: they execute Gipsy and Lower Breton steps with charming daintiness and precision. . . . Night and day there reign such play, good cheer, and freedom as will attract all the world. I had never seen the States before; it is a pretty thing enough. I doubt if there is a province whose assembly has so grand an air as this; it must be very full, I fancy, for there is not one of the members at the war nor at Court; except the little cornet,[2] who perhaps may return here one day like the rest. . . . A multitude of presents, pensions, repairs of highways and towns, fifteen or twenty large tables, a continual round of dancing and gaming, plays three times a week, and a great deal of show and splendour: there you have the States. I have forgot three or four hundred pipes of wine which are drank out here."

The Bretons find it difficult to forgive Madame de Sévigné for her raillery. I am less severe; but I do not like to hear her say, "You speak very pleasantly of our miseries; we are no longer so *roué*:[3] *one* in eight days only, to keep justice going. 'Tis true that a hanging now comes refreshingly to me." This is carrying the agreeable language of the Court to excess: Barère[4] spoke with the same grace of the guillotine.

---

[1] Letter to Madame de Grignan, 5 August 1671.—T.
[2] M. de Sévigné, her son.—*Author's Note.*
[3] A play upon words: a *roué* is a rake and also one broken on the wheel.—T.
[4] Bertrand Barère de Vieuzac (1755-1841), President of the Convention during the trial of Louis XVI., and member of the Committee of Public Safety (1793-1795).—T

In 1793, the drownings at Nantes were called "republican marriages:" the popular despotism reproduced the amenities of style of the royal despotism.

The Paris fops, who accompanied messieurs the King's company to the States, related that we country squires had our pockets lined with tin so that we might take home M. le Commandant's fricassees of chicken to our wives. These jests were dearly paid for. A Comte de Sabran had erewhile lost his life in return for his idle talk. This descendant of the troubadours and of the Provençal kings, as big as a Swiss,[1] allowed himself to be killed by a little hare-hunter of Morbihan, no taller than a Laplander.[2] This "Ker"[3] was not a whit second to his adversary in pedigree: if St. Elzear of Sabran was a near kinsman of St. Louis, St. Corentin,[4] collateral ancestor of the most noble Ker, was Bishop of Quimper under King Gallon II., three centuries before Christ.

The King's revenue, in Brittany, consisted of the benevolences, which varied according to needs; the income from the Crown domains, which might amount to three or four hundred thousand francs; the stamp-duty, &c.

Brittany had her own revenues, which served to meet her expenditure: the "great due" and the "petty due," which were laid on liquor and the liquor traffic, produced two millions a year; and then there were the sums raised by hearth-money. One little suspects the important part played by hearth-money in our history; yet it was to the French Revolution what the stamp-duties were to the Revolution in America.

Hearth-money or *fouage* (*census pro singulis focis exactus*) was a quit-rent, or a sort of villain tax, charged upon the goods of the commonalty for each hearth. This hearth-money, which was gradually increased, went to pay the debts of the province. In time of war, the expenditure amounted to more than seven millions from one session to the next, a sum which exceeded the receipts. A plan had been proposed to create a capital out of the funds provided by hearth-money and to turn it into

---

[1] A *Suisse*, or porter.—T.

[2] This duel took place *circa* 1735 between Jean François de Kératry, a younger son from Cornouaille, not Morbihan, and the Marquis, not Comte, de Sabran.—B.

[3] A large proportion of Breton names commence with Ker: one says a "Ker" of Brittany as who should say a "Tre, Pol, or Pen" of Cornwall or a "Thwaite" of Westmoreland.—T.

[4] St. Corentin was the first titular Bishop of Cornouaille (or Quimper), which see was created by King Gallon, or Grallon, Mur, or the Great, not "three centuries before Christ," but towards the close of the fifth century A.D.—B.

stock for the benefit of the payers of hearth-money: in this
way the tax became only a loan.   The injustice (although it
was an injustice made legal by the wording of the customary
law) lay in making it bear upon the property of the commonalty
alone.   The commons never ceased protesting; the nobles, who
set less store by their money than by their privileges, would not
hear of a duty which would have made them liable to a villain-
tax.   This was the question when the States of Brittany, that
were to prove so bloody, came together in December 1788.

Men's minds were at that time excited by various causes:
the assembly of the Notables, the territorial impost, the traffic
in corn, the approaching sittings of the States-General and
the affair of the Necklace, the Plenary Court and the *Mariage
de Figaro*, the grand bailiwicks and Cagliostro[1] and Mesmer,[2]
a thousand other serious and trivial matters formed subjects
of controversy in every family.

The Breton nobility had, at its own instance, assembled
at Rennes to protest against the establishment of the Plenary
Court.   I went to this diet: it was the first political meeting
I ever attended.   I was bewildered and amused by the cries
I heard.   The members climbed on the tables and chairs;
they gesticulated, and all spoke at one time.   The Marquis de
Trémargat,[3] who had a wooden leg, shouted in stentorian tones:

"Let us all go to the Commandant, M. de Thiard;[4] we will
say to him, 'The nobles of Brittany are at your door; they ask
to speak to you; the King himself would not deny them!'"

At this outburst of eloquence, the cheers shook the rafters.
He commenced again:

"The King himself would not deny them!"

The shouts and stamping redoubled.   We went to M. le
Comte de Thiard, a man of the Court, an erotic poet, a gentle
and frivolous spirit, mortally bored by our uproar; he looked
upon us as so many *hou-hous*, wild-boars, wild beasts; he was
burning to be gone from our Armorica, and had not the
slightest desire to deny us the entrance to his house.   Our
spokesman told him what he wanted, after which we went
back and drew up the following declaration:

---

[1] Giuseppe Balsamo (1743-1795), known as Alessandro Conte di Cagliostro,
the conjurer, and one of the leading spirits in the affair of the Necklace.—T.

[2] Friedrich Anton Mesmer (1734-1815), the discoverer of animal magnetism.—T.

[3] Louis Anne Pierre Geslin, Comte (not Marquis) de Trémargat (*b.* 1749), a
naval officer and knight of St. Louis.—B.

[4] Henri Charles Comte de Thiard-Bissy (1726-1794), a lieutenant-general and
principal equerry to the Duc d'Orléans.   In February 1787 he succeeded M. de
Montmorin in his post of King's Commandant in Brittany.   He was guillotined
on the 26th of July 1794.—B.

"We declare infamous those who are capable of accepting any places, whether in the new administration of justice, or in the administration of the States, which shall not be approved by the constitutional laws of Brittany."

Twelve gentlemen were chosen to carry this document to the King: upon their arrival in Paris, they were locked up in the Bastille, whence they soon emerged in the quality of heroes;[1] they were received with laurel-branches on their return.

We wore coats with large buttons of mother-of-pearl bedecked with ermine, round which buttons was inscribed in Latin the motto, "Death before dishonour." We triumphed over the Court, over which all the world was triumphing, and we fell with it into the same abyss.

It was at this period that my brother, continuing to prosecute his plans, resolved to have me admitted to the Order of Malta. In order to effect this, it was necessary that I should receive the tonsure: this could be given me by M. Cortois de Pressigny,[2] Bishop of Saint-Malo. I therefore went to my native city, where my good mother was living: she no longer had her children with her; she spent her days at church, her evenings knitting. Her absent-mindedness was incredible: I met her one day in the street, carrying one of her slippers under her arm by way of a prayer-book. From time to time some old friends would find their way to her retreat and talk of the good times that were past. When she and I were alone, she would improvise beautiful stories for me in verse. In one of these stories the devil carried off a chimney with an evil-doer in it, and the poet exclaimed:

> Le diable en l'avenue
> Chemina tant et tant,
> Qu'on en perdit la vue
> En moins d'une heur' de temps.[3]

---

[1] The twelve gentlemen sent to the Bastille, 15 July 1788, were the Marquis de La Rouërie, the Comte de La Fruglaye, the Marquis de La Bourdonnaye de Montluc, the Comte de Trémargat, the Marquis de Corné, the Comte Godet de Châtillon, the Vicomte de Champion de Cicé, the Marquis Alexis de Bedée, the Chevalier de Guer, the Marquis du Bois de La Feronnière, the Comte Hay des Nétumières, and the Comte de Becdelièvre-Penhouët. Their captivity was anything but harsh, and lasted under two months, from 15 July to 12 September 1788.—B.

[2] Gabriel Comte Cortois de Pressigny (1745-1823). He emigrated in 1791; on the Restoration he was sent as a special envoy to the Holy See. In 1816 he was created a peer of France, and in 1817 appointed Archbishop of Besançon.—B.

[3] "Along the avenue
The devil went so fast
That he was lost to view
Before an hour had passed."—T.

"I cannot help thinking," said I, "that the devil does not go very fast."

But Madame de Chateaubriand proved to me that I did not know what I was talking about: my mother was charming.

She had a long and plaintive ballad on the subject of the *Récit véritable d'une cane sauvage en la ville de Montfort-la-Cane-lez-Saint-Malo.* A certain lord had imprisoned a young and very beautiful girl in the Castle of Montfort, with the intention of ravishing her. Through a dormer-window she could see the church of St. Nicholas; she prayed to the saint with eyes full of tears, and was miraculously wafted outside the castle. But she fell into the hands of the traitor's servants, who proposed to do by her as they presumed their master had done. The poor girl, distraught, looking to every side in search of help, saw only the wild-duck upon the pond of the castle. Renewing her prayers to St. Nicholas, she besought him to allow these birds to be the witnesses of her innocence, so that, if she was doomed to lose her life, and was unable to accomplish the vows which she had taken to St. Nicholas, the birds themselves would fulfil them in their own way, in her name and on her behalf.

The girl died within the year: and behold, on the Feast of the Translation of the Bones of St. Nicholas, 9 May, a wild-duck, accompanied by its brood of ducklings, came to St. Nicholas' Church. She entered the building, fluttered before the statue of the Blessed Liberator, and acclaimed him by flapping her wings; after which she returned to the pond, leaving one of her little ones as an offering. Some time afterwards, the duckling disappeared unobserved. For two hundred years and more, the duck, always the same duck, returned, on a fixed day, with her hatch, to the church of the great St. Nicholas at Montfort.

The story was written and printed in 1652: the author very justly observes that "a poor wild-duck is not a very considerable thing in the eyes of God; that nevertheless she acts her part in doing homage to His greatness; that St. Francis' grasshopper was of even less account, and that nevertheless its trill charmed a seraph's heart."

But Madame de Chateaubriand followed a false legend: in her ballad, the maiden imprisoned at Montfort was a princess, who succeeded in being changed into a duck in order to escape her captor's violence. I remember only the following lines of one stanza of my mother's ballad:

Cane la belle est devenue,
Cane la belle est devenue,
Et s'envola par une grille,
Dans un étang plein de lentilles.[1]

As Madame de Chateaubriand was a real saint, she obtained the Bishop of Saint-Malo's promise to give me the tonsure, although he had a scruple on the subject: to bestow the mark of an ecclesiastic upon a layman and a soldier appeared to him to be a profanation not far removed from simony. M. Cortois de Pressigny, now Archbishop of Besançon and a peer of France, is a worthy and deserving man. He was young at that time, protected by the Queen, and on the highroad to fortune, which he attained later by a better road: persecution.

Dressed in uniform, and wearing my sword, I went down on my knees at the prelate's feet; he cut two or three hairs from the crown of my head: this was called the tonsure, of which I received a formal certificate. With this certificate, it was possible for an income of 200,000 livres to fall to me, when my proofs of nobility had been admitted in Malta: an abuse, no doubt, in the ecclesiastical order, but a useful thing in the political order of the old constitution. Was it not better that a kind of military benefice should be attached to the sword of a soldier than to the cloak of an abbé who would have spent the revenues of his fat living on the pavement of Paris?

The fact that the tonsure was conferred on me for the foregoing reasons has caused ill-informed biographers to state that I had at one time entered the Church.

This happened in 1788. I kept horses, I rode all over the country, or galloped beside the waves, the moaning friends of my youth: I alighted from my horse and frolicked with them; the whole barking family of Scylla sprang to my knees to fondle me: *Nunc vada latrantis Scyllæ.* I have travelled very far to admire the scenes of nature: I might have contented myself with those which my native land offered to my eyes.

Nothing could be more charming than the country for five or six leagues round Saint-Malo. The banks of the Rance

---

[1] " The beautiful maid became a duck,
Became a duck, became a duck,
And through a lattice off she flew
To a pond where duck-weed grew."—T.

alone, as one ascends the river from its mouth to Dinan, ought to attract the traveller, forming a constant medley of rocks and verdure, of strands and forests, of creeks and hamlets, of the ancient manors of feudal Brittany and the modern habitations of commercial Brittany. The latter were built at a time when the merchants of Saint-Malo were so rich that, on days of merry-making, they heated piastres and flung them red-hot to the people through the windows. These dwellings are very luxurious. Bonnaban, the country-seat of Messieurs de La Saudre,[1] is in part built of marble brought from Genoa, a magnificence of which we in Paris have no idea. The Briantais,[2] the Bosq, the Montmarin,[3] the Balue,[4] the Colombier[5] are, or were, adorned with orangeries, fountains, and statues. In some cases the gardens slope down to the shore behind the arcade formed by a screen of lime-trees, through a colonnade of pine-trees, to the end of a lawn; across a bed of tulips, the sea displays its ships, its calms, and its tempests.

Every peasant, sailor, and husbandman owns a little white cottage with a garden; among the vegetables, the currant-bushes, the roses, the irises, the marigolds of this garden, you find a shoot of Cayenne tea, a stalk of Virginian tobacco, a Chinese flower, some kind of souvenir of other shores and another sun: they compose the chart and the itinerary of the owner. The occupiers of these coast holdings belong to a fine Norman race; the women are tall, slender, active, and wear grey-woollen bodices, petticoats of calamanco and striped silk, white stockings with coloured clocks. Their foreheads are shaded by an ample dimity or cambric head-dress, the flaps of which stand up in the shape of a cap or float like a veil. A number of silver chains hang in a bunch at their left side. Every morning, in the spring, these daughters of the North, stepping from their boats, as though they were coming once again to invade the land, carry to market baskets of fruit and shells filled with curds: when, with one hand, they hold on their

---

[1] Pierre and François Guillaume de La Saudre. The Château de Bonnaban is still one of the finest seats in the neighbourhood of Saint-Malo. It is now the property of the Comte de Kergariou.—B.

[2] The Briantais, at Saint-Servan, on the banks of the Rance, was at that time the property of the Picot de Prémesnil family, and now belongs to M. Lachambre, a late member of the Chamber of Deputies.—B.

[3] The Bosq and the Montmarin faced each other on opposite banks of the Rance: the former at Saint-Servan, the latter at Pleurtuit. Both belonged to the opulent family of Magon.—B.

[4] The Balue, at Saint-Servan, also belonged to the Magons.—B.

[5] The Colombier, at Paramé, was the property, in 1788, of the Eon de Carissan family.—B.

heads black jars full of milk or flowers, when the lappets of their white caps set off their blue eyes, their pink faces, their fair hair pearled with dew, the Valkyrs of the *Edda*, of whom the youngest is the Future, or the Basket-bearers of Athens, were less graceful. Does the picture still resemble the original? Those women, doubtless, no longer exist; nought remains but my recollection of them.

I left my mother and went to see my two elder sisters, who lived near Fougères. I stayed a month with Madame de Chateaubourg. Her two country-houses, Lascardais[1] and Le Plessis,[2] near Saint-Aubin-du-Cormier, famous for its tower and its battle,[3] stood in a country of rocks, moors, and woods. My sister's steward was M. Livoret,[4] formerly a Jesuit, who had met with a strange adventure.

When he was made steward at Lascardais, the Comte de Chateaubourg, the elder, had just died: M. Livoret, who had not known him, was installed as care-taker of the castle. The first night that he slept there alone, he saw a pale old man come into his room, in a dressing-gown and night-cap, and carrying a little light. The apparition went to the hearth, placed the candlestick on the mantel, lit the fire and sat down in a chair. M. Livoret trembled all over his body. After two hours spent in silence, the old man rose, took his light again, and left the room, closing the door behind him.

The next day the steward told his adventure to the farm-people, who, on hearing the description of the spectre, declared that it was their old master. The matter did not end there: if M. Livoret looked behind him in a wood, he saw the ghost; if he had to climb over a stile in a field, the shade set itself astride the stile. One day, the unhappy haunted man venturing to say, "Monsieur de Chateaubourg, leave me," the ghost replied, "No." M. Livoret, a cold and practical man,

[1] The Château de Lascardais was the principal residence of M. and Madame de Chateaubourg. It is in the commune of Mézières, canton of Saint-Aubin-du-Cormier, Arrondissement of Fougères (Ille-et-Vilaine) and is now occupied by Madame la Vicomtesse de Breil de Pontbriand, the Comtesse de Chateaubourg's grand-daughter.—B.

[2] Le Plessis-Pillet is in the commune of Dourdain, canton of Liffré, Arrondissement of Fougères.—B.

[3] Saint-Aubin-du-Cormier is twelve miles S.E. of Fougères. The tower is a very tall one. The battle referred to is that in which La Trémoille defeated the Bretons and the revolted Duc d'Orléans (afterwards Louis XII.) in 1488.—T.

[4] Robert Lambert Livorel (not Livoret) entered the Company of Jesus in 1753, at the age of eighteen. He was a coadjutor brother at Rennes College at the time of the suppression of the Company in 1762.—B.

possessed of very little imagination, repeated his story as often as he was asked, always in the same way and with the same conviction.

A little later I accompanied to Normandy a brave officer attacked with brain-fever. We were lodged in a farm-house: an old tapestry, lent by the lord of the manor, separated my bed from the invalid's. Behind this hanging the patient was bled: to relieve him of his sufferings, they plunged him into ice-baths; he shivered under this torture, with his nails turned blue, his violet face haggard, and his teeth clenched. His head was shaven, and a long beard which came down from his pointed chin served to clothe his bare, wet, lean chest.

When the invalid had a fit of crying, he opened an umbrella, thinking that he was sheltering himself from his tears: if this were a sure protection against weeping, a statue should be raised to the inventor.

My only happy moments were those at which I went to wander in the grave-yard of the village church, built upon a mound. My companions were the dead, a few birds, and the setting sun. I dreamed of Paris society, of my early years, of my phantom, of the Combourg woods, to which I was so near in point of space, though so far removed in point of time. I returned to my poor sick man: it was the blind leading the blind.

Alas, let a blow, a fall, a moral suffering deprive Homer, Newton, Bossuet of their genius, and those divine men, instead of exciting profound pity, bitter and eternal regret, would be the object of a smile! Many people whom I have known and loved have seen their reason troubled while about me, as though I bore with me the germ of the contagion. I can explain Cervantes' masterpiece and its cruel gaiety only by a sad reflection: when one considers existence as a whole, and weighs its good and evil, one feels tempted to long for any accident that brings forgetfulness with it, as a means of escaping from one's self; a joyful drunkard is a happy being. Putting religion aside, happiness lies in not knowing one's self and in reaching death without having felt life.

I brought my friend back completely cured.

Madame Lucile and Madame de Farcy, who had returned with me to Brittany, wished to go back to Paris; but I was detained by the unsettled condition of the province. The States had been summoned for the end of December 1788. The commune of Rennes and, following in its wake, the other communes of Brittany had passed a resolution forbidding their

deputies to take part in any business before the question of
hearth-money had been settled.

The Comte de Boisgelin,[1] who was to preside over the
order of the nobles, hurried to Rennes. The gentry were
convoked by private letters; among them were those who, like
myself, were still too young to have votes in the deliberations.
We might be attacked, strong arms needed counting as well as
votes: we went to our posts.

A number of meetings were held at M. de Boisgelin's
before the opening of the States. All the scenes of confusion
at which I had assisted were renewed. The Chevalier de
Guer, the Marquis de Trémargat, my uncle the Comte de
Bedée, nicknamed Bedée the Artichoke, because of his stoutness, as opposed to another Bedée, long and slim, who was
called Bedée the Asparagus, broke a number of chairs in
climbing on them to deliver their harangues. The Marquis
de Trémargat, a wooden-legged naval officer, made many
enemies for his order. One day they were talking of estab-
lishing a military school for the education of the sons of poor
nobles; a member of the Third Estate cried:

"And what are our sons to have?"

"The almshouse," replied Trémargat.

The phrase fell among the crowd and soon bore fruit.

At these meetings I became aware of a disposition of character in myself which I have since found again in the field of
politics and arms: the more my colleagues or companions grew
inflamed, the calmer I became. I saw the tribune or the gun
fired with indifference: I have never bowed before either words
or cannon-balls.

The result of our deliberations was that the nobles were
to treat general matters first, and not busy themselves with
hearth-money until the other questions had been disposed of; a
resolution directly opposed to that of the commons. The nobles
had no great confidence in the clergy, who often abandoned
them, especially when presided over by the Bishop of Rennes,[2]
a wheedling, circumspect person, who spoke with a slight and
not ungraceful lisp, and nursed his prospects at Court. The
hatred was fomented by a newspaper, the *Sentinelle du Peuple*,
edited at Rennes by a scribbler newly arrived from Paris.

[1] Louis Bruno Comte de Boisgelin (1734-1794), Knight of St. Louis and of the
Holy Ghost, and holder of several Court and military appointments. He was
guillotined on the 7th of July 1794; his wife, a sister of the Chevalier de Boufflers,
ascended the scaffold on the same day.—B.

[2] François Bareau de Girac (1736-1820).—B.

The States were held in the Jacobin Convent on the Place du Palais. We entered the sessions-hall, in the temper which I have described; we had hardly taken our seats before we were besieged by the mob. The 25th, 26th, 27th, and 28th of January 1789 were unlucky days. The Comte de Thiard had few troops under his command; he lacked both vigour and decision, and moved without acting. The School of Law at Rennes, which had Moreau at its head, had sent for the young men of Nantes; they came to the number of four hundred, and in spite of his entreaties, the Commandant was unable to prevent them from invading the town. Meetings held by various factions in the cafés and on the Champ-Montmorin resulted in collisions attended with bloodshed.

Tired of being blockaded in our hall, we resolved to sally forth sword in hand; it was a pretty sight enough. At a signal given by our president, we all drew our swords together, to the cry of "Brittany for ever!" and, like a forlorn garrison, executed a furious sortie in order to fight our way through. The mob received us with yells, with showers of stones, blows of iron-shod sticks, and pistol-shots. We forced a passage through the surging crowd, which closed in upon us. Several gentlemen were wounded, dragged along the ground, lacerated, covered with bruises and contusions. We succeeded with great difficulty in extricating ourselves and reaching our respective lodgings.

Duels followed between the nobles and the law-students and their friends from Nantes. One of these duels took place in public on the Place Royale; the honours remained with old Keralieu,[1] a naval officer, who was attacked, and who fought with incredible vigour amid the applause of his youthful adversaries.

Another mob had formed. The Comte de Montboucher[2] caught sight in the crowd of a student called Ulliac, and said to him:

"Monsieur, this concerns you and me!"

A ring was formed around them; Montboucher disarmed Ulliac and handed him back his sword: they embraced, and the crowd dispersed.

---

[1] The name of Keralieu does not figure upon the lists of the States of 1788-1789, nor is it to be found in the Breton peerages. Doubtless the name should read Kersalaün. A duel did, in fact, take place between M. de Kersalaün and a young citizen of Rennes, Joseph Marie Jacques Blin. Jean Joseph Comte de Kersalaün was the eldest son of the Marquis de Kersalaün, the senior member of the Parliament. He was forty-five, and therefore much "older" than his adversary, who was only twenty-four years of age.—B.

[2] Captain René François Joseph de Montbourcher (1759-1835). His name was pronounced Montboucher, as Chateaubriand spells it.—B.

At least our Breton nobility did not succumb without honour. It refused to send deputies to the States-General, because it had not been convoked in accordance with the fundamental laws of the constitution of the province; it joined the army of the Princes in vast numbers, and was decimated in Condé's Army, or with Charette in the wars of the Vendée. Would it have made any difference in the majority in the National Assembly if it had joined that assembly? That is scarcely likely: in great social transformations, cases of individual resistance, however creditable to personal character, are powerless against facts. Nevertheless it is· difficult to say what might not have been effected by a man of Mirabeau's genius, but of opposite principles, if one had been found in the order of the Breton nobility.

Young Boishue and my schoolfellow Saint-Riveul had been killed in these encounters, on their way to the chamber of the nobles: the former was in vain defended by his father, who served as his second.[1]

Reader, pause: see flow the first drops of blood which the Revolution was to shed. Heaven decreed that they should issue from the veins of a companion of my childhood. Suppose that I had fallen instead of Saint-Riveul; it would have been said of me, merely changing the name, as was said of the victim with whom commenced the great immolation:

"A gentleman called Chateaubriand was killed on his way to the assembly-room of the States."

Those few words would have taken the place of my long history. Would Saint-Riveul have played my part on the earth? Was he destined for fame or for silence?

And now, reader, pass on; cross the river of blood which for all time separates the old world, whence you are issuing, from the new, at the entrance to which you shall die.

The year 1789, so famous in our history and in the history of the human race, found me on the moors of my Brittany; I was not even able to leave the country until rather late, and did not reach Paris until after the sack of the Maison Reveillon,[2] the opening of the States-General,[3] the constitution of the

[1] Louis Pierre de Guehenneuc de Boishue (1767–1789) eldest son of Jean Baptiste René de Guehenneuc, Comte de Boishue. He was therefore only twenty-one years of age when he was killed, on the 27th of January 1789, in the streets of Rennes, at the same time as young Saint-Riveul (on whom see note *ante*).—B.

[2] The sacking of the house of Reveillon, the paper manufacturer of the Rue Saint-Antoine, took place 28 April 1789.—T.

[3] 4 May 1789.—T.

Third Estate into a National Assembly, the oath of the Tennis Court,[1] the Royal Speech of the 23rd of June, and the joining of the clergy and the nobles to the commons.[2]

There was a great stir along my road: in the villages the peasants stopped the carriages, asked to be shown passports, interrogated the travellers. The nearer we approached to the capital, the more the excitement increased. Passing through Versailles, I saw troops quartered in the orangery, trains of artillery parked in the court-yards, the provisional hall of the National Assembly erected on the Place du Palais, and deputies moving to and fro amid sight-seers, people of the palace, and soldiers.

In Paris the streets were blocked by crowds standing before the bakers' shops; the passers-by stood discussing at the street corners, the tradesmen came out of their shops and gave and received the news before their doors; the agitators gathered together at the Palais-Royal: Camille Desmoulins began to distinguish himself in the throng.[3]

I had scarcely alighted,[4] together with Madame de Farcy and Madame Lucile, at a lodging-house in the Rue de Richelieu, when a riot broke out: the mob proceeded to the Abbaye to deliver some French Guards, who had been imprisoned by order of their officers. The non-commissioned officers of an artillery regiment quartered at the Invalides joined the people. The defection of the army was commencing.

The Court, alternately yielding and resisting, a mixture of obstinacy and weakness, of hectoring and fear, allowed itself to be bullied by Mirabeau,[5] who demanded that the troops should be removed to a distance, and yet did not consent to remove them: it accepted the affront and did not remove the cause of it. In Paris a rumour spread that an army was arriving through the Montmartre sewer, that the dragoons were about to force the barriers. It was suggested to take up the street pavements, to carry the paving-stones to the top floors of the houses, in order to hurl them upon the tyrant's satellites: every one set to work. In the midst of this turmoil M. Necker was ordered to resign. The new ministry consisted

[1] 20 June 1789.—T.　　[2] 30 June 1789.—T.
[3] Camille Desmoulins (1760–1794) delivered his famous harangue, at the conclusion of which he distributed leaves from the trees overhead to the rioters as a rallying-token, in the Palais-Royal on the 12th of July 1789. He was guillotined 5 April 1794.—T.　　[4] 30 June 1789.—B.
[5] Honoré Gabriel Riquetti, Comte de Mirabeau (1749–1791), represented the Third Estate of the town of Aix in the National Assembly.—T.

of M. de Breteuil,[1] La Galaizière, the Maréchal de Broglie,[2] La Vauguyon, La Porte[3] and Foullon.[4]   These replaced Messieurs de Montmorin,[5] de La Luzerne,[6] de Saint-Priest[7] and de Nivernais.[8]

A Breton poet, newly landed, had asked me to take him to Versailles.   There are people who will go to see gardens and fountains amid the downfall of empires: scribblers especially possess this faculty of isolating themselves in their hobby during the course of the greatest events; with them, their phrase or their strophe fills the place of everything.

I took my Pindar to the gallery at Versailles at mass-time. The Œil-de-Bœuf was radiant: M. Necker's dismissal had raised the spirits of all; they felt sure of victory: possibly Sanson[9] and Simon[10] were among the crowd, witnessing the delight of the Royal Family.

The Queen passed by with her two children; their fair hair appeared to be waiting for crowns: Madame la Duchesse d'Angoulême,[11] aged eleven, drew all eyes through a virginal pride; beautiful through nobility of birth and maidenly innocence, she seemed to say, like Corneille's orange-blossom in the *Guirlande de Julie*:

J'ai la pompe de ma naissance.[12]

---

[1] Louis Auguste Le Tonnelier, Baron de Breteuil (*b.* 1733) was head of the Royal Household and Governor of Paris when placed at the head of this short-lived ministry.—T.

[2] Victor François Maréchal Duc de Broglie (1718–1804) became Minister of War.   He was a distinguished soldier, and had been created a Prince of the Holy Roman Empire in 1759 by the Emperor of Germany in recognition of his services in the war against Prussia.   The title is still borne by the heads of both branches of the Broglie family.—T.

[3] Arnaud de La Porte(1737–1792), Intendant-General of the Navy.   In 1790 he was appointed Intendant of the Civil List, and distinguished himself by his fidelity and firmness in the King's cause, notably at the time of the arrest at Varennes.   He perished on the scaffold in 1792.—T.

[4] Joseph François Foullon (1715–1789) was appointed Controller-General of Finance on the 12th of July and hanged from a lantern in the Rue de la Verrerie on the 22nd, thus becoming one of the first victims of the Revolution.—T.

[5] Armand Marc Comte de Montmorin-Saint-Hérem (*d.* 1792) was Minister of Foreign Affairs in Necker's cabinet.   In 1791 he received the portfolio of the Interior.   He perished in the massacres of September 1792.—T.

[6] César Guillaume de la Luzerne (1738–1821), Bishop of Langres, created a cardinal in 1817.—T.

[7] François Emmanuel Guignard, Comte de Saint-Priest (1735–1821), Minister of the Interior, created a Peer of France in 1815.—T.

[8] Louis Jules Mancini-Mazarini, Duc de Nivernais (1716–1798).—T.

[9] Charles Henri Sanson (*b.* 1739), appointed public executioner in 1778 by Louis XVI., who died by his hand fifteen years later.—B.

[10] Antoine Simon (*d.* 1794), cobbler and member of the Paris Commune, appointed tutor to Louis XVII., 1 July 1793, guillotined 28 July 1794.—B.

[11] Marie Thérèse of France (1778–1851), daughter of Louis XVI., married in 1799 her cousin the Duc d'Angoulême, second son of the Comte d'Artois, later Charles X.—T.   [12] " Of my birth I have the splendour."—T.

MARIE ANTOINETTE

The little Dauphin[1] walked under his sister's protection, and M. Du Touchet followed his pupil; he noticed me, and obligingly called the Queen's attention to me. Casting a smiling look in my direction, she gave me that gracious bow which she had already made me on the day of my presentation. I shall never forget that look, so soon to be extinguished. Marie Antoinette, when she smiled, outlined so clearly the shape of her mouth, that the recollection of that smile (O horror!) enabled me to recognize the jaw-bone of the daughter of kings when the head of the unhappy woman was discovered in the exhumations of 1815.

The counter-stroke to the blow struck at Versailles resounded in Paris. On my return I came upon a crowd hastening along and carrying the busts of M. Necker and of M. le Duc d'Orléans,[2] covered with crape. They cried, "Long live Necker! Long live the Duc d'Orléans!" and among those cries was heard one bolder and more unforeseen:

"Long live Louis XVII.!"

Long live the child whose very name would have been forgotten in the funeral inscription of his family, if I had not recalled it to the memory of the House of Peers![3] Had Louis XVI. abdicated, Louis XVII. been placed upon the throne, M. le Duc d'Orléans declared Regent, what would have happened?

On the Place Louis XV., the Prince de Lambesc,[4] at the head of the "Royal German" regiment, drove back the crowd into the gardens of the Tuileries and wounded an old man: suddenly the tocsin sounded. The cutlers' shops were broken into, and thirty thousand muskets taken from the Invalides. The people armed themselves with pikes, cudgels, pitchforks, sabres, pistols; they sacked Saint-Lazare, burnt down the barriers. The electors of Paris took in hand the government of the Capital, and in a night sixty thousand

---

[1] Louis Duc de Normandie (1785-1795), second son of Louis XVI., became Dauphin on the death of his elder brother, and was recognised as King of France by the emigrants and the foreign Powers after the execution of his father. He died a wretched death in the Temple, 8 June 1795.—T.

[2] Louis Philippe Joseph, fifth Duc d'Orléans (1747-1793), nicknamed Philippe Égalité, voted for the King's death, and was himself guillotined, 6 November 1793.—T.

[3] In a speech made on the 9th of January 1816, preparatory to the general mourning ordered for the 21st, the anniversary of the execution of Louis XVI.—B.

[4] Charles Eugène of Lorraine, Duc d'Elbeuf, Prince de Lambesc (1754-1825), a kinsman of Marie Antoinette, whom he accompanied to France, becoming colonel of the regiment known as Royal-Allemand. After his trial and acquittal for charging the people at the Tuileries, he emigrated and took service in the Austrian army, rising to the rank of Lieutenant-Field-Marshal in 1796. He continued to live in Vienna after the Restoration, and died there, childless, in 1825, one of the branches of the House of Lorraine dying out with him.—T.

citizens were organized, armed, equipped into National Guards.

On the 14th of July came the fall of the Bastille. I was present, as a spectator, at this assault against a few pensioners and a timid governor: if the gates had been kept closed, the mob could never have entered the fortress. I saw two or three guns fired, not by the pensioners, but by French Guards who had climbed to the towers.

De Launey[1] was torn from his hiding-place, and after undergoing a thousand outrages, was struck down on the steps of the Hôtel de Ville; Flesselles,[2] the provost of the merchants, had his brains blown out by a pistol-shot: this was the spectacle which heartless enthusiasts thought so fine. In the midst of these murders, the people gave themselves up to orgies, as in the troubles in Rome under Otho and Vitellius. "The victors of the Bastille," happy drunkards, declared conquerors by pot-house votes, were driven about in hackney-coaches; prostitutes and sans-culottes commenced to reign and escorted them. The passers-by uncovered, with the respect born of fear, before those heroes, some of whom died of fatigue amidst their triumph. The keys of the Bastille multiplied; they were sent to all the important simpletons in the four quarters of the world. How often have I missed my fortune! If I, a spectator, had inscribed my name on the list of the victors, I should be in receipt of a pension to-day.

The experts hurried to assist at the *post-mortem* examination of the Bastille. Temporary cafés were established under tents; people hastened thither as to the fair at Saint-Germain or to Longchamp; numbers of carriages drove slowly past, or stopped at the foot of the towers, whence the stones were being hurled down amid whirlwinds of dust. Elegantly-dressed women and fashionable young men stood upon different points of the Gothic rubbish, and mingled with the half-naked workmen engaged in demolishing the walls amid the acclamations of the crowd. At this meeting-place were to be seen the most famous orators, the best-known men of letters, the most celebrated painters, the most renowned actors and actresses, the most popular dancers, the most illustrious foreigners, the nobles of the Court and the ambassadors of Europe: old France had come there to end, new France to commence, its existence.

---

[1] Bernard René Jourdan, Marquis de Launey (1740-1789), Captain-Governor of the Bastille.—B.

[2] Jacques de Flesselles (1721-1789), provost of the merchants of Paris.—T.

No event, however wretched or hateful in itself, should be treated lightly when its circumstances are serious, or when it marks an epoch : what should have been seen in the capture of the Bastille (and what was not then seen) was, not the violent act of the emancipation of a people, but the emancipation itself which resulted from that act.

Men admired what they ought to condemn, the accident, and did not seek to discover in the future the accomplishment of a people's destiny, the changes in morals, ideas, political power, a renovation of the human race, of which the capture of the Bastille, like a blood-stained jubilee, inaugurated the era. Brutal anger wrought ruins, and beneath that anger was concealed the intelligence which laid among those ruins the foundations of the new edifice.

But the nation, deceived as to the grandeur of the material fact, was not deceived as to the grandeur of the moral fact : in the eyes of the nation, the Bastille was the trophy of its servitude, and seemed to be erected at the entrance to Paris, opposite the sixteen pillars of Montfaucon,[1] as the gibbet of its liberties.[2] In demolishing a State fortress, the people considered that it was breaking the military yoke, and made a tacit engagement to take the place of the army which it was disbanding : we know what prodigies were wrought by the people turned soldier.

Awakened by the sound of the fall of the Bastille, as though by the premonitory sound of the fall of the throne, Versailles had lapsed from the heights of self-confidence to the depths of despondency. The King hurried to the National Assembly, and delivered a speech from the president's chair; he declared that an order had been given for the withdrawal of the troops, and returned to his palace amid a shower of benedictions. A vain parade! Parties do not believe in the conversion of the opposing parties : the liberty which capitulates, or the power which degrades itself, receives no mercy from its foes.

Eighty deputies set out from Versailles to announce the making of peace to the Capital; illuminations followed. M.

[1] An unsavoury eminence, between the Faubourg Saint-Martin and the Faubourg du Temple, on which stood a number of gibbets, erected early in the fourteenth century.—T.

[2] After a lapse of fifty-two years, fifteen bastilles are being built in order to oppress the liberty in whose name the first Bastille was destroyed.—*Author's Note* (Paris, 1841).

de La Fayette[1] was made Commandant of the National Guard,
M. Bailly,[2] Mayor of Paris: I never knew the poor but
respectable scholar, save through his misfortunes. Revolutions
possess men for each of their several periods; some follow
these revolutions to their finish, others commence but do not
complete them.

A general dispersal ensued; the courtiers left for Bâle,
Lausanne, Luxemburg, and Brussels. Madame de Polignac[3] in
her flight met M. Necker returning. The Comte d'Artois, his
sons,[4] the three Condés[5] emigrated, drawing after them the
higher clergy and a portion of the nobility. The officers of the
army, threatened by their mutinous soldiers, yielded to the
torrent which drifted them down its stream. Louis XVI. alone
remained behind to face the nation with his two children and a
few women: the Queen, "Mesdames,"[6] and Madame Élisabeth.[7]
"Monsieur,"[8] who stayed until the flight to Varennes, was of no
great assistance to his brother: although, by declaring himself
in the Assembly of Notables in favour of the vote by heads, he
had decided the fate of the Revolution, the Revolution distrusted

[1] Marie Paul Joseph Gilbert de Motier, Marquis de La Fayette (1757-1834)
had taken a leading part in the assistance rendered by the French to the American
Revolution. He was outlawed in 1792, fled, was captured by the Austrians, and
imprisoned, for his complicity in the French Revolution, in the citadel of Olmütz,
until 1797. This foreign captivity doubtless saved him from the native guillotine.
He took no part in public affairs until the Restoration, when he sat in the Chamber
of Deputies as a member of the opposition. In 1830, after the Orleanist usurpation he for the second time received the command of the National Guard.—T.

[2] Jean Sylvain Bailly (1736-1793) was a member of the French Academy and
of the Academy of Science, and keeper of the picture-gallery at Versailles. He
became the first president of the National Assembly, having presided at the occasion of the Oath of the Tennis Court, and was the first Mayor of Paris. His
popularity left him in 1791, after his endeavour to suppress the riotous meetings in the Champ-de-Mars; he resigned the mayoralty and quitted Paris. In
1793, he was recognised at Melun, brought back to Paris, and guillotined
(11 November).—T.

[3] Yolande Martine Gabrielle, Duchesse de Polignac (1749-1793), née de
Polastron, wife of the Comte Jules, later Duc de Polignac, governess of the
Children of France, and favourite of Marie Antoinette. She was the mother of
the Prince de Polignac who became minister to Charles X.—T.

[4] Louis Antoine, Duc d'Angoulême (1775-1844), and Charles Ferdinand, Duc
de Berry (1778-1820).—T.

[5] Louis Joseph Prince de Condé (1736-1818), his son Louis Henri Joseph Duc
de Bourbon (1756-1830), and his grandson Louis Antoine Henri Duc d'Enghien
(1772-1804).—T.

[6] The King's aunts, daughters of Louis XV.: Madame Adélaïde (1732-1800)
and Madame Victoire (1733-1799). They emigrated in 1791.—T.

[7] Madame Élisabeth (1764-1794), the King's sister, guillotined 10 May
1794.—T.

[8] Louis Stanislas Xavier Comte de Provence (1755-1824); succeeded to the
Crown in 1795 as Louis XVIII. "Monsieur" is the title of the eldest brother of
the King of France.—T.

him ; he, Monsieur, disliked the King, did not understand the Queen, and was not loved by them.

Louis XVI. went to the Hôtel de Ville on the 17th : a hundred thousand men, armed like the monks of the League, received him. He was harangued by Messrs. Bailly, Moreau de Saint-Méry,[1] and Lally-Tolendal,[2] all of whom wept : the last has remained subject to tears. The King broke down in his turn ; he fixed an enormous tricolour cockade on his hat ; he was then and there declared to be " an honest man, Father of the French, King of a free people," while the said people was preparing, by virtue of its liberty, to lay low the head of that honest man, its father and its King.

A few days after this reconciliation, I was at the windows of my lodgings with my sisters and some Bretons ; we heard cries of " Shut the doors, shut the doors!" A troop of tatterdemalions approached from one end of the street ; from the midst of this troop rose two standards which we could not see clearly at that distance. As they came nearer, we distinguished two dishevelled and disfigured heads, which the forerunners of Marat[3] were carrying, each at the end of a pike : they were the heads of Messrs. Foullon and Bertier.[4] The others all drew back from the windows ; I remained. The assassins stopped in front of me, stretched the pikes towards me, singing, capering, jumping up in order to bring the pale effigies nearer to my face. One eye in one of these heads had started from its socket, and fell upon the dead man's lurid face ; the pike projected through the open mouth, the teeth of which bit upon the iron.

" Brigands ! " I cried, filled with indignation which I was unable to contain. " Is that how you understand liberty ? "

Had I had a gun, I should have fired at those wretches as

---

[1] Médéric Louis Élie Moreau de Saint-Méry (1750–1819), chairman of the electors of Paris. He was arrested after the 10th of August 1792, but succeeded in making good his escape.—B.

[2] Trophine Gérard Marquis de Lally-Tolendal (1751–1830), delegate of the nobles of Paris to the States-General. He too escaped from the Abbaye after his arrest in August, and took refuge in England, whence he wrote to the Convention in order to obtain the honour (eventually awarded to Malesherbes) of defending Louis XVI. He was created a peer of France under the Restoration, and made a member of the French Academy ; in 1817 he received his marquisate, the original title of the family being Comte de Lally and Baron Tollendal in Ireland.—T.

[3] Jean Paul Marat (1744–1793), the famous demagogue of the Terror.—T.

[4] Louis Bénigne François Bertier de Sauvigny (1742–1789), Intendant of Paris, and son-in-law to Foullon. He was hanged from a lantern after being made to kiss the head of his father-in-law, who had just met with the same fate.—T.

at a pack of wolves. They shouted and yelled; they beat long
at the doors of the gate-way, in the hope of breaking them down
and adding my head to those of their victims. My sisters
fainted; the poltroons of the lodging-house overwhelmed me
with reproaches. The murderers, who were being pursued,
had not time to break into the house, and passed on. Those
heads, and others which I saw soon afterwards, changed my
political tendencies; I held the banquets of cannibals in ab-
horrence, and the idea of leaving France for some distant
country began to take root in my mind.

Recalled to office on the 25th of July, installed and received
with festivities, M. Necker, the third successor, after Calonne
and Taboureau,[1] of Turgot,[2] was soon left behind by events,
and lapsed into unpopularity. It is one of the singular facts
of the time that so serious a person should have been raised
to the post of minister through the tact of a man noted for
such mediocrity and levity as the Marquis de Pezay.[3] The
Compte rendu,[4] which replaced in France the system of taxation
by that of loans, stirred people's ideas : women talked of receipts
and expenditure; for the first time one saw, or thought one
saw, something in the mechanism of figures. These calcula-
tions, painted in colours laid on *à la Thomas*,[5] had first
established the reputation of the director-general of finance.
The banker was a clever accountant, but a resourceless econo-
mist; a noble but turgid writer; an honest man, but devoid of
the loftier virtues. He was like the character which speaks the
prologue in a classical play, and which disappears at the rise of
the curtain, after explaining the piece to the audience. M. Necker

[1] Taboureau des Réaux, Intendant of Valenciennes, was Controller-General
from October 1776 to June 1777.—B.
[2] Anne Robert Jacques Turgot, Baron de L'Aulne (1727–1781), Controller-
General from 1774 to 1776.—T.
[3] Alexandre Frédéric Jacques Masson, Marquis de Pezay (1741–1777), commenced life as an officer of Musketeers, and made his name known by means
of some trivial drawing-room verse and of his inferior prose translations of
Tibullus, Catullus, and Propertius. He was charged with the duty of instructing
Louis XVI., then Dauphin, in elementary tactics, managed to insinuate himself
into the Prince's intimacy, and eventually succeeded in bringing about the fall of
Terray and the rise of Necker.—T.
[4] The *Compte rendu au Roi* was a sort of specimen budget published by Necker
in 1780, from which public opinion was for the first time enabled to form an
opinion of the working of the administration of the public revenues, till then
kept secret. The *Compte rendu* caused a prodigious sensation.—B.
[5] Antoine Léonard Thomas (1732–1785), a member of the French Academy,
and a man of letters noted for rhetoric and over-emphasis of style. Chateaubriand's
allusion is to the excessive optimism of the *Compte rendu*, which showed a very
large surplus.—T.

was the father of Madame de Staël :[1] his vanity hardly permitted him to believe that his true title to the recollection of posterity lay in the fame achieved by his daughter.

The monarchy was demolished, in imitation of the Bastille, at the evening sitting of the National Assembly on the 4th of August. They who, from hatred of the past, decry the nobility to this day, forget that it was a member of that body, the Vicomte de Noailles,[2] supported by the Duc d'Aiguillon[3] and Matthieu de Montmorency,[4] who upset the edifice which was the object of the revolutionary onslaughts. Upon the motion of the feudal delegate were abolished all feudal rights : rights of hunting and preserving feathered and ground game, tithes and champerty, the privileges of the orders, of the towns and provinces, personal servitude, manorial jurisdiction, purchase of offices. The severest blows struck against the ancient constitution of the State were delivered by noblemen. The patricians began the Revolution, the plebeians completed it : just as old France owed her glory to the French nobility, even so does young France owe to it her liberty, if liberty there be for France.

The troops encamped around Paris had been sent away, and by one of those contradictory counsels which vexed the will of the King, the Flanders Regiment was summoned to Versailles. The Bodyguards invited the officers of that regiment to dinner ;[5] heads grew excited ; the Queen appeared in the middle of the banquet, with the Dauphin ; toasts were drunk to the health of the Royal Family ; the King came in

[1] Anne Louise Germaine Baronne de Staël-Holstein (1766–1817), the most famous of women-writers. She married the Baron de Staël-Holstein, Swedish Ambassador to France, in 1786. He died in 1802, and eight years later she was married for the second time, but secretly, to a young officer, M. de Rocca. In 1815 she obtained two million francs from Louis XVIII., by way of a restitution of moneys due to her father.—T.

[2] Louis Marie Vicomte de Noailles (1756–1804), second son of Philippe de Noailles, Maréchal Duc de Mouchy, and brother-in-law of La Fayette. He took part in the French expedition to the United States, and pronounced himself in favour of the Revolution in 1789. He sat in the States-General as deputy for the nobility of the bailiwick of Nemours.—T.

[3] Armand Désiré de Wignerod-Duplessis-Richelieu, Duc d'Aiguillon (1731–1800), representative of the nobility of the seneschalty of Agen in the States-General, and son of the Duc d'Aiguillon, Prime Minister to Louis XV.—T.

[4] Matthieu Jean Félicité Vicomte, later Duc de Montmorency-Laval (1767–1826), had also imbibed his revolutionary opinions in the American Campaign. He abandoned them, however, at the Restoration, under which he became a peer of France, Minister of Foreign Affairs, a member of the French Academy, and a duke. In January 1826 he was appointed governor to the Duc de Bordeaux, but died a few weeks later.—T.

[5] In the Opera-house, 1 October 1789.—T.

his turn; the military band played the touching and favourite air, " *Ô Richard! ô mon roi!* "[1] No sooner was this news spread through Paris, than it was seized upon by the opposite opinion; people cried that Louis was refusing his sanction to the Declaration of Rights with the intention of escaping to Metz with the Comte d'Estaing.[2] Marat propagated this rumour: he was already writing the *Ami du peuple.*[3]

The 5th of October arrived. I did not witness the events of that day. The accounts of what had occurred reached the Capital early on the 6th. We were told at the same time to expect a visit from the King. I was as bold in public places as I was timid in drawing-rooms: I felt myself made for solitude or the forum. I hastened to the Champs-Élysées: first appeared guns, upon which harpies, thieves' doxies, women of the town rode astride, uttering the most obscene speeches, making the most filthy gestures. Next, surrounded by a horde of people of every age and sex, marched on foot the Bodyguards, who had exchanged hats, swords, and bandoliers with the National Guards: each of their horses carried two or three fish-fags, dirty bacchantes, drunk and indecently clad. After them came the deputation from the National Assembly; the royal carriages followed, rolling in the dusty darkness of a forest of pikes and bayonets. Tattered rag-men, butchers with their blood-stained aprons hanging from their thighs, their bare knives from their belts, their shirt-sleeves turned up, walked beside the carriage-doors; other sinister guards had climbed upon the roof; others hung on to the foot-board, lolled upon the box. They fired muskets and pistols; they cried:

"Here are the baker, the baker's wife, and the baker's boy!"

By way of oriflamme, they carried before the descendant of St. Louis, in mid-air, upraised on Swiss halberts, the heads of two Bodyguards, powdered and curled by a Sèvres hair-dresser.

[1] When Louis XVI. entered the hall, M. de Canecaude, commissary of the King's Military Household, ordered the band-master to play Grétry's " *Où peut-on être mieux qu'au sein de sa famille?* " "Where is greater happiness found than in one's family circle?" The band-master replied that he had not the music, and played, " *Ô Richard! ô mon Roi, l'univers t'abandonne:* " "O Richard, O my King, the world is forsaking thee," from *Richard Cœur-de-Lion* by the same composer.—B.

[2] Vice-Admiral Charles Hector Comte d'Estaing (1729–1794) was a member of both forces, and had seen much service both on sea and land. He embraced the side of the Revolution, and was at this time Commandant of the National Guard. He was guillotined 28 April 1794.—T.

[3] Marat's paper was first published 12 September 1789, with the title the *Publiciste parisien.* With the sixth issue, that is, on 17 September 1789, the title was changed to the *Ami du peuple, ou le Publiciste parisien.*—B.

Bailly the astronomer told Louis XVI. at the Hôtel de Ville that the "humane, respectful and faithful" people had "conquered" its King, and the King on his side, "greatly touched and greatly pleased," declared that he had come to Paris "of his free will:" unworthy insincerities pertaining to the violence and fear which at that time dishonoured all men and all parties. Louis XVI. was not insincere: he was weak; weakness is not an insincerity, but it takes its place and fulfils its functions: the respect with which the virtues and misfortunes of the sainted and martyred King must needs inspire us render any expression of human judgment almost sacrilegious.

The deputies left Versailles and held their first sitting on the 19th of October in one of the halls of the archbishop's palace.   On the 9th of November they moved into the Riding-hall, near the Tuileries.   The remainder of the year 1789 witnessed the decrees which despoiled the clergy, destroyed the old magistracy, and created the *assignats ;*[1] the resolution of the Commune of Paris in favour of the first committee of research; and the order of the judges for the prosecution of the Marquis de Favras.[2]

The Constituent Assembly, in spite of all with which it can be reproached, remains nevertheless the most illustrious popular assemblage that has ever appeared among the nations of the world, both because of the magnitude of its transactions 'and the immensity of their results.   There is no political question, however lofty, which it did not discuss and suitably solve.   What would it not have been, had it kept to the *cahiers*[3] of the States-General and not endeavoured to go beyond them !   All that human experience and intelligence had conceived, discovered and elaborated during three centuries is to be found in these instructions.   The various abuses of the old monarchy are there pointed out and remedies proposed ; every kind of liberty is claimed, even the liberty of the press ; every form of improvement demanded for industries, manufactures, commerce, public roads, the army, taxation, finance, the schools, public education, and the rest.   We have

[1] The paper money of the French Republic, "assigned" upon the spoils of the clergy, &c.—T.

[2] Thomas Mahi, Marquis de Favras (1744-1790), was accused of conspiring to assassinate La Fayette, Necker, and Bailly, and to carry off Louis XVI. in order to place him at the head of an anti-revolutionary army.   He was condemned to be hanged, and executed 19 February 1790.—T.

[3] The so-called *cahiers* or note-books consisted of the official instructions of the electors to the deputies to the States-General.—T.

passed across abysses of crime and accumulations of glory to
no profit; the Republic and the Empire have served no
purpose: the Empire merely regulated the brute force of the
arms which the Republic had set in motion; it has left us
centralization, a vigorous form of administration which I consider an evil, but which alone, perhaps, was able to replace the
local systems of administration at a time when these were
destroyed, and when anarchy combined with ignorance filled all
men's heads.   With that exception, we have not moved a step
forward since the Constituent Assembly: its labours are like
those of the great physician of antiquity, which at the same
time extended and settled the boundaries of science.   Let us
speak of some of the members of this Assembly, and in
particular of Mirabeau, in whom they are all summed up, by
whom they are all governed.

Connected, thanks to the disorders and the chances of his
life, with the greatest events and with the lives of malefac-
tors, ravishers, and adventurers, Mirabeau, the tribune of the
aristocracy, the deputy of the democracy, had in his com-
position something of Gracchus and Don Juan, of Catiline and
Guzman de Alfarache, of the Cardinal de Richelieu and the
Cardinal de Retz, of the *roué* of the Regency and the savage of
the Revolution: moreover he had something of the Mirabeaus, the
exiled Florentine family, which retained a trace of those armed
palaces and of those great factionists celebrated by Dante; the
naturalized French family, in which the republican spirit of the
Italian middle-ages and the feudal spirit of our own middle-
ages were united in a succession of uncommon men.
Mirabeau's ugliness, laid on over the substratum of beauty
special to his race, produced a sort of powerful figure from the
"Last Judgment" of Michael Angelo, the fellow-countryman
of the Arrighettis.[1]   The scars dug into the orator's face by
the small-pox had rather the semblance of gaps left by the fire.
Nature seemed to have moulded his head for empire or the
gallows, and to have hewn his arms to clasp a nation or carry
off a woman.   When he shook his mane as he looked at the
mob, he stopped it; when he raised his paw and showed his
claws, the plebs ran furiously.   I have seen him in the tribune,
amid the awful disorder of a sitting, sombre, ugly and motionless: he reminded one of Milton's Chaos, shapeless and
impassive in the centre of his own confusion.

---

[1] The original name of the Riquettis de Mirabeau was Arrighetti.—T.

Mirabeau took after his father [1] and his uncle,[2] both of whom, like Saint-Simon,[3] wrote, off-hand, pages that became immortal. Speeches were written for him to deliver from the tribune: he took from them what his mind was able to amalgamate with its own substance. If he adopted them in their entirety, he delivered them badly; his hearers perceived that they were not his own, through words which he inserted at random and which betrayed him. He derived his energy from his vices; those vices did not spring from a chilly temperament, but were supported by deep, burning, tempestuous passions. Cynicism of manners, by annihilating the moral sense, brings back into society a sort of barbarians; these barbarians of civilisation, while equipped for destruction, like the Goths, have not their power of creating: the latter were the enormous children of a virgin nature, the former are the monstrous abortions of a nature that is depraved.

I twice met Mirabeau at a banquet, once at the house of Voltaire's niece, the Marquise de Villette,[4] and on another occasion at the Palais-Royal, with some members of the Opposition to whom Chapelier[5] had introduced me: Chapelier went to the scaffold in the same tumbril with my brother and M. de Malesherbes.

Mirabeau talked much, and, above all, much of himself. This lion's whelp, himself a lion with a chimera's head, this man so positive where facts were concerned, was all romance, all poetry, all enthusiasm in imagination and language: one recognized the lover of Sophie,[6] exalted in sentiment, capable of sacrifice.

[1] Victor Riquetti, Marquis de Mirabeau (1715-1789). He joined the economists, advocated liberty, and called himself the Friend of Men, after the title of his principal work, the *Ami des hommes*: nevertheless he proved himself the tyrant of his family, a bad husband, and a bad father. He died on the eve of the capture of the Bastille, 13 July 1789.—T.

[2] Jean Antoine Joseph Charles Elzéar de Riquetti (1717–1794). He adopted the title of *bailli* in 1763, on becoming a grand-cross of the Order of Malta, and was thenceforth known as the Bailli de Mirabeau.—B.

[3] Louis de Rouvroy, Duc de Saint-Simon (1675-1755), author of the famous Memoirs.—T.

[4] Reine Philiberte Marquise de Villette (*d.* 1822), *née* Roupt de Varicourt, was adopted by Voltaire at the instance of his niece, Mme. Denis. She called him uncle; he called her "*Belle et bonne*," and married her in 1777 to the Marquis de Villette (*vide infra*, p. 178).—T.

[5] Isaac René Guy Le Chapelier (1754-1794), one of the most capable members of the Constituent Assembly, and a founder of the Club Breton, later the Club des Jacobins. He was guillotined 22 April 1794.—T.

[6] Sophie Marquise de Monnier (1760-1789), *née* Ruffei. For eloping with her, Mirabeau was imprisoned for nearly four years, 1777-1780, at Vincennes by *lettre-de-cachet* obtained at his father's instance. His letters to Sophie from Vincennes, written in a style of exalted sentiment, were published in 1792 in 4 vols. 8vo. The lady herself was locked up in a convent until the death of her husband, a man

"I discovered her," he said, "that adorable woman. . . . I knew what her soul was, that soul shaped by nature's hands in a moment of magnificence."

Mirabeau delighted me with stories of love, with desires for retirement, among which he interspersed barren discussions. He interested me, moreover, in another direction: like myself, he had been treated sternly by his father, who, like mine, had kept up the inflexible tradition of absolute paternal authority.

My great table-companion enlarged upon foreign politics, and hardly spoke of politics at home, although it was the latter which occupied him; but he let fall a few words of sovereign contempt for those men who proclaim themselves superior by reason of the indifference which they affect for misfortunes and crimes. Mirabeau was by nature generous, sensible to friendship, ready to forgive injuries. Notwithstanding his immorality, he had not been able to warp his conscience; he was only corrupt for himself: his firm and upright mind did not treat murder as a sublime effort of the intelligence; he had no sort of admiration for the sewer or the slaughter-house.

Nevertheless, Mirabeau was not wanting in arrogance; he was an outrageous boaster; although he had become a cloth-merchant in order to be elected by the Third Estate (the order of the nobility having committed the honourable folly of rejecting him), he was in love with his birth: "a refractory hawk," says his father, "whose nest was laid among four towers." He did not forget that he had figured at Court, ridden in the coaches, and hunted with the King. He insisted upon being addressed by his title of count; he adhered to his colours, and put his servants into livery when every one else ceased to do so. In and out of season, he referred to "his kinsman," Admiral de Coligny. The *Moniteur* having spoken of him as Riquet:[1]

"Are you aware," he said angrily to the journalist, "that with your 'Riquet' you have set Europe at cross-purposes for three days?"

He repeated that impudent and well-known jest:

"In any other family, my brother the viscount would be the wit and the worthless fellow; in my family, he is the fool and the good man."

very much her senior. She eventually committed suicide because of the infidelity of one of her lovers.—T.

[1] Riquetti, not Riquet, instead of Mirabeau. It was in the account of the sitting in which titles of nobility were abolished that the journalist, in conformity with that abolition, dropped Mirabeau's territorial title, and wrote of him by his patronymic of Riquetti.—B.

... sort
... he
... he ... a club-
... estate ... order
... towards the folly of
... has ... a refractory
... was laid among four
... that figured at Court,
... the King. He insisted
...; he adhered to his
... when every one else
... referred to "his
... having spoken

... to the journalist, "that
... purposes for

... viscount would be
... my family, he is the fool

... of the infidelity

... it was on the account of the
... an indemnity
... were of family his

H. G. MIRABEAU

Some biographers ascribe the phrase to the viscount, comparing himself humbly with the other members of the family.

The ground-work of Mirabeau's opinions was monarchical; he once uttered these fine words:

"I have tried to cure the French of the superstition of monarchy and to substitute its cult."

In a letter intended to be laid before Louis XVI. he wrote:

" I should not like to have worked only for a vast destruction."

This, nevertheless, is what happened to him: Heaven, to punish us for making a bad use of our talents, gives us occasion to repent of our successes.

Mirabeau moved public opinion with two levers: on the one side, he placed his fulcrum in the masses, of whom he had constituted himself the defender, while despising them; on the other, although he was a traitor to his order, he retained its sympathy through caste affinity and common interest. This would not happen to a plebeian who should become the champion of the privileged classes: he would be abandoned by his own party, without winning over the aristocracy, which is naturally ungrateful and not to be won by those not born within its ranks. The aristocracy, moreover, is not able to make a noble without notice, since nobility is the daughter of time.

Mirabeau created a school. Men imagined that by shaking off the moral shackles they were turning themselves into statesmen. These imitations produced only petty miscreants: this one who flatters himself that he is corrupt and a robber is only debauched and a cheat; that other who thinks himself vicious is only vile; a third who boasts of being a criminal is merely infamous.

Too early for himself, too late for the Court, Mirabeau sold himself to the Court, and the Court bought him. He staked his reputation for a pension and an embassy: Cromwell was on the verge of bartering his future for a title and the Order of the Garter. Notwithstanding his haughtiness, Mirabeau did not rate himself high enough. Nowadays, when the abundance of cash and places has raised the price of consciences, there is not a street-boy but costs hundreds of thousands of francs and the leading honours of the State to buy. The grave released Mirabeau from his promises, and shielded him from the perils which he would probably not have been able to conquer: his life would have shown his weakness in good; his death left him in possession of his strength in evil.

At the end of dinner, the discussion turned upon Mirabeau's enemies; I found myself by his side and had not spoken a word. He looked me in the face with his eyes of pride, vice and genius, and laying his hand upon my shoulder, said:

"They will never forgive me my superiority!"

I still feel the pressure of that hand, as though Satan had touched me with his fiery claw. When Mirabeau fixed his look upon a young mute, had he a presentiment of my future condition? Did he think that he would one day figure in my recollections? I was destined to become the historian of great personages: they have defiled before me without my hanging to their mantles to make them drag me with them to posterity.

Mirabeau has already undergone the metamorphosis which is wrought in those whose memory is destined to survive: carried from the Pantheon to the sewer, and back from the sewer to the Pantheon, he has raised himself to the full height of that time which to-day forms his pedestal. We no longer behold the real Mirabeau, but the idealized Mirabeau, the Mirabeau as the painters depict him, in order to make him the symbol or the myth of the period which he represents: he thus becomes both more false and more true. From among so many reputations, so many actors, so many events, so many ruins, there will remain but three men, attached to each of the three great revolutionary epochs: Mirabeau for the aristocracy, Robespierre for the democracy, Bonaparte for the despotism; the monarchy has none: France has paid dear for three reputations which virtue is unable to acknowledge!

The sittings of the National Assembly offered a spectacle of an interest which our "Chambers" are far from approaching. One rose early to find room in the crowded galleries. The deputies arrived eating, talking, gesticulating; they formed groups in the various parts of the house, according to their opinions. The orders of the day were read; after that, the subject agreed upon was set forth, or else an extraordinary motion. There was no question of any insipid point of law; rarely did some scheme of destruction fail to form part of the proceedings. The members spoke for or against; each spoke extempore as best he could. The debates grew stormy; the galleries joined in the discussion, applauded and cheered, hissed and hooted the speakers. The president rang his bell, the deputies apostrophized each other from bench to bench. Mirabeau the Younger[1] took his competitor by the collar; Mirabeau the Elder cried:

[1] André Boniface Louis Riquetti, Vicomte de Mirabeau (1754-1792), the Comte de Mirabeau's younger brother, nicknamed Mirabeau-Tonneau, because of his stoutness, to distinguish him from his brother, Mirabeau-Tonnerre.—T.

"Silence, the 'thirty votes'!"

One day I was seated behind the royalist opposition; before me was a Dauphiné nobleman, swarthy of visage, short of stature, who jumped upon his seat with rage and said to his friends:

"Let us fall upon those ragamuffins, sword in hand!"

He pointed in the direction of the majority. The ladies of the markets, who sat knitting in the galleries, heard him, rose from their seats, and all cried at once, their stockings in their hands, and foaming at the mouth:

"To the lantern with them!"

The Vicomte de Mirabeau, Lautrec,[1] and some younger nobles proposed to take the galleries by assault.

Soon this tumult was drowned by another: petitioners, armed with pikes, appeared at the bar:

"The people are starving," they said: "it is time to take measures against the aristocrats and to rise 'to the level of the situation.'"

The president assured these citizens of his respect:

"We have our eye upon the traitors," he replied, "and the Assembly will see justice done."

Thereupon a fresh din; the deputies of the Right cried that they were making for anarchy; the deputies of the Left replied that the people was free to express its will, that it had the right to complain of the abettors of despotism, seated in the very midst of the national representatives: they spoke thus of their colleagues to that sovereign people which was waiting for them under the street lamps.

The evening sittings surpassed the morning sittings in scandalousness: people speak better and more boldly by candle-light. At such times the Riding-hall became a veritable play-house, in which was enacted one of the greatest tragedies in the world. The leading characters still belonged to the old order of things: their terrible substitutes, hidden behind them, spoke little or not at all. At the end of a violent discussion, I saw a common-looking deputy ascend the tribune, a man with a grey and impassive face, his hair neatly dressed, decently clad like the steward in a good house, or like a village attorney careful of his appearance. He read a long and tedious report; he was not listened to; I asked his name: it was Robespierre.[2] The men in leathern shoes were ready to

[1] M. de Lautrec de Saint-Simon was not a member of the Constituent Assembly, but acted as one of Mirabeau-Tonneau's seconds in his duel with the Duc de Liancourt.—B.

[2] Maximilien Marie Isidore Robespierre (1759–1794), the leader of the Terror.—T.

leave the drawing-rooms, and already the wooden shoes were kicking at the door.

When, before the Revolution, I read the history of public disturbances among various nations, I could not conceive how it was possible to live in those times; I was surprised that Montaigne was able to write with such spirit in a castle which he could not go round without running the risk of being taken prisoner by bands of Leaguers or Protestants.[1]

The Revolution made me understand the possibility of existence under such conditions. Moments of crisis produce a reduplication of life in men. In a society which is dissolving and recomposing itself, the struggle of two geniuses, the clash of the past and the future, the mixture of old manners and new manners form a transient combination which does not leave a moment for weariness. Passions and characters, when at liberty, display themselves with an energy which they do not possess in the well-regulated State. The breaches of the laws, the emancipation from duties, social usages, and seemly manners, the very dangers, all add to the interest of this disorder. The human race making holiday perambulates the streets, having got rid of its schoolmasters and returned for a moment to a state of nature, and does not begin again to feel the need of social restraint until it bears the yoke of the new tyrants engendered by licence.

I cannot better depict society in 1789 and 1790 than by comparing it with the architecture of the time of Louis XII. and Francis I., when the Greek orders began to be grafted upon the Gothic style, or rather by likening it to the collection of ruins and tombs of all ages heaped pell-mell, after the Terror, in the cloisters of the Petits-Augustins: only, the ruins of which I speak were alive and constantly changing. In every corner of Paris were literary sets, political societies, and spectacles; future celebrities wandered unrecognized in the crowd, like the souls on the shore of Lethe, before enjoying the light. I saw Marshal Gouvion-Saint-Cyr[2] play a part in

---

[1] The Château de Montaigne stood on a hill near the village of Saint-Michel, five leagues from Bergerac, in Guyenne. Montaigne was on one occasion captured by marauders and likely to be shot. His good-humour won not only his release but the restoration of the property of which he had been robbed (*Cf.* MONTAIGNE, Booke III. chap. 12: *Of Physiognomy*).—T.

[2] Laurent Maréchal Marquis Gouvion-Saint-Cyr (1764–1830), later a distinguished officer in the armies of the Republic and the Empire. He would appear to have achieved no great success as either an amateur or professional actor.—T.

Beaumarchais' *Mère Coupable*[1] at the Théâtre du Marais. One
went from the Club des Feuillants to the Club des Jacobins,
from the public ball-rooms and gaming-houses to the meetings in
the Palais-Royal, from the gallery of the National Assembly to
the gallery in the open air. The streets were filled with popular
deputations, cavalry pickets, infantry patrols passing to and fro.
Behind a man in a French coat, with powdered hair, a sword,
a hat carried under his arm, pumps and silk stockings, walked
a man wearing his hair short and without powder, an English
frock and an American neck-cloth. At the theatres the actors
gave out the news; the pit shouted patriotic ditties. Topical
pieces drew crowds : an abbé appeared upon the stage ; the audience cried, "Jack-priest! Jack-priest!" and the abbé answered :
 "Gentlemen, long live the nation!"

People trooped to hear Mandini and his wife, Viganoni and
Rovedino,[2] sing at the *Opera Buffa*, after hearing *Ça ira* roared
in the streets; they went to admire Madame Dugazon,[3] Madame
Saint-Aubin,[4] Carline,[5] little Olivier,[6] Mademoiselle Contat,
Molé, Fleury, Talma at the commencement of his career, after
seeing Favras hanged.

The walks on the Boulevard du Temple and the Boulevard
des Italiens, or de Coblentz, the paths of the Tuileries Gardens
were inundated with smartly dressed women : three young
daughters of Grétry's[7] shone there, white and pink as their
costumes ; they soon died, all three.

"She fell asleep for ever," said Grétry, speaking of his eldest
daughter, "seated on my knees, as beautiful as in life."

A multitude of carriages ploughed across the muddy spaces
in which the *sans-culottes* plodded on foot, and one saw the
beautiful Madame de Buffon[8] sitting alone in a phaeton

---

[1] *L'Autre Tartufe, ou, la Mère Coupable*, a prose drama in five acts, produced
6 June 1792.—B.

[2] The four leading and accomplished singers in the Italian *Opera Buffa* company which first played in the Salle des Machines at the Tuileries and later,
when the Royal Family came to occupy the palace, at the Théâtre de Monsieur,
renamed Théâtre de la Rue Feydeau.—B.

[3] Louise Rosalie Lefèvre (1755-1821), wife of the actor Dugazon, a brilliant
performer of *amoureuses* or leading ladies at the Théâtre Italien, later Opéra
Comique, in the Rue Favart.—T.

[4] Jeanne Charlotte Dame d'Herbey (1764-1850), *née* Schrœder, known as
Madame Saint-Aubin, a player of *ingénues'* parts at the Opéra Comique.—B.

[5] Marie Gabrielle Malagrida (1763-1818), known as Carline, and married to
Nivelon, the dancer at the Opera. She played *soubrettes* charmingly at the Théâtre
Italien, but her acting was better than her singing : she had a very small voice.—B.

[6] Chateaubriand is mistaken here. He is writing of the theatres in 1789 and
1790, whereas Mademoiselle Olivier died in 1787.—B.

[7] André Ernest Modeste Grétry (1741-1813), the famous composer.—T.

[8] Marguerite Françoise Comtesse de Buffon (1767-1808), *née* de Bouvier de

belonging to the Duc d'Orléans, waiting at the door of some club.

All that was elegant and in good taste in aristocratic society met at the Hôtel de La Rochefoucauld,[1] at the *soirées* of Mesdames de Poix, d'Hénin, de Simiane, de Vaudreuil, in the few *salons* that remained open of the upper magisterial circle. At M. Necker's, at M. le Comte de Montmorin's, at the houses of the different ministers gathered (in addition to Madame de Staël, the Duchesse d'Aiguillon, Mesdames de Beaumont[2] and de Sérilly)[3] all the new lights of France and all the liberties of the new manners. The shoemaker knelt to take the measure of your foot in the uniform of an officer of the National Guard; the monk who on Friday trailed his white or black gown along the ground appeared on Sunday in a round hat and a lay coat; the shorn Capuchin read the paper in the public-house, and in the midst of a circle of frivolous women, a nun appeared gravely seated: it was an aunt or a sister turned out of her monastery. The crowd visited these convents thrown open to the world like the travellers who, at Grenada, wander through the deserted halls of the Alhambra, or, at Tivoli, linger beneath the columns of the Sibyl's temple.

For the rest, many duels and love-affairs, prison attachments and political friendships, mysterious meetings among ruins, under a tranquil sky, amid nature's peace and poetry; silent, remote, solitary walks, mingled with undying oaths and indefinable affections, to the dull tumult of a fleeing world, to the distant noise of a crumbling society, which threatened in its fall to crush the happiness set at the foot of events. Those who had lost sight of each other for twenty-four hours were not sure of ever meeting again. Some went the revolutionary way; others contemplated civil war; others set out for Ohio, sending ahead plans for country-houses to be built among the savages; others went to join the Princes: all this cheerfully,

Cépoy, and wife of Georges Louis Marie Leclerc, Comte de Buffon, son of the great writer. She was the mistress of Philippe Égalité, to whom she bore a son who was killed when fighting in the English army in the Peninsula. The Comte de Buffon was guillotined 10 July 1794. In 1798 his widow married M. Renouard de Bussières, a Strasburg banker.—B.

[1] The town-house of Louis Alexandre Duc de La Rochefoucauld (1735-1792).—T.

[2] Pauline Marie Michelle Frédérique Ulrique Comtesse de Beaumont (1768-1803), *née* de Montmorin-Saint-Hérem, wife of the Comte Christophe François de Beaumont.—B.

[3] Anne Louise Dame de Sérilly, *née* Thomas, wife of Antoine Jean François de Megret de Sérilly. Her husband and brother-in-law were guillotined in 1794. Her own death-sentence was commuted owing to the fact that she was pregnant. In 1795 she married François de Pange, who died in September 1796.—B.

often without a sou in their pockets, the Royalists declaring that the thing would come to an end one of these mornings by a decree of Parliament, the patriots, quite as airy in their hopes, foretelling the reign of peace and happiness together with that of liberty.   People sang :

> La sainte chandelle d'Arras,
> Le flambeau de la Provence,
> S'ils ne nous éclairent pas,
> Mettent le feu dans la France ;
> On ne peut pas les toucher,
> Mais on espère les moucher.[1]

And that was how people spoke of Robespierre and Mirabeau !

"It is as little within the power of any earthly faculty," wrote L'Éstoile,[2] "to keep the French people from talking as to hide the sun in the ground or bury it in a hole."

The Palace of the Tuileries, a great gaol filled with sentenced prisoners, rose erect amid these festivals of destruction. The condemned themselves made merry while waiting for the "cart," the "shears," and the "red shirt" which had been put out to dry; and through the windows one saw the dazzling illuminations of the Queen's circle.

Pamphlets and newspapers swarmed in thousands; the satires and poems, the songs of the *Actes des Apôtres*[3] replied to the *Ami du peuple*, or to the *Modérateur*[4] of the Club Monarchien, edited by Fontanes; Mallet Du Pan,[5] on the political side of the *Mercure*, was in opposition to La Harpe and Chamfort on the literary side of the same journal.   Champ-

---

[1] " Arras' candle so sacred and bright,
    The torch that from far Provence came,
    Although they afford us no light,
    Are setting our fair France aflame ;
    We cannot touch them, no doubt,
    But hope to snuff both of them out."

Robespierre was deputy for Arras, Mirabeau for Aix, the old capital of Provence.—T.

[2] Pierre de L'Éstoile (1540-1611) Grand-Crier to the French Chancery, and author of a valuable diary of the times of Henry III. and Henry IV.—T.

[3] The *Actes des Apôtres* was published from November 1789 to October 1791 ; 311 numbers were issued in all.   Its principal contributors were Peltier, Rivarol, Champcenetz, Mirabeau the younger, the Marquis de Bonnay, François Suleau, Montlosier, Bergasse, &c.—B.

[4] The *Journal de la Ville et des Provinces, ou, le Modérateur*, edited by M. de Fontanes, first appeared 1 October 1789.—B.

[5] Jacques Mallet-Dupan (1749-1800), political editor of the *Mercure de France*. He left France in 1792, returned first to his native city, Geneva, and then settled in London, where he founded the *Mercure britannique* (1799).—T.

cenetz,[1] the Marquis de Bonnay, Rivarol,[2] Mirabeau the Younger (the Holbein of the sword, who levied on the Rhine the legion of the Hussars of Death), Honoré Mirabeau the Elder amused themselves by drawing caricatures at dinner and composing the *Petit almanach des grands hommes* : Honoré would subsequently go off to move martial law or the seizure of the property of the clergy. He spent the night at Madame Le Jay's,[3] after declaring that he would not leave the National Assembly unless driven out at the point of the bayonet. Égalité consulted the devil in the Montrouge stone-quarries, and returned to the Jardin de Monceau to preside over the orgies prepared by Laclos.[4] The future regicide proved himself worthy of his race : he was twice prostituted ; debauchery handed him over exhausted to ambition. Lauzun,[5] already worn out, supped in his pleasure-house at the Barrière du Maine with dancers from the Opera, carressed indifferently by Messrs. de Noailles, de Dillon,[6] de Choiseul, de Talleyrand[7] and other elegants of the time, of whom two or three mummies still survive.

The majority of the courtiers celebrated for their immorality at the end of the reign of Louis XV., and during the reign of Louis XVI., were enlisted under the tricolour banner : almost all of them had been through the American war and had besmirched their ribbons with the Republican colours. The Revolution employed them so long as it remained at a middling height ; they even became the first generals of its armies. The Duc de Lauzun, the romantic lover of the Princess Czartoriska, the woman-hunter of the high-road, the Lovelace who "had" this one and then "had" that one, in the chaste and noble cant of the Court ; the Duc de Lauzun, becoming Duc de Biron, and

[1] The Chevalier de Champcenetz (1759–1794), one of the wittiest Royalist partisans under the Revolution ; arrested and murdered in 1794.—T.
[2] Antoine Comte de Rivarol (1753–1801), a brilliant and caustic wit.—T.
[3] The wife of Le Jay the bookseller, Mirabeau's publisher.—B.
[4] Pierre Ambroise François Choderlos de Laclos (1741–1803), author of *Les Liaisons dangereuses*, editor of the *Journal des amis de la Constitution*, and secretary to the Duc d'Orléans. He served as an artillery-general in the Army of Italy.—T.
[5] Armand Louis de Gontaut-Biron, Duc de Lauzun (1747–1793), son of the Duc de Biron, to whose title he succeeded in 1788. He fought on the American side in the War of Independence, and served as a general in the republican armies until his arrest and execution, 31 December 1793.—T.
[6] The two brothers Arthur Comte de Dillon and Théobald de Dillon, both fought in the republican campaigns. Arthur was executed in 1794, Théobald killed in 1792 by his soldiers, who believed that he was betraying them.—T.
[7] Charles Maurice de Talleyrand-Périgord (1754–1838), Bishop of Autun, created Prince de Bénévent by Bonaparte in 1806, Duc de Talleyrand and Duc de Dino by Louis XVIII. in 1817.—T.

commanding the forces of the Convention in the Vendée: the pity of it! The Baron de Besenval,[1] the lying and cynical revealer of the corruption of the upper classes, the fly on the wheel of the puerilities of the expiring old monarchy; that ponderous baron, compromised in the affair of the Bastille, and saved by M. Necker and Mirabeau only because he was a Swiss: the disgrace of it! What had such men to do with such events? When the Revolution had attained its full height, it scornfully abandoned these frivolous apostates from the throne: it had needed their vices, it now needed their heads; it disdained no blood, not even that of the Du Barry.[2]

The year 1790 brought to completion the measures outlined by the year 1789. The property of the Church, first placed in the hands of the nation, was confiscated, the civil constitution of the clergy decreed, the nobility abolished.

I did not attend the Federation of July 1790: a somewhat serious illness made me keep my bed; but before that I had been much amused by the sight of the wheel-barrows on the Champ de Mars. Madame de Staël has written a wonderful description of that scene.[3] I shall always regret not to have seen M. de Talleyrand say Mass, served by the Abbé Louis,[4] as I regret not to have seen him, sword at side, give audience to the Ambassador of the Grand Turk.

Mirabeau forfeited his popularity in the year 1790; his relations with the Court were obvious. M. Necker resigned office and withdrew into private life, none caring to restrain him.[5] Mesdames, the King's aunts, left for Rome with a passport from the National Assembly.[6] The Duc d'Orléans returned from England and declared himself the King's most humble and most obedient servant. Societies of Friends of the Constitution multiplied upon the soil and connected themselves with the parent society, receiving its suggestions and executing its orders.

[1] Pierre Victor Baron de Besenval (1722-1791), whose Memoirs were published in 1805-1807 by the Vicomte de Ségur, but were disowned by the baron's family.—T.
[2] Jeanne Vaubernier, Comtesse Du Barry (1744-1794), the last mistress of Louis XV., was guillotined 30 June 1794, having ventured to return to France from England in order to rescue her personal belongings.—T.
[3] *Considérations sur les principaux événements de la Révolution française*, II. 16: *De la Fédération du 14 juillet* 1790.—B.
[4] Joseph Dominique Baron Louis (1755-1837). He had taken minor orders and served as deacon at Talleyrand's Mass in the Champ de Mars. He was several times Minister of Finance under the Restoration and under Louis-Philippe.—T.
[5] 4 September 1790.—B.   [6] 20 February 1791.—B.

Public life met with a favourable disposition in my character: I was attracted by what happened in public, because, in the crowd, I beheld my loneliness and had no occasion to combat my shyness. Nevertheless, the *salons*, sharing as they did in the universal agitation, had become a little less foreign to my mood, and I had made new acquaintances in spite of myself.

The Marquise de Villette I had met casually. Her husband,[1] who bore a slandered reputation, wrote with Monsieur, the King's brother, in the *Journal de Paris*. Madame de Villette, still charming, lost a daughter of sixteen, more charming than her mother, upon whom the Chevalier de Parny wrote some verses worthy of the Anthology.[2]

My regiment, which was in garrison at Rouen, preserved its discipline pretty late. It had an encounter with the mob on the subject of the execution of the actor Bordier,[3] who underwent the last sentence pronounced by the parliamentary power; hanged one day, he would have been a hero the next, had he lived twenty-four hours longer. But at last the insurrection showed itself among the soldiers of the Navarre Regiment. The Marquis de Mortemart emigrated; his officers followed him. I had neither adopted nor rejected the new opinions; I was as little disposed to attack as to serve them, was unwilling either to emigrate or to continue in the military career, and I resigned my commission.

Freed from all bonds, I had, on the one side, somewhat animated discussions with my brother and the Président de Rosanbo; on the other, discussions no less embittered with Ginguené, La Harpe, and Chamfort. From my early youth, my political impartiality pleased nobody. Besides, I attached importance to the questions then raised only through general ideas concerning the liberty and dignity of the human race; personal politics bored me; my real life lay in higher regions.

The streets of Paris, blocked with people night and day, were no longer suited to my lounging inclinations. To recover the desert, I took refuge in the theatre: I ensconced myself at the back of a box and allowed my thoughts to wander to the sound of Racine's[4] verses, Sacchini's[5] music,

---

[1] Charles Michel Marquis de Villette (1736-1793). At the trial of Louis XVI., he voted for imprisonment and for banishment at the conclusion of the war.—B.

[2] I omit a poetical quotation from Parny.—T.

[3] Bordier was a comedian well known in Paris for his performances of the character of Harlequin. He and Jourdain, an advocate from Lisieux, placed themselves at the head of a riot on the night of 3 August 1789 and were eventually taken and hanged.—B.

[4] Jean Racine (1639-1699), the greatest of the French tragic poets.—T.

[5] Antoine Marie Gaspard Sacchini (1735-1786), the " Racine of music," com-

or the Opera ballets. I must have had the courage to
see *Barbe-bleue*[1] and the *Sabot perdu*[2] twenty times in succession at the Italiens, courting tedium in order to dispel
it, like an owl in a hole in a wall; while the monarchy
fell, I heard neither the cracking of the venerable vaults nor
the screeching of the vaudeville, neither Mirabeau's voice
thundering in the tribune nor Colin's singing to Babet on
the stage :

> Qu'il pleuve, qu'il vente ou qu'il neige,
> Quand la nuit est longue, ou l'abrège. ·

Madame Ginguené sometimes sent M. Monet, the director of
mines, and his young daughter to disturb my unsociable mood :
Mademoiselle Monet took her seat in the front of the box; I
sat, half pleased, half grumbling, behind her. I do not know
whether she attracted me, whether I liked her; but I was very
much afraid of her. When she was gone, I regretted her,
while rejoicing at no longer seeing her. Still, I sometimes
went, with the perspiration standing on my brow, to fetch her
for a walk: I gave her my arm, and I believe I pressed hers
a little.

One idea governed me, the idea of going to the United
States: a useful object was wanting for my voyage; I proposed, as I have said in the Memoirs and in several of my
works, to discover the North-West Passage. This plan·was
not out of keeping with my poetic nature. No one troubled
himself about me; I was at that time, like Bonaparte, a slim
sub-lieutenant, entirely unknown; both of us emerged from
obscurity at the same period, I to seek renown in solitude, he
to seek glory among mankind. I had not attached myself to
any woman, and my sylph still possessed my imagination. I
placed before myself the bliss of realizing my fantastic wander-
ings in her company in the forests of the New World. Through
the influence of a new manifestation of nature, my flower of
love, my nameless phantom of the woods of Armorica, grew
into *Atala* beneath the shady groves of Florida.

poser of a number of brilliant operas. His merits were never fully appreciated,
owing to the disputes between the adherents of Gluck and Piccini, which absorbed
public attention at the time.—T.

[1] A comedy in three acts, interspersed with songs; words by Michel Jean
Sedaine (1719–1797).—B.

[2] A comic opera in one act, words and the greater part of the music by Jean
Cazotte (1720–1792).—B.

[3] "Fall rain, or fall snow, or blow wind,
To shorten long nights we've a mind."—T.

M. de Malesherbes excited me on the subject of this voyage. I went to see him in the mornings: we sat, with our noses glued to maps; we compared the different plans of the Arctic Circle; we calculated the distances between Behring's Straits and the furthermost part of Hudson's Bay; we read the different narratives of the travellers and navigators, English, Dutch, French, Russian, Swedish, Danish; we enquired into the roads to be followed on land to reach the shores of the Polar Sea; we discussed the difficulties to be overcome, the precautions to be taken against the rigours of the climate, the attacks of wild animals, the scarcity of food. This illustrious man said to me:

"If I were younger, I would go with you, I would spare myself the sight of all the crimes, meannesses and madnesses which I see about me. But, at my age, a man must die where he stands. Do not fail to write to me by every ship, to keep me informed of your progress and your discoveries: I will commend them to the ministers. It is a great pity that you know no botany."

After these conversations, I would peruse Tournefort,[1] Duhamel,[2] Bernard de Jussieu,[3] Grew,[4] Jacquin, Rousseau's[5] Dictionary, the *Flores élementaires;* I ran to the Jardin du Roi, and before long thought myself a very Linnæus.[6]

At last, in January 1791, I seriously made up my mind. The chaos was increasing: it was sufficient to bear an "aristocratic" name to be exposed to persecution: the more moderate and conscientious your opinions the more were you liable to suspicion and annoyance. I therefore resolved to strike my tents: I left my brother and my sisters in Paris, and made for Brittany.

At Fougères I met the Marquis de La Rouërie: I asked him to give me a letter for General Washington.[7] "Colonel Armand" (the name by which the marquis was known in

---

[1] Joseph Pitton de Tournefort (1656–1708), author of an early classification of botanical *genera* and species.—T.
[2] Henri Louis Duhamel du Monceau (1700–1782), Inspector-General of the Navy, and an eminent agricultural and arboricultural expert.—T.
[3] Bernard de Jussieu (1699–1777), the most learned member of a family comprising no less than four distinguished botanists.—T.
[4] Nehemiah Grew (*circa* 1628–1711), author of the *Anatomy of Plants*, and an early Fellow of the Royal Society (1673).—T.
[5] Jean Jacques Rousseau (1712–1778): the work referred to is his *Dictionnaire botanique.*—T.
[6] Charles Linnæus (1707–1778), the great Swedish botanist.—T.
[7] George Washington (1732–1799), first President of the United States (1789–1793 and 1793–1797).—T.

America) had distinguished himself in the American War
of Independence. He made himself famous in France through
the royalist conspiracy which made such touching victims
in the Desilles[1] family. He having died while organizing
this conspiracy, his body was disinterred and recognized,
and caused the misfortune of his hosts and of his friends.
The rival of La Fayette and Lauzun, the predecessor of
La Rochejacquelein, the Marquis de La Rouërie was a more
spirited person than they: he had fought oftener than the
first; he had carried off opera-singers like the second; he
would have become the companion in arms of the third. He
swept the woods in Brittany in company with an American
major,[2] and with a monkey seated on his horse's crupper.
The Rennes law-students loved him for his boldness of
action and his liberty of ideas: he had been one of the twelve
Breton nobles sent to the Bastille. His figure and manners
were elegant, his appearance smart, his features charming,
and he resembled the portraits of the young lords of the
League.

I selected Saint-Malo as my port of embarkation, in order
to embrace my mother. I have told you in the third book
of these Memoirs how I passed through Combourg and of
the sentiments that oppressed me. I stayed two months at
Saint-Malo, busying myself with preparations for my departure,
as I had done before, when I was thinking of departing for
the Indies.

I struck a bargain with a captain called Dujardin,[3] who
was to carry to Baltimore the Abbé Nagault,[4] superior of
the seminary of Saint-Sulpice, and several seminarists under
the conduct of their head. These travelling companions would
have been more to my liking four years earlier: from being

---

[1] Angélique Françoise Dame de La Fonchais (1769–1793), sister to André Desilles, the hero of Nancy, was guillotined 13 June 1793, at the same time as her brother-in-law, Michel Julien Picot de Limoëlan, displaying admirable courage on the scaffold.—B.

[2] Major Chafner, *vide supra*, p. 66.—B.

[3] Captain Dujardin Pinte-de-Vin of the brig *Saint-Pierre*, bound for the islands of Saint-Pierre and Miguelon, whence she was to make for Baltimore.—B.

[4] François Charles Nagot (d. 1816), not Nagault, was the superior, not of the seminary of Saint-Sulpice, but of the community of Robertines in Paris, one of the annexes of the seminary of Saint-Sulpice. He left for Baltimore in order to become the superior of a Sulpician seminary in that city, accompanied by three young priests of the Company. The Abbé Nagot arrived at Baltimore 10 July 1791, and in the September following established St. Mary's Seminary, the first and best-known seminary in the United States. In 1822 Pope Pius VII. erected St. Mary's College into a Catholic university.—B.

a zealous Christian I had become "a man of strong mind,"[1] in other words a man of weak mind. This change in my religious opinions had been brought about by reading philosophical books. I believed in good faith that a religious mind was in part paralyzed, that there existed truths which it was unable to comprehend, superior though it might be in other respects. This blessed pride imposed upon me; I inferred in the religious mind that very absence of a faculty which exists precisely in the philosophic mind: the narrow intelligence thinks that it sees everything because it keeps its eyes open; the superior intelligence consents to close its eyes, because it sees everything within. Lastly, one thing finished me: the groundless despair which I carried at the bottom of my heart.

A letter from my brother has fixed the date of my departure in my memory: he wrote to my mother from Paris, informing her of the death of Mirabeau.[2] Three days after the arrival of this letter, I joined the ship lying in the roads;[3] my luggage was already on board. The anchor was weighed, a solemn moment with mariners. The sun was setting when the coasting pilot left us, after putting us through the channels. The weather was overcast, the wind slack, and the swell beat heavily upon the rocks at a few cables' length from our vessel.

My eyes remained fixed upon Saint-Malo, where I had left my mother in tears. I saw the steeples and domes of the churches where I had prayed with Lucile, the walls, the ramparts, the forts, the towers, the beach where I had spent my childhood with Gesril and my other play-fellows; I was abandoning my distracted country at the moment when she had lost a man who could never be replaced. I was going away in equal uncertainty as to my country's destinies and my own: which of us was to perish, France or I? Should I ever see France and my family again?

With nightfall came a calm which kept us lying at the mouth of the roads; the lights of the town and the beacons were kindled: those lights which twinkled beneath my paternal roof seemed at once to smile to me and bid me farewell, while lighting me amid the rocks, the darkness of the night, and the blackness of the waves.

I carried with me only my youth and my illusions: I was deserting a world whose dust I had trod and whose stars I had counted for a world of which the soil and the sky were both unknown to me. What was to become of me if I attained

---

[1] *Esprit fort*, a free-thinker or latitudinarian.—T.
[2] 2 April 1791.—T.　　　　　[3] 8 April 1791.—B.

the object of my voyage? While I roamed upon the polar shores, the years of discord which have crushed so many generations with so loud a noise would have fallen silently over my head; society would have renewed its aspect in my absence. It is probable that I should never have had the misfortune to write; my name would have remained unknown, or would have won only a peaceful renown of the kind which is less than glory, which is scorned by envy and left to happiness. Who knows whether I would have recrossed the Atlantic, whether I would not have settled down among the solitudes explored and discovered at my peril and risk, like a conqueror in the midst of his conquests!

But no, I was to return to my native land, there to undergo altered miseries, to become something quite different from what I had been! The sea in whose lap I was born was about to become the cradle of my second life; she bore me upon my first voyage as though in the bosom of my foster-mother, in the arms of the confidant of my first tears and my first pleasures.

The ebb-tide, in the absence of the wind, carried us out to sea; the lights of the shore grew smaller and smaller, and disappeared. Exhausted with my reflections, with vague regrets, with even vaguer hopes, I went below to my cabin: I lay down to rest, rocked in my hammock to the sound of the billows which caressed the side of the vessel. The wind rose; the unfurled sails, which hung flapping about the masts, filled out, and when, next morning, I went up on deck, the land of France was out of sight.

Here my destinies changed: "Again to sea!" as Byron sings.

BOOK VI[1]

ONE-AND-THIRTY years after embarking, as a simple sub-lieutenant, for America, I embarked for London with a passport conceived in these terms:

"Pass His Lordship the Vicomte de Chateaubriand, Peer of France, Ambassador of the King to His Britannic Majesty," and so on.

No description: my greatness was such as to make my face known wherever I went. A steamboat chartered for my sole use conveyed me from Calais to Dover. On setting foot upon English soil, on the 5th of April 1822,[2] I was saluted by the guns of the fort. An officer came on behalf of the commandant to offer me a guard of honour. On alighting at the Shipwright Inn,[3] the land-

---

[1] This book was written in London between April and September 1822, and revised December 1846.—T.

[2] The 5th of April was the date of Chateaubriand's arrival in London. He landed at Dover from the French packet *Antigone*, on the evening of the 4th (*Moniteur*, 11 April 1822).—B.

[3] This should read the Ship Inn, also known as Wright's Hotel.—T.

lord and waiters received me with hanging arms and bareheaded.
The Mayoress invited me to an evening party in the name of
the fairest ladies of the town.   M. Billing,[1] who was attached
to my embassy, awaited me.   A dinner of huge fishes and
enormous pieces of beef restored Monsieur l'Ambassadeur, who
had no appetite and was not at all fatigued.   The crowd gathered
beneath my windows rent the air with hurrahs.   The officer
returned and, despite my wishes, posted sentries at my door.
The next morning, after lavishly distributing the money of the
King my master, I set out for London, to the roar of artillery,
in a light carriage drawn by four fine horses driven at full trot
by two smart postillions.   My staff followed in other coaches;
couriers wearing my livery accompanied the cavalcade.   We
passed through Canterbury, attracting the eyes of John Bull
and of the occupants of the vehicles we passed.   At Blackheath,
a common formerly haunted by highwaymen, I found a newly-
built village.   Soon there loomed before me the immense cap
of smoke which covers the city of London.

Plunging into the gulf of black mist, as though into one
of the jaws of Tartarus, and crossing the entire town, whose
streets I recognized, I reached the Embassy in Portland Place.
The *chargé d'affaires*, M. le Comte Georges de Caraman,[2]
the secretaries of embassy, M. le Vicomte de Marcellus,[3]
M. le Baron E. de Cazes, M. de Bourqueney,[4] and the *attachés*
of the embassy received me with dignified politeness.   All the
ushers, doorkeepers, footmen, and flunkeys of the house stood
gathered upon the pavement.   I was handed the cards of the
English ministers and of the foreign ambassadors, who had
been informed beforehand of my coming.

On the 17th of May in the year of grace 1793, I disembarked
at Southampton for London, an obscure and humble traveller

[1] Baron A. Billing, *attaché* to the French Embassy in London (1822), and afterwards *chargé d'affaires* at Naples (1834).—B.

[2] The Comte Georges de Caraman, son of the Duc de Caraman, Ambassador to Vienna.—B.

[3] Marie Louis Jean André Charles Demartin du Tyrac, Comte de Marcellus (1795-1865). While secretary of embassy in 1820, he discovered the Venus of Milo, now at the Louvre. He was *chargé d'affaires* in London during Chateaubriand's absence at the Congress of Verona, and was appointed Under-Secretary for Foreign Affairs in the Polignac Ministry. Marcellus was the author of, among other works, a valuable volume on the subject of these Memoirs, entitled, *Chateaubriand et son temps.*—B.

[4] François Adolphe Comte de Bourqueney (1799-1869). Here signed upon Chateaubriand's dismissal in 1824. In 1840 he was again secretary of embassy in London, *chargé d'affaires* in 1841, Ambassador to Constantinople in 1844, and Ambassador to Vienna under the Second Empire. Louis-Philippe created him a baron (1842), and Napoleon III. a count (1859).—B.

from Jersey. No mayoress took note of my passage ; the mayor
of the town, William Smith, handed me on the 18th a way-bill
for London to which was added an extract from the Alien Bill.
My description ran in English :

"François de Chateaubriand, French officer in the emigrant
army, five feet four inches high, thin shape, brown hair and
whiskers."

I modestly shared the cheapest conveyance with some sailors
on leave ; I changed horses at the meanest inns ; poor, sick, and
unknown, I entered a wealthy and famous city in which Mr. Pitt
held sway ; I took a lodging at six shillings a month under the
laths of a garret which a cousin from Brittany had prepared for
me at the end of a little street off the Tottenham Court Road.

> Ah ! *Monseigneur*, que votre vie,
> D'honneurs aujourd'hui si remplie,
> Diffère de ces heureux temps.[1]

Still an obscurity of another kind envelopes me in London.
My political position casts into shade my literary fame : not
a fool in the three kingdoms but prefers the ambassador of
Louis XVIII. to the author of the *Génie du Christianisme*.
I shall see how the matter turns after my death, or when I shall
have ceased to fill M. le Duc Decazes'[2] place at the Court of
George IV.,[3] a succession as incongruous as the rest of my life.

Now that I have arrived in London as French Ambassador,
one of my chief pleasures is to leave my carriage at the corner
of some square, and on foot to traverse the back-streets which
I frequented in former days, the cheap popular suburbs, where
misfortune takes refuge under the protection of a kindred
suffering, the nameless shelters which I haunted with my
companions in distress, not knowing whether I should have
bread to eat on the morrow, I whose table to-day is covered
with three or four courses. At all those narrow and necessitous
doors which were once open to me, I see none but strange faces.
I no longer meet my fellow-countrymen roaming, recogniz-
able by their gestures, their gait, the shape and age of their
clothes. I no longer perceive those martyred priests, wearing

---

[1] "Ah, my Lord, how your Lordship's life,
  In which such honours now are rife,
  Differs from those happy days ! "—T.

[2] The Duc Decazes was French Ambassador in London from 17 February
1820 to 9 February 1822.—B.

[3] George IV. (1762–1830) came to the throne in 1820, after being Prince Regent
since 1811.—T.

the clerical collar, the big three-cornered hat, the long, black, threadbare frock, whom the English used to salute as they passed.   Wide streets, lined with palaces, have been cut, bridges built, walks planted with trees: Regent's Park, near Portland Place, occupies the space of the old meadows filled with herds of cows.   A cemetery which formed the prospect from the dormer-window of one of my attics has disappeared within the circumference of a factory.   When I call upon Lord Liverpool,[1] I find it difficult to pick out the spot where stood the scaffold of Charles I.; new buildings, closing in upon the statue of Charles II.,[2] have come forward, with forgetfulness, to cover up memorable events.

How much do I regret, in the midst of my insipid grandeur, that world of tribulations and tears, those times in which I mingled my sorrows with those of a colony of unfortunates! It is true, then, that all changes, that misfortune itself comes to an end, like prosperity! What has become of my brothers in emigration?   Some are dead, others have undergone various destinies: they have, like me, beheld the loss of their kinsmen and friends; they are less happy in the land of their birth than they were on foreign soil.   Had we not on that soil our meetings, our amusements, our merry-makings, and, above all, our youth? Mothers of families and young girls commencing life in adversity brought the weekly fruit of their toil, to revel in some dance of their country.   Attachments were formed in the course of the evening chit-chat after work, on the grass at Hampstead or Primrose Hill.   In chapels adorned with our own hands, in old tumble-down buildings, we prayed on the 21st of January and on the anniversary of the Queen's death,[3] and were much moved by a funeral oration pronounced by the emigrant curate of our village. We strolled beside the Thames, now to see the vessels laden with the world's riches entering dock, and again to admire the country-houses at Richmond, we so poor, we who had lost the shelter of the paternal roof-tree: all these things constitute true happiness!

[1] Robert Banks Jenkinson, second Earl of Liverpool (1770–1828), Prime Minister from 1812 to 1827.—T.

[2] Chateaubriand refers to the statue of James II., not Charles II., which stood until recent years in Whitehall Gardens, behind Whitehall, and was entirely hidden from view by the United Service Institute.   This very beautiful statue has now been placed in a more conspicuous position in a garden standing back from the Whitehall pavement, beside Gwydyr House.—T.

[3] Marie Antoinette was guillotined 16 October 1793; 21 January was the date of the execution of Louis XVI.—T.

When I come home in 1822, instead of being received by my friend, shivering with cold, who opens the door of our garret to me, calls me "thee" and "thou," sleeps on a pallet beside mine, covering himself with his thin coat and having the moonlight for a lamp, I pass by the light of candles between two rows of lackeys, ending in half-a-dozen respectful secretaries. Overwhelmed along my road with the words, "*Monseigneur,* my Lord, your Excellency, *Monsieur l'Ambassadeur,*" I come to a drawing-room upholstered in silk and gold.

"I beg you, gentlemen, to leave me! A truce to these my lords! What use do you think I have for you? Go and laugh in the *chancellerie,* as though I were not here. Do you imagine you will make me take this masquerade seriously? Do you think me fool enough to believe that I have changed my nature by changing my coat? The Marquess of Londonderry is coming, you say;[1] the Duke of Wellington[2] has asked for me; Mr. Canning[3] is looking for me; Lady Jersey[4] expects me to dinner, to meet Mr. Brougham;[5] Lady Gwydyr[6] hopes to see me at ten o'clock in her box at the Opera; Lady Mansfield[7] at midnight at Almack's?"[8]

Mercy! Where can I hide? Who will deliver me? Who will save me from this persecution? Return to me, fair days of misery and loneliness! Come back to life, companions of my exile! Come, old comrades of the pallet and the camp-bed, let

[1] Robert Stewart, second Marquess of Londonderry, K.G. (1769–1822), Secretary of State for Foreign Affairs in the Liverpool Ministry. He bore the title of Viscount Castlereagh until the death of his father in 1821. He cut his throat on the 13th of August of this same year 1822.—T.

[2] Arthur Wellesley, first Duke of Wellington, K.G. (1769–1852) became Premier in 1828.—T.

[3] George Canning (1770–1827) became Foreign Secretary upon the suicide of Castlereagh.—T.

[4] Sarah Child Villiers, Countess of Jersey (1787–1867), was Lady Sarah Fane, eldest daughter of the tenth Earl of Westmorland, and grand-daughter of Robert Child the banker, whose fortune she inherited. She married George Villiers, fourth Earl of Jersey, who assumed the additional surname of Child in 1812, and became one of the reigning queens of London society.—T.

[5] Henry Brougham, first Lord Brougham and Vaux (1778–1868), had lately made his name as counsel for Queen Caroline at her trial (1820). He became Lord Chancellor and a peer in 1834.—T.

[6] Priscilla Barbara Elizabeth Lady Gwydyr (1761–1828) *née* Bertie, widow of the first Lord Gwydyr, and Baroness Willoughby de Eresby in her own right.—T.

[7] Louisa Murray, Countess of Mansfield (*d.* 1843), was the Honourable Louisa Cathcart, daughter of the ninth Baron Cathcart, and became Countess of Mansfield in her own right. In 1776 she married her cousin David, seventh Viscount Stormont and second Earl of Mansfield. He died in 1793, and in 1797 she married the Honourable Fulke Greville, retaining her title as Countess of Mansfield.—T.

[8] Almack's, the ball-room in King Street, St. James's, retained its vogue from 1765 to 1840. Lady Mansfield was one of the lady patronesses of Almack's.—T.

us go into the country, into the little garden of some despised tavern, and drink a cup of bad tea on a wooden bench, while we talk of our mad hopes and our ungrateful country, discuss our troubles, and seek means to assist each other or to succour one of our kinsmen in yet worse plight than ourselves!

That is how I feel, that is how I speak to myself in these first days of my embassy in London. I escape from the melancholy which besets me beneath my roof only by saturating myself with a less weighty melancholy in Kensington Gardens. These gardens, at least, have not changed; the trees alone have grown taller; in them, ever solitary, the birds build their nests in peace. It is no longer even the fashion to meet there, as in the days when the loveliest of Frenchwomen, Madame Récamier,[1] used to walk there followed by the crowd. From the edge of the deserted lawns of Kensington, I love to watch, across Hyde Park, the crowd of horses, the carriages of the fashionable world, among which figures my empty tilbury; while I, once more a poor little emigrant noble, walk along the path in which the exiled confessor was wont to say his breviary.

It was in Kensington Gardens that I projected the *Essai historique;* that, on reading over the diary of my travels beyond sea, I drew from it the loves of *Atala;* it was there too, after wandering far away in the fields beneath a lowering sky, which assumed a golden hue and became, as it were, pervaded with polar light, that I jotted down in pencil the first sketch of the passions of *René.* At night I deposited in the *Essai historique* and the *Natchez* the harvest of my dreams of the day. The two manuscripts marched abreast, although I often wanted money to buy paper for them, and was obliged, for lack of thread, to fasten the sheets together with splinters torn from the mantel-boards of my garret.

These spots where I received my first inspirations impress me with a sense of their power; they reflect upon my present the gentle light of my recollections; I feel in the mood to resume my pen. So many hours are wasted in embassies! I have as much spare time here as in Berlin to continue my Memoirs, the edifice which I am building up out of ruins and dead bones. My secretaries in London ask leave to go to

---

[1] Julie Récamier (1777-1849), *née* Bernard, wife of Récamier the banker. A woman of great beauty and charm; she was painted by David and Gérard, and sat to Canova for his bust of Beatrix. Chateaubriand became and remained until his death the most intimate and assiduous of her friends.—T.

picnics in the morning, to balls at night: by all means! The men in their turn, Peter, Valentine, Lewis, go to the ale-house, and the maids, Rose, Peggy, Mary, for a walk through the streets : I am delighted. They leave me the key of the hall-door : *monsieur l'ambassadeur* is left in charge of his own house ; if any one knocks, he will open the door. Everybody has gone out ; I am alone : let us get to work.

Twenty-two years ago, as I said, I was sketching, in London, the outlines of the *Natchez* and of *Atala;* I have now, in my Memoirs, come to just the period of my travels in America: that fits in perfectly. Let us wipe out those two-and-twenty years, as they are, in fact, wiped out from my life, and start for the forests of the New World: the story of my embassy shall come at its own date when God pleases ; but provided I remain here a few months, I shall have the pleasure of coming from the Falls of Niagara to the army of the Princes in Germany, and from the army of the Princes to my retirement in England. The Ambassador of the King of France will be able to tell the story of the French Emigrant in the very spot where the latter spent his exile.

The last book ended with my embarkation at Saint-Malo. Soon we left the Channel, and the immense swell from the west told us that we had reached the Atlantic.

It is difficult for people who have never been to sea to imagine the feelings which one experiences when looking over the side of a ship and seeing nothing but the grave face of the deep on every hand. The dangerous life of the sailor has about it an independence which comes from the absence of land: the passions of mankind are left behind on shore ; between the world which one is quitting and that for which one is making, one has no love and no country save the element upon which one is borne. No more duties to fulfil, no more visits to pay, no more newspapers, no more politics. The very language of the sailors is not the ordinary language: it is the language spoken by the ocean and the sky, the calm and the tempest. You inhabit a watery universe among creatures whose garments, tastes, manners, and faces are different from those of the autochthonic peoples ; they combine the rudeness of the sea-wolf with the lightness of the bird. The cares of society are not seen upon their brow ; the wrinkles which cross it resemble the folds of the lowered sail and are hollowed out less by age than by the north wind, as in the waves. The skin of these creatures, impregnated with salt, is red and hard, like the surface of the surge-swept rock.

The sailors become enamoured of their ship; they weep with regret on leaving her, with affection on rejoining her. They are unable to stay at home with their families; after swearing a hundred times that they will not again expose themselves to the sea, they find it impossible to live without it, like a youth who is unable to tear himself from the arms of a moody and faithless mistress.

In the docks of London and Plymouth, it is not unusual to find sailors born on board ship: from their childhood to their old age they have never set foot on shore; spectators of the world which they have never entered, they have seen the land only from the side of their floating cradle. In this life reduced to so small a space, beneath the clouds and upon the depths, all things become life-like to the mariner: an anchor, a sail, a mast, a gun are persons that excite his attachment and that have each their history.

The sail was torn off the coast of Labrador; the master sail-maker put in that patch which you see there.

The anchor saved the ship when she had dragged her other anchors among the coral-reefs of the Sandwich Islands.

The mast was broken in a squall off the Cape of Good Hope; it was all in one piece; it is much stronger since it has consisted of two pieces.

The gun is the only one which was not dismounted in the fight of the *Chesapeake*.

The news on board is most interesting: they have just heaved the log; the ship is making ten knots.

The sky is clear at mid-day: they have taken the altitude; we are at latitude so-and-so.

We have taken our reckoning: we have made so many miles in our course.

The variation of the compass is so many degrees: we have gone up north.

The sand is running badly through the hour-glass: we shall have rain.

They have seen stormy petrels in the wake of the vessel: we must look out for a squall.

Flying-fish have been showing in the south: the weather will settle down.

A clear spot has formed in the clouds in the west: that's a sign of wind; the wind will blow from that side to-morrow.

The water has changed colour; pieces of wood and wrack

have been seen floating by; there were ducks and gulls in sight; a small bird came and perched on the yards: we must heave to sea, for we are approaching land, and it is not good to come alongside at night.

In the hen-coop is a favourite and, so to speak, sacred cock, which has survived all the others; he is famous for having crowed during a fight, as though he were in a farm-yard in the midst of his hens. Below decks lives a cat: a greenish tabby, with a hairless tail and bushy whiskers, firm on his paws, able to bring a back-balance and side-balance to play against the pitching and the rolling of the ship; he has been twice round the world and has saved himself from shipwreck by climbing on a barrel. The ship-boys give the cock biscuits soaked in wine, and Tom has the privilege of sleeping, when he pleases, in the second mate's fur-coat.

The old sailor is like the old ploughman. True, their manner of harvesting is different: the sailor has led a wandering life, the ploughman has never left his fields; but they both know the stars and foretell the future while ploughing their furrows. Both have their prophets: one, the lark, the redbreast, the nightingale; the other, the petrel, the curlew, the halcyon. They retire to rest at night, one in his cabin, the other in his hut: frail dwelling-houses in which the hurricane which shakes them does not disturb peaceful consciences.

> If the wind a tempest's blowing,
>   Still no danger they descry;
> The guiltless heart, its boon bestowing,
>   Soothes them with its lullaby.

The sailor does not know where Death will overtake him, upon what shore he will leave his life: perhaps, when he has mingled his last breath with the wind, he will be cast into the bosom of the waves, fastened to two oars, to continue his voyage; perhaps he will be buried on a desert island, which none shall ever see again, and sleep as he slept in mid-ocean, in his lonely hammock.

The vessel is a sight in herself: sensible to the smallest movement of the helm, winged horse or hippogriff that she is, she obeys the hand of the pilot as a horse does that of its rider. The grace of the masts and rigging, the nimbleness of the sailors laying out on the yards, the various aspects under which the ship displays herself, whether listing, borne down by a contrary blast, or scudding before a favourable wind, cause this intelligent machine to become one of the marvels of human genius. At one time the swell and its foam break and burst against the keel; at another the peaceful waves separate submissively before the stem. The flags, the pennants, the sails complete the beauty of this palace of Neptune: the courses, spread in their width, swell out like huge cylinders; the top-sails, confined at their waist, resemble a syren's breasts. Driven by a stiff breeze, the ship noisily ploughs the seas with her keel as with a plough-share.

On this ocean highway, along which one sees no trees, nor villages, nor towns, nor towers, nor steeples nor tomb-stones; on this road without posts or milestones, which has no boundaries save the waves, no relays save the winds, no lights save the stars, the finest adventure, when one is not travelling in search of unknown lands and seas, is the meet-ing of two vessels. They are mutually discovered on the horizon through the spy-glass; they turn each in the direction of the other. The crew and the passengers hasten on deck. The two ships approach each other, hoist their ensigns, clew up some of their sails, heave-to. When all is silence, the two captains take their stand upon the quarter-deck and hail each other through the speaking-trumpet:

"The ship's name? From what port? Name of the cap-tain? Where is he from? How many days out? What is the latitude and longitude? Good-bye, let go!"

They let go the reefs; the sails fall down again. The sailors and passengers of the two ships watch each other flee from sight, without a word: one crew goes to seek the sun of Asia, the other the sun of Europe, both of which will see them die. Time carries off and separates travellers on earth even more rapidly than the wind carries them off and separates them on the ocean; they make a sign to each other at a distance:

"God speed you, and a prosperous journey!"

The common port is Eternity.

And what if the vessel encountered were that of Cook[1] or La Pérouse?

The boatswain of my Saint-Malo ship was an old super-cargo called Pierre Villeneuve, whose very name pleased me, because of the good Villeneuve of my childhood. He had served in India, under the Bailli de Suffren, and in America under the Comte d'Estaing; he had been present at a number of engagements. Leaning against the bow of the ship, near

[1] Captain James Cook (1728-1779). His discoveries were still fresh in the public mind in 1792.—T.

the bowsprit, like a veteran seated under the vine-arbour of his little garden in the moat of the Invalides, Pierre, chewing a plug of tobacco which filled out his cheek like a swelling, described to me the clearing of the decks, the effect of the gun-fire below decks, the damage done by the cannon-balls in ricochetting against the gun-carriages, the guns, the timber-work. I made him talk of the Indians, the negroes, the planters. I asked him how the people were dressed, how the trees were shaped, what was the colour of the earth and sky, the taste of the fruits; whether pine-apples were better than peaches, palm-trees finer than oaks. He explained all this by means of comparisons taken from things I knew : the palm-tree was a large cabbage; the robe worn by a Hindoo was like my grandmother's; the camels were like a hump-backed donkey; all the peoples of the East, and notably the Chinese, were cowards and robbers. Villeneuve came from Brittany, and we never failed to end with praises of the incomparable beauty of our native country.

The bell interrupted our conversations; it struck the watches, the time for dressing, for the roll-call, for meals. In the morning, at a signal, the crew mustered on deck, stripped off their blue shirts, and put on others which were drying in the shrouds. The discarded shirts were forthwith washed in tubs in which this school of seals also soaped their brown faces and tarred paws. At the mid-day and evening meals, the sailors, seated in a circle around the mess-platters, one after the other, regularly and without any attempt at fraud, dipped their tin spoons into the soup which splashed to the roll of the ship. Those who were not hungry sold their ration of biscuit or salt junk to their messmates for a screw of tobacco. The passengers took their meals in the captain's room. In fine weather, a sail was spread over the stern of the vessel, and we dined in sight of a blue sea, flecked here and there with white marks where it had been struck by the breeze.

Wrapped in my cloak, I stretched myself at night upon deck. My eyes contemplated the stars above my head. The inflated sail threw back upon me the coolness of the breeze which rocked me beneath the dome of heaven : half dozing and pushed on by the wind, I was wafted towards new skies and new dreams.

The passengers on board ship afford a different sort of society from that of the crew: they belong to another element; their destinies are of the land. Some travel in search of fortune, others of rest; these are returning home, those leaving

it; others cross the seas in order to become acquainted with
the manners of nations, to study science and art. People
have time to know one another in this wandering hostelry
which travels with the traveller, to have many adventures, to
breed antipathies, to contract friendships. When those young
women come and go, born of mixed English and Indian blood,
who add to the beauty of Clarissa the delicacy of Sacontala,
then are formed chains which are bound and unbound by the
fragrant breezes of Ceylon, sweet and light as themselves.

Among my fellow-passengers was an Englishman. Francis
Tulloch[1] had served in the artillery: he was a painter, a
musician, a mathematician; he spoke several languages. The
Abbé Nagault, Superior of the Sulpicians, had met the Anglican
officer and made him a Catholic: he was taking his neophyte
to Baltimore.

I became intimate with Tulloch: as I was at that time a
profound "Philosopher," I invited him to return to his parents.
The spectacle that lay before our eyes transported him with
admiration. We used to rise at night, when the deck was given
up to the officer of the watch and a few sailors who smoked their
pipes in silence: *Tuta æquora silent.*[2] The vessel rolled at the
will of the slow and silent waves, while gleams of fire ran with
a white foam along her sides. Thousands of stars shining in
the sombre azure of the celestial dome, a boundless sea, infinity
in the sky and on the waves! Never has God confused me
with His greatness more than during those nights when I had
immensity over my head and immensity beneath my feet.

Westerly winds, interspersed with calms, delayed our
progress. On the 4th of May, we had reached only the level
of the Azores. On the 6th, at about eight o'clock in the
morning, we came in sight of the Isle of the Peak; this volcano
long commanded unnavigated seas:[3] a useless beacon by night,
an unseen landmark by day.

There is something magical in seeing the land rise from the
depths of the sea. Christopher Columbus, surrounded by a
mutinous crew, preparing to return to Europe without having

---

[1] Chateaubriand met Francis Tulloch in 1826, after writing this portion of his
Memoirs. He does not tell us much about him even in the *Essai sur les Révolutions*, where he speaks of Tulloch at some length. It would appear, according to
Chateaubriand, that he was the son of an English father and a Scotch mother, and
that he did not eventually take orders, but remained in the world and married.—T.

[2] VIR., Æ. I. 164. The correct quotation runs: *Æquora tuta silent.*—T.

[3] The Azores were known to the Carthaginians, but fell out of the map until
rediscovered in 1431.—T.

attained the object of his voyage, perceives a small light upon
a beach which the darkness had hidden from him. The flight
of the birds had guided him to America; the gleam from the
hut of a savage reveals to him the presence of a new world.
Columbus must have experienced the sort of feeling which
the Scriptures attribute to the Creator when, having out of
nothing brought forth the world, He saw that His work was
good: "And God saw that it was good."[1] Columbus created a
world. One of the first lives of the Genoese pilot is that which
Giustiniani,[2] when editing a Hebrew psalter, placed in the
form of a "note" at the foot of the psalm, *Cæli enarrant
gloriam Dei.*[3]

Vasco da Gama must have marvelled no less when, in 1498,
he approached the coast of Malabar. Thereupon all things
change on the face of the globe: a new revelation of nature is
given; the curtain which for thousands of ages has concealed
one part of the earth is raised, discovering the birthplace of
the sun, the spot whence he issues each morning "as a bride-
groom, as a giant;"[4] we see in all its nudity the wise and
brilliant East, whose mysterious history was intermixed with
the journeys of Pythagoras, the conquests of Alexander, the
memory of the Crusades, and whose perfumes came to us
across the plains of Arabia and the seas of Greece. Europe
sent to the East a poet to salute it: the Swan of Tagus made
his sad and beautiful voice heard upon the shores of India;
Camoëns[5] borrowed their lustre, their fame and their misfortune; he left them only their riches.

When Gonzalo Villo, Camoëns' maternal grandfather, discovered a portion of the Archipelago of the Azores, he ought,
had he foreseen the future, to have reserved for himself a concession of six feet of ground to cover the bones of his grandson.

We anchored in a bad roadstead, with a rocky bottom, in
five-and-forty fathoms of water. The island of Graciosa, before
which we were moored, displayed its hills a little swollen in

[1] GEN. i. 10.—T.

[2] Agostino Pantaleone Giustiniani (1470-1531), Bishop of Nebbis in Corsica,
and author of the *Psalterium hebraicum, græcum, arabicum, chaldaicum, cum tribus
latinis interpretationibus et glossis,* the first work of its kind published. Giustiniani
was drowned in crossing from Genoa to Corsica.—T.

[3] Ps. xviii.—T.

[4] *Ibid.* 6.—T.

[5] Luiz de Camoëns (1517 or 1525-1579), author of the *Lusiad,* which treats of
the exploits of Vasco da Gama, spent many years in India and in exile in Macao,
where he wrote his principal poem. On his return from banishment, he was
wrecked off the coast of Cochin China, where he is said to have lost all he
possessed, except the manuscript of the *Lusiad.*—T.

outline like the ellipses of an Etruscan amphora; they were draped in the green of their cornfields and emitted an agreeable odour of wheat peculiar to the harvests of the Azores. In the midst of these carpets, one saw the dividing lines of the fields, formed of volcanic stones, half black and half white, piled one upon the other. On the summit of a mound stood an abbey, the monument of an old world upon new soil; at the foot of this mound, the red roofs of the town of Santa-Cruz were mirrored in a pebbly creek. The whole island, with its indentations of bays, capes, bights and promontories, reflected its inverted landscape in the sea. For outer girdle it had a belt of rocks jutting from the surface of the waves. In the background of the picture, the cone of the volcano of the Peak, planted upon a cupola of clouds, pierced the perspective of the air beyond Graciosa.

Tulloch, the second mate and I decided to go on land; the long-boat was lowered and rowed towards the shore, which lay about two miles away. We saw some movement on the beach; a pram put out in our direction. So soon as she had come within speaking distance, we distinguished a number of monks. They hailed us in Portuguese, in Italian, in English, in French, and we replied in all four languages. Alarm prevailed, our vessel was the first ship of large tonnage that had ventured to anchor in the dangerous roadstead where we were going with the tide. On the other hand, the islanders now saw the tricolour flag for the first time; they did not know whether we hailed from Tunis or Algiers: Neptune had not recognized the standard so gloriously borne by Cybele. When they saw that we had human shapes and that we understood what was said to us, their delight was extreme. The monks took us up in their boat, and we rowed merrily towards Santa-Cruz, where we landed with some difficulty because of a rather violent surf.

The whole island came running up. Four or five *alguasils*, armed with rusty pikes, took possession of us. His Majesty's uniform attracted the honours in my direction, and I was taken for the leading member of the deputation. We were led to the Governor's house, or hovel, where His Excellency, dressed in a worn green uniform, which had once been gold-laced, received us in solemn audience: he gave us leave to replenish our stores of provisions.

Our monks took us to their convent, a roomy and well-lighted building, surrounded with balconies. Tulloch had discovered a fellow-countryman: the principal brother, who did all the bustling about for us, was a sailor from Jersey whose ship had gone down with all hands off Graciosa. The solitary survivor of the shipwreck, and not lacking in intelligence, he had become an apt pupil of the catechists; he learnt Portuguese and a few words of Latin; the fact of his being an Englishman militated in his favour, and they converted him and made a monk of him. The Jersey sailor found it much pleasanter to be lodged, boarded, and clothed at the altar than to take in the top-gallant sail in a storm. He had not forgotten his old trade: it was long since he had heard his language spoken, and he was delighted to meet some one who knew it; he laughed and swore like a true pilot's apprentice. He showed us over the island.

The houses in the villages, built of wood and stone, were adorned with outer galleries which gave an air of neatness to these cottages, because of the quantity of light that prevailed. The peasants, almost all vine-dressers, were half-naked and bronzed by the sun; the women, short, yellow as mulattoes, but sprightly, were frank coquettes, with their posies of syringa-blossoms and their beads worn by way of crowns or chains.

The hill-slopes glowed with vine-stocks, the wine from which resembled that of Fayal. Water was scarce, but wherever a spring welled, there grew a fig-tree, there rose an oratory with a frescoed portico. The ogives of the portico framed views of the island and portions of the sea. On one of these fig-trees, I saw a flock of blue teal settle, not of the web-footed variety. The tree had no leaves, but bore red fruit set like crystals. When adorned with the cerulean birds, which let fall their wings, its fruits appeared to be of a brilliant purple, while the tree seemed suddenly to have shot forth an azure foliage.

It is probable that the Azores were known to the Carthaginians; it is certain that Phœnician coins have been dug up in the island of Corvo. The modern navigators who first landed at this island are said to have found an equestrian statue pointing with outstretched arm to the west, provided always that this statue is not the imaginary engraving which adorns the old books of seaports.

In the manuscript of the *Natchez*, I have made Chactas, returning from Europe, land at the island of Corvo, where he comes across the mysterious statue. He thus expresses the feelings which filled my mind at Graciosa, when I recalled the legend:

"I approached that extraordinary monument. On its base,

bathed by the foam of the ocean, were carved unknown characters: the moss and the saltpetre of the sea corroded the surface of the time-honoured bronze; the halcyon, perched upon the helmet of the colossus, uttered at intervals its plaintive note; shell-fish clung to the courser's flanks and mane of brass, and one's ear, when approached to its open nostrils, seemed to hear confused murmurs."

We were served with a good supper by the monks after our excursion, and we spent the night in drinking with our hosts. The next day, at noon, our provisions having been taken on board, we returned to the ship. The monks took charge of our letters for Europe. The vessel had been in danger through the rising of a stiff south-easterly wind. We heaved the anchor; but it was caught in the rocks, and we lost it, as we expected. We set sail: the wind continued to freshen, and we had soon passed the Azores.

> Fac pelagus me scire probes, quo carbasa laxo.

> "Muse, help me to show that I know the sea over which I spread my sails."

Thus, six hundred years ago, wrote Guillaume-le-Breton,[1] my fellow-countryman. Restored to the sea, I began anew the contemplation of my solitude; but across the ideal world of my dreams, stern monitors appeared to me: France and the events of reality. My lurking-place during the day, when I wished to avoid my fellow-passengers, was the main-top, to which I climbed nimbly amid the applause of the sailors. I there sat and commanded the waves.

The vast expanse, doubly hung with azure, had the appearance of a canvas prepared to receive the future creations of a mighty painter. The colour of the water was like that of liquid glass. Long and steep undulations opened within their hollows vistas of the ocean deserts: those wavering landscapes made clear to my eyes the comparison drawn in the Scriptures of the earth reeling before the Lord, like a drunken man.[2] Sometimes one might have pronounced the space narrow and restricted, for want of a vanishing point; but if a wave happened to raise its crest, a billow to curve in imitation of a distant coast, a shoal of dog-fish to pass along the horizon, then one had a

---

[1] Guillaume le Breton (circa 1165–circa 1220), the historian of Philip Augustus. The quotation is from his chronicle entitled, *Philippides libri duodecime, sive Gesta Philippi Augusti, versibus heroïcis descripta.*—T.

[2] Ps. cvii. 27.—T.

scale to measure by. The expanse was revealed still more when a mist, creeping to the ocean's surface, seemed to enlarge the very immensity.

On descending from the eyrie of the mast, as when, in former days, ever reduced to a solitary existence, I climbed down from my nest in the willow-tree, I supped on a ship-biscuit, a little sugar, and a lemon; I then lay down, either wrapped in my cloak on deck, or in my cot below: I had but to stretch my arm to reach from my bed to my coffin. ·

The wind compelled us to bear to the North, and we came alongside of the bank of Newfoundland. Floating icebergs roamed in the midst of a pale, cold mist.

The men of the trident have sports which are handed down to them from their ancestors: when you cross the Line, you must make up your mind to receive "baptism;" the same ceremony occurs beneath the Tropics, the same ceremony on the bank of Newfoundland, and whatever the spot, the leader of the masquerade is always "the Old Man of the Tropics." To the sailors, tropical and hydropical are interchangeable terms: the Old Man of the Tropics therefore has an enormous paunch; he is dressed, even when beneath his native Tropics, in all the sheepskins and all the furred jackets that the crew can supply. He sits squatting in the main-top and roaring from time to time. Every one looks at him from below: he begins to climb down the shrouds, moving heavily like a bear, and stumbling like Silenus. As he sets foot on deck, he utters fresh roars, gives a bound, seizes a pail, fills it with sea-water, and empties it over the chief of those who have not crossed the Equator or who have not reached the line of ice. You fly beneath the decks, you spring upon the hatches, you clamber up the masts: Old Father Tropics is after you; all this ends in a generous gift of drink-money: games of Amphitrite which Homer would have celebrated, even as he sang Proteus, if old Oceanus had been known in his entirety in the time of Ulysses; but, in those days, only his head was visible at the Pillars of Hercules: his body lay hidden and covered the world.

We steered for the islands of Saint-Pierre and Miquelon, in search of a new port. When we came in sight of the former, one morning between ten and twelve o'clock, we were almost upon it; its coast showed like a black hump through the fog.

We anchored in front of the capital of the island: we could not see it, but we heard the sounds on land. The passengers hastened to disembark; the Superior of Saint-Sulpice, who had been constantly racked with sea-sickness, was so weak that he had to be carried on shore. I took a separate lodging; I waited until a gust of wind tore the mist asunder and showed me the place in which I was living and, so to speak, the faces of my hosts in this land of shadows.

The port and roadstead of Saint-Pierre are situated between the east coast of the island and a long-shaped islet called the *Île aux Chiens*, or Isle of Dogs. The port, known as the *Barachois*, or Little Inlet, cuts into the land and ends in a brackish pool. Small, barren mountains crowd together in the centre of the island; some are detached and overhang the coast; others have at their feet a skirt of flat and turfy moorland. The look-out hill is visible from the market-town.

The Governor's house faces the wharf. The church, the vicarage, the provision warehouse are situated at the same spot; next come the houses of the naval commissary and the harbour-master. From there, the one street of the town runs over the shingles along the beach.

I dined two or three times with the Governor, a very polite and obliging officer. On a sloping bank he grew a few European vegetables. After dinner he showed me what he called his garden. A delicate and fragrant odour of heliotrope was exhaled from a small patch of flowering beans; it was not wafted to us by a gentle breeze from home, but by a wild New-foundland wind, having no connection with the exiled plant, no sympathy of remembrance or delight. In this perfume no longer inhaled by beauty, purified in its breast, or diffused upon its path, in this perfume of a changed dawn, cultivation and world, lurked all the several melancholies of regrets, absence, and youth.

From the garden we mounted towards the hills, and stopped at the foot of the flag-staff of the look-out. The new French flag waved over our heads; like Virgil's women, we looked at the sea, *flentes:* it separated us from our native land! The Governor was uneasy: he belonged to the defeated opinion; he was bored, moreover, in this sequestered spot, which was suited to a visionary like myself, but which was a thankless habitation for a man interested in affairs and not endowed with the all-filling passion which causes the rest of the world to disappear from view. My host inquired after the Revolution; I asked him for news of the North-West Passage. He was in the van of the wilderness, but he knew nothing of the Esquimaux and from Canada received nothing save partridges.

One morning I had gone alone to the *Cap-à-l'Aigle*, or Eagle Head, to see the sun rise in the direction of France. There, a wintry brook formed a cascade which with its last leap reached the sea. I sat down upon a projecting rock, my feet hanging over the water which broke into foam at the bottom of the cliff. A young fisher-girl appeared on the upper slopes of the hillside; she was bare-legged, in spite of the cold, and walked in the dew. Her black hair was carelessly twisted under the figured silk kerchief bound round her head; over this kerchief she wore a hat made out of the reed-grass of the country and shaped like a cradle or boat. A bunch of purple heather peeped out from her bosom, which was outlined beneath the white material of her shift. From time to time she stooped to gather the leaves of an aromatic plant known in the island as " home-grown tea." With one hand she dropped these leaves into a basket which she carried in the other. She saw me: without being frightened, she came and sat down by me, placed her basket within reach, and began like myself to look at the sun, her legs swinging over the sea.

We remained some minutes without speaking; at last I proved myself the bolder, and asked:

"What are you gathering there? The season for bilberries and atocas is over."

She opened two large, dark, shy, but proud eyes, and answered:

"I was picking tea."

She showed me her basket.

"Are you taking the tea home to your father and mother?"

"My father is away fishing with Guillaumy."

"What do you do in the island in the winter?"

"We make nets; we fish in the lakes by breaking the ice; on Sundays we go to Mass and Vespers or we sing hymns; and then we play in the snow and watch the boys hunting the polar bears."

"Will your father be back soon?"

"Oh no: the skipper is taking the ship to Genoa with Guillaumy."

"But Guillaumy will come home again?"

"Oh yes, next season, when the fishermen return. He is going to bring me a striped silk bodice in his stock, a muslin skirt, and a black necklace."

"And you will be decked out for the wind, the mountains, and the sea. Would you like me to send you a bodice, a skirt, and a necklace?"

"Oh no!"

She rose, took up her basket, and ran down a steep path, along a fir-grove. In a loud voice she sang a Mission hymn :

> Tout brûlant d'une ardeur immortelle,
> C'est vers Dieu que tendent mes désirs.[1]

She scattered to flight, as she went, those pretty birds called egrets, from the tuft on their heads ; she looked as though she were one of their number. When she reached the sea, she leapt into a boat, unfurled the sail, and seated herself at the rudder ; one might have taken her for Fortune ; she sailed away from me.

"Oh yes ; oh no ; Guillaumy:" the picture of the young sailor seated on a yard among the winds changed the hideous rock of Saint-Pierre into a land of delights :

> L'isole di Fortuna, ora vedete.[2]

We spent a fortnight in the island. From its desolate shores one discerns the yet more desolate coasts of Newfoundland. The hills in the interior put out diverging chains of which the highest extends towards Rodriguez Creek. In the dales, the granite rock, mixed with red and green mica, is covered with a thick cushion of sphagnum, lichens, and dicranum.

Small lakes are nourished by the tribute brought by the streams from the *Vigie*, or Look-Out ; the Courval ; the *Pain-de-Sucre*, or Sugarloaf ; the Kergariou ; the *Tête-Galante*, or Gallant Head. These pools are known by the names of the *Étangs-du-Savoyard*, or Savoyard's Ponds ; the *Cap-Noir*, or Black Head ; the Ravenel ; the *Colombier*, or Dove-cot ; the *Cap-à-l'Aigle*, or Eagle Head. When the whirlwinds strike upon these pools, they rend the shallow waters, laying bare, in places, portions of submarine meadows, which are as suddenly covered over by the newly-woven veil of the waters.

The *flora* of Saint-Pierre is the same as that of Lapland and Magellan's Straits. The number of plants diminishes as one proceeds towards the Pole ; in Spitzbergen we find only forty species of phanerogamous plants. In changing their habitation, races of plants become extinct : some which dwell in the frozen steppes in the North become daughters of the mountain in the South ; others which thrive in the peaceful atmosphere of the thickest forests decrease in strength and

---

[1] " Burning with immortal ardour,
    'Tis to God my hopes are turned."—T.
[2] TASSO, *Gerusalemme Liberata*, xv. 27.—B.

size until at last they expire on the stormy strands of the ocean. At Saint-Pierre, the marsh myrtle (*vaccinium fugilinosum*) is reduced to the condition of creeping grasses; it will soon be buried in the wadding and cushions of the mosses which serve as its soil. Myself a passenger plant, I have taken my precautions to disappear by the sea-shore, the site of my birth.

The slope of the hillocks of Saint-Pierre is laid over with balsam-trees, medlars, dwarf palms, larches, black firs, the gems of which are used for brewing an antiscorbutic beer. These trees do not exceed a man's stature. The ocean wind pollards them, shakes them, bends them like so many ferns; then, gliding beneath these forests of shrubs, it raises them again; but it finds no trunks there, nor branches, nor arches, nor echoes to wail among, and it makes no more noise than on a heath.

These rickety woods form a contrast with the great forests of Newfoundland, whose fir-trees bear a silver lichen (*alectoria trichodes*): the polar bears seem to have torn their fur against the branches of those trees, of which they are the strange creepers. The swamps of Jacques Cartier's[1] island contain roads beaten by these bears: it is as though one saw rustic footpaths in the neighbourhood of a sheep-fold. The whole night re-echoes with the cries of these famished beasts; the traveller is comforted only by the no less mournful sound of the sea: those waves, so unsociable and so rude, become friends and companions.

The northernmost point of Newfoundland touches the latitude of Cape Charles I. in Labrador; a few degrees higher, the polar landscape commences. If we are to believe the travellers, a charm lies upon those regions: in the evening the sun, touching the earth, seems to stay motionless, and subsequently reascends the sky instead of sinking beneath the horizon. The snow-clad mountains, the valleys carpeted with white moss upon which the reindeer browse, the seas covered with whales and strewn with ice-bergs, this whole scene glitters, lighted as it were at one time by the gleam of the setting sun and the light of dawn: one knows not whether he is assisting at the creation or the end of the world. A little bird, similar to that which sings in our woods at night, utters a plaintive warbling. Then love leads the Esquimaux to

[1] Jacques Cartier (1494–*circa* 1554), the discoverer of Newfoundland and of the greater part of Canada.—T.

the icy rock where his mate awaits him : those human nuptials at the extreme boundaries of the earth lack neither dignity nor happiness.

When we had shipped stores and replaced the anchor which we had lost at Graciosa, we left Saint-Pierre. Sailing south before the wind, we reached the latitude of 38°. The calm delayed us at a short distance from the coasts of Maryland and Virginia. The misty sky of the northerly regions had been succeeded by the clearest weather; the land was not in sight, but the odour of the pine-forests was wafted to our nostrils. The dawn and the early morning, the rising and setting sun, the twilight and the night were alike admirable. I was never satisfied with gazing at Venus, whose rays seemed to envelop me like the tresses of my sylph of former days.

One day I was reading in the captain's room; the bell struck for prayers; I went and mingled my prayers with those of my companions. The officers and passengers filled the quarter-deck; the chaplain, book in hand, stood a little before them, near the helm; the sailors were crowded promiscuously on deck; we stood with our faces turned towards the ship's bows. All sails were furled. The disk of the sun, preparing to plunge into the sea, appeared through the rigging of the vessel in the midst of the boundless space : it was as though, with the rocking of the poop, the radiant luminary at each moment changed its horizon. When I drew this picture, which you can see in its entirety in the *Génie du Christianisme*,[1] my religious sentiments were in harmony with the scene; but alas, when I was present at it in person, I had not yet put off the old man : it was not God alone that I contemplated in the waves, in all the magnificence of His works. I beheld an unknown woman and the miracles worked by her smile; the beauties of the heavens seemed to open out at her breath; I would have bartered Eternity for one of her caresses. I pictured her to myself throbbing behind the veil of the universe which hid her from my gaze. Ah, why was it not in my power to tear aside that curtain to press the idealized woman to my heart, to be consumed upon her breast with that love which was the source of my inspirations, of my despair, and of my life! While I abandoned myself to these impulses so well suited to my future career as a *coureur des bois*,

---

[1] *Génie du Christianisme*, Part I. book v. chap. 12: *Deux perspectives de la Nature.*—B.

an accident occurred which very nearly put an end to my plans
and to my dreams.

The heat was overpowering; the vessel, lying in a dead
calm, with furled sails and overweighted by the masts, rolled
heavily: burning upon deck and wearied by the motion, I
longed to bathe, and although we had no boat out, I dived
into the sea from the bowsprit. All went well at first, and
several passengers followed my example. I swam without
looking at the ship; but when I came to turn my head, I saw
that the current had dragged her some distance. The sailors,
alarmed, had slipped a rope to the other swimmers. Sharks
appeared in the ship's waters, and the men fired at them to
drive them away. The swell was so heavy that it delayed
my return by exhausting my strength. I had an eddy below
me, and at any moment the sharks might carry off one of my
arms or legs. On board, the boatswain was trying to lower a
boat, but it was necessary to fix the tackling, and all this
took time.

By the greatest good fortune, an almost imperceptible
breeze sprang up; the vessel answered her helm a little and
approached me; I was just able to catch hold of the rope, but
my companions in rashness were clinging to it; when we were
pulled to the ship's side, I was at the extremity of the line, and
they bore upon me with all their weight. We were thus
fished up one by one, which took long. The rolling continued;
at each roll, we were either plunged six or seven feet into the
water, or hung up as many feet in the air, like fish at
the end of a line: at the last immersion, I felt ready to faint
away; one roll more and it would have been over. I was
hoisted on deck half dead: had I been drowned, what a good
riddance for me and the rest!

Two days after this accident, we came in sight of land. My
heart beat fast when the captain pointed it out to me: America!
It was barely indicated by the crowns of a few maple-trees
standing above the water. The palms at the mouth of the Nile
have since indicated the coast of Egypt for me in the same
manner. A pilot came on board; we entered Chesapeake Bay.
In the evening a boat was sent on shore to fetch fresh provisions.
I joined the party, and soon trod American soil.

Turning my looks around me, I remained for some moments
motionless. This continent, perhaps unknown during the whole
course of antiquity and a large number of modern centuries;
the first wild destinies of that continent and its second destinies
after the arrival of Christopher Columbus; the sway of the

European monarchies shaken in this new world; the old society ending in young America; a republic of a hitherto unknown character ushering in a change in the human mind; the part which my country had played in these events; those seas and shores owing their independence in part to French blood and the French flag; a great man issuing from the midst of discord and the desert; Washington inhabiting a flourishing city in the same spot where William Penn [1] had bought a patch of forest-land; the United States handing on to France the revolution which France had supported with her arms; lastly, my own destinies, the virgin muse which I had come to abandon to the passion of a new revelation of nature; the discoveries which I desired to attempt in the deserts which still extended their broad kingdom behind the narrow empire of a foreign civilization: such were the thoughts that revolved through my mind.

We walked towards a dwelling-house. Woods of balsam-trees and Virginian cedars, mocking-birds and cardinal-birds proclaimed by their aspect and shade, their song and colour, that we were in a new clime. The house, which we reached in half-an-hour, combined the characteristics of an English farm-house and a West-Indian cabin. Herds of European cattle grazed in pastures surrounded by glades, in which played striped squirrels. Blacks were sawing logs of wood, whites cultivating tobacco-plants. A negress of thirteen or fourteen years of age, nearly naked and of singular beauty, opened the gate of the enclosure to us, like a young figure of Night. We bought cakes of Indian corn, chickens, eggs, milk, and returned to the ship with our demi-johns and baskets. I gave my silk handkerchief to the little African: a slave welcomed me to the soil of liberty.

We weighed anchor in order to make the roads and port of Baltimore: as we approached, the waters grew narrow; they were smooth and motionless; we appeared to be ascending a lazy stream lined with avenues. Baltimore presented itself to us as though at the further end of a lake. Opposite the town rose a wooded hill, at the foot of which they were commencing to build. We moored alongside the quay. I slept on board and did not go on shore till the next day. I went to stay at the inn with my luggage; the seminarists retired to the establishment prepared for them, whence they have since dispersed over America.

---

[1] William Penn (1644–1718), the Quaker. He commuted a claim upon the Crown for a grant of land in North America, where he founded the colony of Pennsylvania (1682), laying out Philadelphia as the capital.—T.

What became of Francis Tulloch? The following letter was handed to me in London on the 12th of April 1822:

"Thirty years have elapsed, my dear viscount, since the 'epoch' of our journey to Baltimore, and it is very doubtful whether you will remember as much as my name; but if I may judge from the feelings of my heart, which has always been loyal and true to you, this is not so, and I flatter myself that you would not be displeased to see me again. Although we are living almost opposite each other (as you will see by the date of this letter), I am only too well aware how many things separate us. But should you show the smallest wish to see me, I shall be eager to prove to you, in so far as I can, that I am ever, as I always have been, your faithful and devoted,

"FRANCIS TULLOCH.

"*P.S.*—The distinguished rank which you have won and which you have earned by so many claims has not escaped me; but the memory of the Chevalier de Chateaubriand is so dear to me that I cannot write to you (this time, at least) as Ambassador, &c., &c. So pardon the style for the sake of our old alliance.

"30 PORTLAND PLACE,
Friday, 12 *April.*"

And so Tulloch was in London; he did not become a priest; he is married; his romance ended as did mine. This letter testifies to the truthfulness of my Memoirs and the faithfulness of my recollections. Who would have given evidence of the "alliance" and "friendship" formed thirty years ago upon the sea, if the other contracting party had not appeared upon the scene? And what a sad and retrogressive perspective this letter unfolds before me! Tulloch, in 1822, was again living in the same city as myself, in the same street; the door of his house was opposite mine, as when we met on the same ship, upon the same deck, cabin facing cabin. How many of my other friends I shall never meet again! Every night, on retiring to rest, a man can count his losses: there is naught save his years that does not leave him, although these pass; when he reviews them and calls their numbers, they reply, "Here!" Not one but answers the roll-call.

Baltimore, like all the other capitals of the United States, had not the dimensions which it now possesses: it was a pretty little Catholic town, neat and lively, with customs and a society

closely resembling the customs and society of Europe. I paid
the captain my passage-money and gave him a farewell dinner.
I booked my seat in the stage-coach which ran three times a
week to Pennsylvania. I climbed up to it at four o'clock in the
morning, and found myself rolling along the high-roads of the
New World.

The road we followed was marked out rather than made,
and crossed a somewhat flat tract of country : there were hardly
any trees, some straggling farms, and thinly-scattered villages.
The climate was French : swallows flew over the water as on
the pond at Combourg.

As we drew nearer to Philadelphia, we met country-folk
going to market, public carriages and private carriages. Philadelphia struck me as a fine town, with wide streets, some of which
were planted with trees, intersecting each other at right angles in
regular order from north to south and east to west. The Delaware runs parallel to the street which follows its west bank.
This river would be considered a large one in Europe : it is not
spoken of in America ; its banks are low and unattractive.

At the period of my journey (1791), Philadelphia had not
yet spread as far as the Schuylkill ; the ground running towards
that tributary was divided into lots, upon which houses were
being built at intervals.

Philadelphia presents a monotonous aspect. In general,
the Protestant cities of the United States fall short in great
works of architecture : the Reformation, young in years, and
sacrificing nothing to the imagination, has rarely erected those
domes, those aerial naves, those twin towers with which the
old Catholic religion has crowned Europe. No monument, in
Philadelphia, in New York ; at Boston, one pyramid rising
above the mass of walls and roofs : the eye is saddened by
this uniform level.

First alighting at an inn, I next took a room in a boarding-
house in which were staying planters from San Domingo and
Frenchmen who had emigrated with other ideas than mine. A
land of liberty offered an asylum to those who were fleeing from
liberty : nothing better proves the high value of generous institutions than this voluntary exile of the partisans of absolute
power in a pure democracy.

A man who had landed in the United States as I had, filled
with enthusiasm for the classic races, a colonist who sought
on every side the rigidity of the early Roman manners, was
necessarily much scandalized to find on every hand the luxury
of private carriages, frivolity of conversation, inequality of

fortunes, the immorality of banking and gaming-houses, the excitement of theatres and ball-rooms. In Philadelphia I might have thought myself in Liverpool or Bristol. The appearance of the inhabitants was agreeable : the Quakeresses with their grey gowns, their uniform little bonnets and their pale features seemed attractive.

At that period of my life, I had a great admiration for republics, although I did not believe them possible at the stage of the world's history which we had reached : my idea of liberty was that conceived by the ancients, liberty the daughter of the manners of a new-born society ; but I knew nothing of the liberty which is the daughter of enlightenment and of an old civilization, a form of liberty which the representative republic has proved to be real : God grant that it may be lasting ! A man, to be free, is not obliged himself to plough his small field, to storm at arts and sciences, to wear hooked nails and a dirty beard.

General Washington was not in Philadelphia when I arrived there ; I was obliged to wait a week. I saw him go past in a carriage drawn by four prancing horses, driven four-in-hand. Washington, according to my then ideas, was necessarily Cincinnatus ; Cincinnatus in a chariot somewhat upset my republic of 296 B.C. Could Washington the Dictator be anything save a boor, driving his oxen with a goad and holding the tail of his plough ? But when I went to carry my letter of recommendation to him, I found once more the simplicity of the ancient Roman.

A small house, resembling the neighbouring houses, was the palace of the President of the United States : no sentries, no footmen even. I knocked, and a young maid-servant opened the door. I asked if the general was at home ; she replied that he was in. I said I had a letter for him. The servant asked my name, which is difficult to pronounce in English and which she could not remember. She then said softly, "Walk in, sir," and led the way down one of those narrow passages which serve as an entrance-hall to English houses : she showed me into a parlour where she asked me to wait until the general came.

I felt no agitation ; greatness of mind or fortune in no way overawe me : I admire the first without being crushed by it ; the second calls forth my pity rather than my respect : no man's countenance will ever disconcert me.

After a few minutes, the general entered the room : tall in stature, of a calm and cold rather than noble bearing, he resembled his engraved portraits. I handed him my letter in

...
...would carry my letter
...see from the simplicity of

...the new boarding houses, was
...the United States sentries,
...want opened
...was at home, she replied
...for him. The servant
...language in English and
...she said, "Walk in,
...those narrow passages which
...she showed me into
...until the general came.
...mind or fortune in
...without being crushed by
...than my respect no
...

...enter the room, tall in
stature, of a crim... noble bearing,
...I handed him my letter

GENERAL WASHINGTON

silence; he opened it and glanced at the signature which he read aloud, exclaiming:

"Colonel Armand!"

This was the name by which he knew the Marquis de La Rouërie and by which the latter had signed himself.

We sat down. I explained to him as best I could the object of my journey. He replied in monosyllables in English and French, and listened to me with a sort of astonishment. I remarked this and said to him, with some little animation:

"But it is less difficult to discover the North-West Passage than to create a people, as you have done."

"Well, well, young man!" he exclaimed, giving me his hand. He invited me to dinner for the next day, and we parted.

I took care to keep the appointment. We were only five or six guests at table. The conversation turned upon the French Revolution. The general showed us a key from the Bastille. These keys, as I have already said, were rather silly toys which passed from hand to hand at that time.] The consigners of locksmiths' wares might, three years later, have sent to the President of the United States the bolt of the prison of the monarch who bestowed liberty upon France and America. If Washington had seen the "victors of the Bastille" disporting themselves in the gutters of Paris, he would have felt less respect for his relic. The seriousness and strength of the Revolution did not spring from those blood-stained orgies. At the time of the revocation of the Edict of Nantes, in 1685, the same mob from the Faubourg Saint-Antoine demolished the Protestant temple at Charenton with as much ardour as when it laid waste the church of Saint-Denis in 1793.

I left my host at ten o'clock in the evening, and never saw him again; he went away the next day, and I continued my journey.

Such was my meeting with the citizen soldier, the liberator of a world. Washington descended to the grave before a vestige of fame had become attached to my footsteps; I passed before him as the most unknown of beings; he was in all his lustre, I in all my obscurity; my name perhaps did not linger one whole day in his memory: well for me, nevertheless, that his looks fell upon me! I have felt warmed by them for the rest of my life: there is virtue in a great man's looks.

Bonaparte is but lately dead.[1] As I have just knocked at Washington's door, it is natural that the parallel between the

[1] Bonaparte died 5 May 1821.—T.

founder of the United States and the Emperor of the French should occur to my mind : the more so since, at the time when I am writing these lines, Washington himself is no more. Ercilla,[1] singing and battling in Chili, stops in the middle of his journey to describe the death of Dido ; why should not I stop at the commencement of my ramble through Pennsylvania to compare Washington with Bonaparte ? I might have delayed my notice of them until I came to the time at which I met Napoleon ; but should I happen to sink into the grave before reaching the year 1814 in my chronicle, the reader would never know what I had to say on the subject of the two mandataries of Providence. I remember the case of Castelnau :[2] he was Ambassador to England like myself, and like me wrote a part of his life in London. On the last page of Book VII., he says to his son, " I will treat of this fact in the Eighth Book," and the Eighth Book of Castelnau's Memoirs does not exist : that is a warning to me to take advantage of life while it lasts.

Washington does not, like Bonaparte, belong to the race that surpasses human stature. There is nothing astonishing attached to his person ; he is not placed upon a vast stage ; he is not engaged in a struggle with the ablest captains and the most powerful monarchs of the time ; he does not rush from Memphis to Vienna, from Cadiz to Moscow : he defends himself with a handful of citizens in a land not yet famous, within the narrow circle of the domestic hearth. He delivers none of those battles in which the triumphs of Arbela and Pharsalia are renewed ; he overturns no thrones to build up others from their ruins ; he does not send word to the kings at his gate :

> Qu'ils se font trop attendre, et qu'Attila s'ennuie.[3]

A certain silence covers the actions of Washington ; he acts slowly ; it is as though he felt that he was entrusted with

---

[1] Alonso d'Ercilla y Zuñiga (*circa* 1525–*circa* 1600), a famous Spanish poet and warrior. He began life as a page to Philip II., whom he accompanied in his travels to France, Italy, Germany, and England. In 1547 he joined the Chilian expedition, covered himself with glory in the campaign against the Araucanians, and celebrated his own exploits in the *Araucana*, an epic poem of very great merit.—T.

[2] Michel de Castelnau, Sieur de La Mauvissière (*circa* 1520–1592), was five times Ambassador to England under Charles IX. and Henry III. His Memoirs run from 1559 to 1570.—T.

[3] CORNEILLE, *Attila*, Act I. scene I. :

> " Ils ne sont pas venus, nos deux rois ; qu'on leur die
> Qu'ils se font trop attendre, et qu'Attila s'ennuie."

> " Our two kings have not come ; go out to them and say
> That Attila is wearied, and brooks not such delay."—T.

the liberty of the future and feared to compromise it. It is not his own destiny that a hero of this kind carries in his hand : it is that of his country ; he does not suffer himself to stake that which does not belong to him ; but from this profound humility see how great a light arises ! Seek the woods in which flashed Washington's sword : what do you find ? Tombstones ? No : a world ! Washington left the United States as a trophy on his battle-field.

Bonaparte has none of the features of this grave American : he fights noisily upon an old world ; he seeks to create nothing but his fame ; he entrusts himself with nothing but his own lot. He seems to know that his mission will be short, that the torrent which descends from so great a height will soon flow away ; he hastens to enjoy and to misuse his glory, as though it were a fleeting season of youth. Like Homer's gods, he wishes to reach the end of the world in four steps. He appears on every shore ; precipitously he inscribes his name upon the annals of every nation ; he tosses crowns to his family and his soldiers ; he makes haste with his monuments, his laws, his victories. Bending over the world, with one hand he fells the kings to the ground, while with the other he lays low the revolutionary giant ; but in crushing anarchy, he stifles liberty, and ends by losing his own upon his last field of battle.

Each is rewarded according to his works : Washington raises a nation to independence ; a peaceful magistrate, he falls asleep beneath his roof-tree amid the regrets of his fellow-countrymen and the veneration of the nations. Bonaparte robs a nation of its independence : a fallen emperor, he is hurled into exile, where the affrighted earth does not think him sufficiently closely imprisoned, even when guarded by the ocean. He dies : the news, posted on the gate of the palace before which the conqueror has caused so many funerals to be proclaimed, does not delay nor astonish the passer-by : what had the citizens to mourn for ?

Washington's republic is in existence ; Bonaparte's empire is destroyed. Washington and Bonaparte issued from the bosom of democracy : both were born of liberty ; the first was faithful to her, the second betrayed her.

Washington was the representative of the needs, the ideas, the judgment, the opinions of his day ; he seconded, rather than opposed, the changes in men's minds ; he desired what he was bound to desire, the very thing for which he had been called : hence the coherent and perpetual character of his work.

This man who strikes the imagination little, because he is in proportion, merged his existence in that of his country: his glory is civilization's inheritance; his fame towers like one of those public sanctuaries from which flows a fertile and inexhaustible spring.

Bonaparte had it equally in his power to enrich the commonwealth; he worked upon the most intelligent, the most gallant, the most brilliant nation on earth. How high would be the rank held by him to-day, if he had added magnanimity to the heroism which was his, if, Washington and Bonaparte in one, he had appointed liberty the universal legatee of his glory! But this giant did not link his destinies with those of his contemporaries; his genius belonged to modern times: his ambition was of a by-gone age; he did not perceive that the miracles of his life surpassed a diadem in value, and that that Gothic ornament would become him badly. Now he flung himself into the future, again he drew back towards the past; and according to whether he reascended or followed the course of time, thanks to his prodigious force, he drew with him or pushed back the waves. Men, in his eyes, were but a means of power; no sympathy was established between their happiness and his; he had promised to deliver them, and he enchained them; he isolated himself from them, and they withdrew from him. The Kings of Egypt placed their funeral pyramids, not among thriving pastures, but in the midst of barren deserts; those great tombs rise like eternity in the solitude: Bonaparte built the monument of his fame in their image.

I was impatient to continue my journey. I had not come to see the Americans, but something quite different from the men I knew, something more in harmony with the habitual order of my ideas; I burned to throw myself into an enterprise for which I had nothing prepared except my imagination and my courage.

At the time when I formed the project of discovering the North-West Passage, it was not known whether North America extended towards the Pole and joined Greenland, or whether it terminated in some sea adjoining Hudson's Bay and Behring's Straits. In 1772, Hearne had discovered the sea at the mouth of the Copper Mine River in latitude 71° 15' N. and longitude 119° 15' W. of Greenwich.[1]

On the Pacific coast, the efforts of Captain Cook and sub-

---

[1] These measurements have since been rectified as being too high in both cases. —*Author's Note* (Geneva, 1832).

sequent travellers had left doubts. In 1787, a vessel was said to have entered an inland sea of North America; according to the story told by the captain of this ship, all that had been taken for uninterrupted coast to the north of California consisted merely of a closely-knit chain of islands. The British Admiralty sent Vancouver[1] to verify these reports, which proved to be false. Vancouver had not yet made his second voyage.

In 1791, people in the United States were beginning to discuss the road taken by Mackenzie: starting from Fort Chippeway on Mountains Lake,[2] 3 June 1789, he descended to the Arctic Ocean by the river to which he gave his name.

This discovery might have changed my direction and caused me to take my route due north; but I should have scrupled to alter the plans agreed upon between M. de Malesherbes and myself. I proposed, therefore, to travel westwards, so as to strike the north-west coast above the Gulf of California; from there, following the outline of the continent, and always keeping the sea in sight, I intended to explore Behring's Straits, double the northernmost cape of America, descend on the east along the shores of the Arctic Ocean, and return to the United States by way of Hudson's Bay, Labrador, and Canada.

What means had I to carry out this prodigious peregrination? None at all. Most of the French travellers have been isolated men, left entirely to their own resources; it is but rarely that the government or any company has employed or assisted them. Englishmen, Americans, Germans, Spaniards, Portuguese, thanks to the concurrence of the national volition, have accomplished the things which, with us, destitute individuals have begun in vain. Mackenzie and many others after him have, to the profit of the United States and Great Britain, made conquests upon the immensity of America, with which I had dreamed of aggrandizing my native land. In case of success, I should have had the honour of bestowing French names upon unknown regions, of endowing my country with a colony upon the Pacific Ocean, of taking away the rich fur-trade from a rival Power, and of preventing that Power from opening out a shorter road to the Indies, by placing France herself in possession of that road. I have stated these projects in the

---

[1] George Vancouver (1750–1798) accompanied Cook in his second and third voyages round the world, and subsequently served under Rodney. He was despatched on the expedition in question in 1790.—T.

[2] This appears to be an error for Lake Athabasca, on which Fort Chippeway is situated, and which communicates by means of the Slave River with Great Slave Lake and the Mackenzie River.—T.

Essai historique, published in London in 1796, and these projects were taken from the manuscript of my Travels written in
1791.   These dates prove that I was ahead, both in thought and
work, of the latest explorers of the Arctic ice-fields.

I received no encouragement in Philadelphia.   I foresaw
from then that the object of this first journey would be missed,
and that my expedition would be but the precursor of a second
and longer journey.   I wrote in this sense to M. de Malesherbes,
and while looking forward to the future, I promised to poetry
what should be lost to science.   In fact, if I did not find in
America what I had come to seek, the Arctic world, I did find
there a new muse.

A stage-coach, similar to that which brought me from
Baltimore, took me from Philadelphia to New York, a gay,
populous, commercial town, which was nevertheless far from
being what it is to-day, far from what it will be in a few
years; for the United States grow faster than does this
manuscript.   I made a pilgrimage to Boston to salute the first
battlefield of American liberty.   I saw the plains of Lexington;
I there sought, as I since sought at Sparta, the tomb of the
warriors who died " in obedience to the sacred laws of their
country."[1]   A noteworthy instance of the concatenation of
human affairs : a finance bill passed by the English Parliament
in 1765 erects a new empire upon the earth in 1782, and causes
one of the oldest kingdoms of Europe to disappear from the
world in 1789!

I embarked at New York in the packet which sailed for
Albany, situated on the upper reaches of the Hudson River.
The company was numerous.   On the evening of the first day
we were served with a collation consisting of fruits and milk;
the women sat on the benches on deck, the men on the deck
at their feet.   Conversation was not long maintained : at the
sight of a beautiful natural picture, one involuntarily lapses
into silence.   Suddenly some one or other exclaimed :

" There is the place where Asgill[2] was arrested."

[1] Chateaubriand, in a footnote to the *Itinéraire,* confesses his mistake in
searching for the stone lion which, according to Herodotus, marks the tomb of
Leonidas and his companions, at Sparta instead of at Thermopylæ.—B.

[2] Sir Charles Asgill (1760–1823), an English general serving under Cornwallis.
He was taken prisoner by the insurgents and picked out by lot to be shot by way
of reprisals.   He was saved through the intervention of the French Government,
and an act of the American Congress revoked the sentence of death.   Asgill visited
Versailles to thank Louis XVI. and Marie Antoinette, who had actively interceded
on his behalf.   The episode furnished a subject for a number of popular novels
and plays.—B.

A Quakeress from Philadelphia was asked to sing the ballad known as *Asgill.* We were passing between mountains; the fair passenger's voice died away on the water, or rang out when we hugged the bank more closely. The fate of a young soldier, a lover, a poet and a hero, honoured by the interest of Washington and the generous intervention of an unfortunate queen, lent additional charm to the romance of the scene.] The friend whom I have lost, M. de Fontanes, let fall some courageous words in memory of Asgill at the time when Bonaparte was preparing to ascend the throne upon which Marie Antoinette had sat.] The American officers appeared touched by the song of the fair Pennsylvanian: the memory of the past troubles of their country made them appreciate more highly the calm of the present moment. They gazed with emotion upon those spots but lately filled with troops, resounding with the clash of arms, and now wrapped in profound peace; those spots gilded with the fading light of day, enlivened with the singing of the cardinal-birds, the cooing of the ring-doves, the song of the mocking-birds, while the inhabitants, leaning against their fences fringed with trumpet - flowers, watched our bark pass below them.

On arriving at Albany I went in search of a Mr. Swift, for whom I had been given a letter. This Mr. Swift traded in furs with the Indian tribes enclosed in the territory ceded to the United States by England; for the civilized Powers in America, republican and monarchical alike, unceremoniously share among themselves land which does not belong to them. After listening to what I had to say, Mr. Swift made some very reasonable objections. He told me that I could not undertake a journey of this importance at first sight, alone, without assistance, without support, without letters of recommendation to the English, American, and Spanish stations by which I should be obliged to pass; that if I had the good fortune to cross so many solitary tracts of country, I should arrive at frozen regions where I should perish of hunger; he advised me to begin by acclimatizing myself, suggested that I should learn the Sioux, Iroquois, and Esquimaux languages, and live among the *coureurs* and the agents of the Hudson's Bay Company. Having gained this preliminary experience, I might then, in four or five years, with the assistance of the French Government, proceed on my hazardous mission.

This advice, whose justice, in my heart of hearts, I admitted, annoyed me. Had I trusted to my own judgment, I should have set out then and there to go to the Pole, as I might go

from Paris to Pontoise. I concealed my vexation from Mr.
Swift, and asked him to find me a guide and horses to take me
to Niagara and Pittsburg: from Pittsburg I would go down the
Ohio and gather ideas for my future plans. I still had my
first project in my head. Mr. Swift engaged a Dutchman on
my behalf, who spoke several Indian dialects. I bought two
horses and left Albany.

The whole stretch of country between the territory surrounding that town and Niagara is now inhabited and cleared; the
New York Canal crosses it; but at that time a great part of
the district was unfrequented. When, after crossing the
Mohawk, I entered woods which had never known the axe, I
was seized with a sort of intoxication of independence; I went
from tree to tree, left and right, saying to myself:

"Here are no more roads, no more cities, no more monarchies, no more republics, no more presidents, no more kings,
no more men!"

And, in order to test whether I was really reinstated in
my original rights, I indulged in acts of will which infuriated
my guide, who in his heart believed me mad.

Alas, I imagined myself to be alone in that forest in which I
was carrying my head so high! Suddenly I almost broke my
nose against a shed. Under that shed, my amazed eyes beheld
the first savages I had seen in my life. There were a score of
them, men and women, all bedaubed like wizards, with half-
naked bodies, slit ears, crows' feathers on their heads, and
rings through their nostrils. A little Frenchman, all powdered
and curled, in an apple-green coat, a drugget vest, and a muslin
frill and ruffles, was scraping a pocket fiddle and making those
Iroquois dance *Madelon Friquet*. M. Violet (that was his
name) was the savages' dancing-master. They paid him for
his lessons in beaver-skins and bear's hams. He had been
a scullion in the service of General Rochambeau[1] during the
American War. He remained in New York after the departure
of our army, and resolved to instruct the Americans in the fine
arts. His views widened with success, and the new Orpheus
carried civilization to the savage hordes of the New World.
In speaking to me of the Indians, he always said:

[1] Jean Baptiste Donatien de Viveur, Comte de Rochambeau (1725–1807), was
sent to America with 6000 men to assist the insurgents and contributed towards
effecting the capitulation of Cornwallis in 1781. He returned to France when
peace was declared, became Governor of Picardy and Artois, and was created a
Marshal of France in 1791, and given the command of the Northern Army. He
vainly endeavoured to restore discipline and resigned his command in 1792. He
was condemned to death by Robespierre, but made his escape.—T.

"Those savage ladies and gentlemen."

He took great pride in the nimbleness of his pupils; indeed I never saw such capers before or since. M. Violet, holding his little violin between his chest and his chin, tuned the fatal instrument; he cried to the Iroquois:

"Take your places!"

And the whole troop leaped about like a band of demons.

Was it not an overwhelming thing for a disciple of Rousseau, this introduction to savage life through a ball which General Rochambeau's late scullion was giving to the Iroquois? I had a great longing to laugh, but I felt cruelly humiliated.

I bought a complete outfit of the Indians: two bearskins, one to serve as a demi-toga, the other as a bed. I added to my new equipment the red ribbed-cloth cap, the cloak, the belt, the horn to call in the dogs, the bandoleer of the *coureurs des bois*. My hair hung over my bare neck; I wore a long beard: I had something of the savage, the hunter, and the missionary. I was invited to a hunt which was to take place the next day to track a wolverine.

This race of animals is almost entirely destroyed in Canada, as are the beavers. We took boat before daybreak to go up a river which issued from the wood in which the wolverine had been seen. There were some thirty of us, both Indians and American and Canadian *coureurs*: one part of the troop walked alongside of the flotilla with the dogs, and the women carried our provisions. We did not find the wolverine; but we killed lynxes and musk-rats. Formerly the Indians used to go into deep mourning when they had inadvertently killed any of the latter animals; for the female of the musk-rat is, as everybody knows, the mother of the human race. The Chinese, with their finer powers of observation, know to a certainty that the rat changes into a quail, the mole into a loriot.

Our table was abundantly furnished with river-side birds and fish. The dogs are trained to dive; when they are not hunting, they go fishing: they plunge into the streams and seize the fish down at the bottom of the water. The women prepared our meals at a large fire around which we took our places. We had to lie flat down, with our faces against the ground, to protect our eyes from the smoke, the clouds of which floated above our heads and indifferently preserved us from the stings of the mosquitoes.

Seen through the microscope, the various carnivorous insects are formidable animals; they were once perhaps those

winged dragons whose skeletons are sometimes found : de-
creasing in size in proportion as their matter decreased in
energy, these hydras, griffins and others would to-day be reduced to the condition of insects.   The antediluvian giants are
the little men of our time.

M. Violet offered me his credentials for the Onondagas, the
remnant of one of the six Iroquois nations.   I first came to the
Lake of the Onondagas.   The Dutchman selected a suitable
spot at which to pitch our camp : a river issued from the lake ;
our gear was set up in the curve of the river.   We drove two
forked stakes into the ground, at a distance of six feet one from
the other ; in the forks of these stakes we hung, horizontally, a
long pole.   Strips of birch bark, one end resting on the ground,
the other on the transversal pole, formed the sloping roof of
our mansion.   Our saddles served as pillows, our cloaks as
blankets.   We fastened bells to our horses' necks and
turned them loose in the woods near our camp : they did not
wander far.

Fifteen years later, when I was bivouacking in the sand of the
Saba Desert, at a few steps from the Jordan on the banks of
the Dead Sea, our horses, those swift sons of Araby, looked as
though they were listening to the tales of the sheik and taking
part in the story of Antar and of the horse in Job.[1]

It was hardly four o'clock in the afternoon when we were
hutted.   I took my gun and went for a stroll round about.
There were few birds.   A solitary pair alone fluttered before
my eyes, like the birds which I had followed in my paternal
woods ; by the colour of the male, I recognised the white
sparrow, the *passer nivalis* of the ornithologists.   I also heard
the osprey, very clearly characterized by its note.   The flight
of the "screamer" had led me to a dale hemmed in by tall and
rocky heights ; on a mountain-side stood a poor hut ; a lean
cow roamed in a field below.

I like small shelters : "*A chico pajarillo chico nidillo*: a little
bird, a little nest."   I sat down on the slope facing the hut
planted on the hillside opposite.   In a few minutes, I heard
voices in the valley : three men were driving five or six fat
cows ; they put them to graze and drove away the lean cow
with blows of a switch.   An Indian woman came out of the hut,
went towards the frightened beast, and called it.   The cow ran
to her, stretching out its neck with a little low.   The planters

[1] JOB, xxxix. 19-25.—T.

shook their fists at the Indian woman, who returned to her hut. The cow followed her.

I got up, climbed down the declivity of the hillside, crossed the glen, and climbing the opposite hill, reached the hut. I uttered the greeting I had been taught:

"*Siegoh!* I have come!"

The Indian woman, instead of returning my greeting by the customary repetition, "You have come," made no reply. Then I petted the cow: the Indian woman's yellow and saddened face showed signs of softening. I was touched by these mysterious relations of misfortune: there is sweetness in lamenting ills that none have lamented beside.

My hostess looked at me a little longer, with a remnant of doubt lingering in her eyes, and then came forward and passed her hand over the forehead of her companion in misery and solitude. Encouraged by this mark of confidence, I said in English, for I had exhausted my Indian:

"She is very lean."

The Indian woman replied, in broken English:

"She eats very little."

"They drove her away roughly," I added.

And the woman replied:

"We are both accustomed to that."

I asked:

"Does not this meadow belong to you then?"

She answered:

"This meadow belonged to my husband, who is dead. I have no children, and the pale-faces drive their cows into my meadow."

I had nothing to offer this creature of God. We parted. My hostess said a number of things to me which I did not understand; they were doubtless wishes for prosperity; if they have not been heard by Heaven, it is not the fault of her who prayed, but the infirmity of him for whom the prayer was offered. All souls have not an equal aptitude for happiness, just as all lands do not bear equal harvests.

I returned to my wigwam, where a collation consisting of potatoes and Indian corn awaited my arrival. The evening was splendid: the lake, smooth as a flawless mirror, showed not a ripple; the murmuring river bathed our peninsula, which the calycanthuses perfumed with the scent of apple-blossom. The whip-poor-will uttered its song: we heard it, now nearer, now farther away, according as the bird changed the spot of its amorous calls. No one called me. Weep, poor Will!

The next day I went to pay a visit to the sachem of the Onondagas; I reached his village at ten o'clock in the morning. I was at once surrounded by young savages, who spoke to me in their language, mixed with English phrases and a few words of French; they were very noisy and wore an air of light-heartedness, like the first Turks whom I saw, later, at Koroni, when landing on the soil of Greece. These Indian tribes, enclosed in the clearings made by the whites, own horses and cattle; their huts are filled with utensils purchased at Quebec, Montreal, Niagara, and Detroit on the one side, and in the markets of the United States on the other.

The explorers of the interior of North America found in a state of nature, among the different savage tribes, the several forms of government known to the peoples of civilization. The Iroquois belonged to a race which seemed destined to conquer the Indian races, if strangers had not come to exhaust his veins and stop the progress of his genius. That fearless man was not astonished at fire-arms when these were first used against him; he stood fast amid the hiss of the bullets and the roar of the cannon, as though he had heard them all his life; he seemed to pay no more heed to them than to the storm. So soon as he was able to procure a musket, he made better use of it than the European. He did not abandon for it the tomahawk, the scalping-knife, the bow and arrow; but to these he added the carbine, the pistol, the dagger, and the axe: he seemed never to have enough arms to satisfy his valour. Doubly equipped with the murderous instruments of Europe and America, his head decked with plumes, his ears slit, his face streaked with various colours, his arms tattooed and smeared with blood, this champion of the New World became as redoubtable in appearance as in battle, on the shores which he defended foot by foot against the invaders.

The Onondaga chief was an old Iroquois in the fullest sense of the word; he kept up in his person the ancient traditions of the desert. The English narratives never fail to speak of the Indian sachem as "the old gentleman." Now, the old gentleman is perfectly naked; he wears a feather or a fish-bone in his pierced nostrils, and sometimes covers his head, which is smooth and round as a cheese, with a laced three-cornered hat, as an European sign of honour. Has not Velly[1]

---

[1] The Abbé Paul François Velly (1709–1759) wrote the first seven or eight volumes of the History of France in thirty volumes known as the *Histoire de Velly, Villaret et Garnier*. These first eight volumes which cover the period to the reign

depicted history with the same veracity? The Frankish chieftain Khilpérick[1] rubbed his hair in sour butter, *infundens acido comam butyro*, stained his cheeks with woad, and wore a party-coloured jerkin or a greatcoat made of the skin of some beast; he is represented by Velly as a prince magnificent to the point of ostentation in his furniture and equipage, voluptuous to the point of debauchery, and scarcely believing in God, whose ministers formed the subject of his raillery.

The sachem of the Onondagas received me well and made me sit down on a mat. He spoke English and understood French; my guide knew Iroquois: conversation was easy. Among other things, the old man told me that, although his nation had always been at war with mine, he had always respected it. He complained of the Americans; he thought them greedy and unjust, and regretted that, in the division of the Indian territories his tribe had not gone to swell the lot of the English. The women served us with a meal. Hospitality is the last virtue left to the savages in the midst of European civilization; their hospitality is well known of old; the hearth had all the power of the altar. When a tribe was driven from its woods, or when a man came to demand hospitality, the stranger began what was called the dance of the supplicant. The child touched the door-sill and said:

"Here is the stranger."

And the chief replied:

"Child, bring the man into the hut."

The stranger entered, under the protection of the child, and sat down by the ashes on the hearth. The women sang the song of consolation:

> The stranger has found a mother and a wife; the sun will rise
> and set for him as of old.

These customs seem borrowed from the Greeks: Themistocles, visiting Admetus, kisses the Penates and his host's young son (I have possibly at Megara trod upon the poor wife's hearthstone beneath which Phocion's cinerary urn lay concealed);[2] and Ulysses, visiting Alcinous, implores Arete:

"Noble Arete, daughter of Rhexenor, after suffering cruel ills, I throw myself at your feet."[3]

---

of Philip the Fair, are the weakest of the whole compilation, especially the two first, which embrace the history of the Frankish kings.—T.

[1] Khilpérick or Chilperic I. (*d.* 584), King of Soissons, later King of the Franks, youngest son of Clotaire I., King of the Franks.—T.

[2] *Cf.* Plutarch's Life of Phocion.—B.   [3] *Odyssey*, VII.—B.

Having spoken these words, the hero goes towards the hearth and seats himself by the ashes.

I took leave of the old chief. He had been present at the capture of Quebec. In the shameful years of the reign of Louis XV., the episode of the Canadian War comes to our consolation as though it were a page from our ancient history discovered in the Tower of London.

Montcalm,[1] left to defend Canada unaided against forces often relieved and four times his own in number, fights successfully for two whole years; he defeats Lord Loudon[2] and General Abercromby.[3] At last fortune forsakes him; he falls wounded beneath the walls of Quebec, and two days later breathes his last: his Grenadiers bury him in a hole dug by a shell, a grave worthy of the honour of our arms! His noble enemy Wolfe[4] dies facing him; he pays with his own life for Montcalm's life and for the glory of expiring upon a few French flags.

Once more my guide and I mounted our horses. Our road became more difficult and was marked only by some felled trees. The trunks of these trees served as bridges over the streams or as hurdles in the bogs. The American population was at that time moving towards the Genesee grants. These grants were sold at prices more or less high according to the goodness of the soil, the quality of the trees, the current and abundance of the water.

It has been observed that colonists are often preceded in the woods by bees: these are the van-guard of the tillers of the soil, and the symbols of the industry and civilization whose coming they proclaim. Foreign to America, these peaceful conquerors came in the wake of Columbus' sails, and have robbed a new world of flowers of those treasures only of whose use the natives were ignorant; nor have they employed those treasures other than to enrich the soil whence they derived them.

---

[1] Louis Joseph Marquis de Montcalm (1712–1759), entrusted with the defence of Canada against the English in 1756.—T.

[2] John Campbell, fourth Earl of Loudon (1705–1782), Governor-General of Virginia and Commander-in-Chief of the Forces in America (1756), but recalled in 1757.—T.

[3] Sir Robert Abercromby (1740–1827), younger brother of the more famous Sir Ralph Abercromby. He had distinguished himself, as a volunteer, by his gallantry at the battle of Ticonderoga in 1758, after which he was appointed an ensign, and was present at the Battle of Niagara and the capture of Montreal.—T.

[4] General James Wolfe (1727–1759), although only thirty-two years of age at the time of his glorious death, had been present at the battles of Dettingen, Fontenoy, Falkirk, and Culloden, and served in the expedition against Rochefort.—T.

The clearings along both sides of the road which I travelled displayed a curious mixture of the state of nature and the state of civilization. In one corner of a wood which had never known any sound save the yells of the savage and the belling of the stag, one came across a ploughed field; one saw from the same point of view the wigwam of an Indian and the dwelling of a planter. Some of these dwellings, when completed, reminded one of the neatness of the Dutch farm-houses; others were only half finished, and had nothing but the sky for a roof.

I was welcomed in these dwellings, the results of a morning's work; often I would find a family displaying European elegancies, mahogany furniture, a piano, carpets, mirrors, at a few steps from the hut of an Iroquois. In the evening, when the farm-servants returned from working in the woods or fields with the axe or the hoe, the windows were opened. My host's daughters, with their beautiful fair hair dressed in ringlets, would sing, to the accompaniment of the piano, the duet from Paisiello's[1] *Pandolfetto* or some *cantabile* by Cimarosa,[2] all in full view of the wilderness, and sometimes to the murmuring sound of a waterfall.

Small market-towns rose in the better districts. The spire of a new steeple shot up from the midst of an old forest. The English are accompanied by English customs wherever they go: after crossing districts containing no trace of habitation, I came upon the sign of an inn swinging from the bough of a tree. Hunters, planters, and Indians mingled at these caravansaries: the first time I rested there, I swore that it should be the last.

It so happened that, on entering one of these hostelries, I stood dumfoundered at the sight of a huge bed set up in a circle around a post: each traveller took a place in this bed, with his feet against the post in the centre and his head on the circumference of the circle, so that the sleepers were arranged symmetrically, like the spokes of a wheel or the sticks of a fan. After a momentary hesitation, I got into this affair because I saw no one there. I was just falling asleep, when I felt something sliding against me: it was the leg of my big Dutchman;

---

[1] Giovanni Paisiello (1741–1816), composer of a number of operas, most of which were written during his long residence at St. Petersburg, and of some meritorious sacred music.—T.

[2] Domenico Cimarosa (1754–1801), composer of over 120 grand and comic operas, of which the *Matrimonio segreto* is the best known.—T.

I never in my life experienced a greater fright. I sprang out
of the hospitable work-basket, cordially cursing the customs
of our good ancestors. I went and slept in my cloak by the
moonlight: this companion of the traveller's bed had at least
nothing but was agreeable, and fresh, and sweet.

On the bank of the Genesee we found a ferry-boat. A
troop of colonials and Indians crossed the river with us.
We camped in meadows bright with butterflies and flowers.
With our varied costumes, grouped around our several fires,
and our horses tethered or grazing, we looked like a caravan.
I there first met the rattlesnake, which allows itself to be
bewitched by the sound of a flute. The Greeks would have
turned my Canadian into Orpheus; the flute into a lyre; the
snake into Cerberus, or, possibly, Eurydice.

We rode towards Niagara. When we had come within a
distance of eight or nine leagues of our destination, we perceived, in an oak grove, the camp-fire of some savages, who
had settled down on the bank of a stream where we ourselves
were thinking of bivouacking. We took advantage of their
preparations: after grooming our horses and dressing ourselves
for the night, we accosted the band. With legs crossed tailor-
wise, we sat down among the Indians around the blazing pile,
and began to roast our maize cakes.

The family consisted of two women, two infants at the breast,
and three braves. The conversation became general, that is to
say, interspersed with a few words on my side and many
gestures; after that, each fell asleep in the place where he sat.
I alone remained awake, and went to sit by myself on a root
trailing by the bank of the stream.

The moon showed above the tops of the trees; a balmy
breeze, which the Queen of the Night brought with her from
the East, seemed to go before her through the forests, as though
it were her cool breath. The solitary luminary climbed higher
and higher in the sky, now pursuing her even way, again sur-
mounting clusters of clouds, which resembled the summits of a
snow-clad mountain-chain. All would have been silence and
repose, but for the fall of a few leaves, the passing of a sudden
gust of wind, the hooting of the wood-owl; in the distance was
heard the dull roar of the Falls of Niagara, which, in the calm of
night, extended from waste to waste and expired in the lonely
forests. It was during those nights that an unknown muse
appeared to me; I gathered some of her accents; I marked
them on my tables, by the light of the stars, as a vulgar musician

might write down the notes dictated to him by some great master of harmony.

The next day, the Indians armed themselves, the women collected the baggage. I distributed a little gunpowder and vermilion among my hosts. We parted, touching our foreheads and breasts; the braves shouted the order to march and walked in front; the women went behind, carrying the children, who, slung in furs on their mothers' backs, turned their heads to look at us. I followed this progress with my eyes until the whole band had disappeared among the trees of the forest.

The savages of the Falls of Niagara in the English dominion were entrusted with the police service of the frontier on that side. This outlandish constabulary, armed with bows and arrows, prevented our passage. I was obliged to send the Dutchman to the fort of Niagara for a permit in order to enter the territory of the British government. This saddened my heart a little, for I remembered that formerly France had ruled in both Upper and Lower Canada. My guide returned with the permit : I still have it; it is signed, "Captain Gordon." Is it not strange that I should have found the same English name on the door of my cell in Jerusalem ? "Thirteen pilgrims had inscribed their names on the door and walls of the chamber: the first was called Charles Lombard, who visited Jerusalem in 1669; the last was John Gordon, and the date of his passage is 1804."[1]

I stayed two days in the Indian village, whence I wrote another letter to M. de Malesherbes. The Indian women busied themselves with different occupations; their nurslings were slung in nets from the branches of a tall purple beech. The grass was covered with dew, the wind issued all perfumed from the woods, and the cotton-plants of the country, throwing back their capsules, looked like white rose-trees. The breeze rocked the cradles in mid-air with an almost imperceptible movement; the mothers stood up from time to time to see if their children were asleep and had not been awakened by the birds.

From the Indian village to the cataract was some three or four leagues : it took my guide and me as many hours to reach it. Already at six miles' distance, a column of vapour indicated the situation of the weir to my eyes. My heart beat with joy mingled with terror, as I entered the wood that concealed from my view one of the grandest spectacles which nature has offered to mankind.

[1] *Itinéraire de Paris à Jérusalem*, Book II.—B.

We dismounted. Leading our horses by the bridle, we passed through heaths and thickets until we came to the bank of the Niagara River, seven or eight hundred paces above the falls. As I never ceased going forward, the guide caught me by the arm; he stopped me on the very edge of the water, which passed with the swiftness of an arrow. It did not seethe, but glided in one sole mass to the slope of the rock; its silence before its fall contrasted with the uproar of the fall itself. The Scriptures often compare a people to the mighty waters : here it was a dying people which, deprived of its voice by the agony of death, went to hurl itself into the abyss of eternity.

The guide continued to hold me back, for I felt, so to speak, drawn on by the stream, and I had an involuntary longing to fling myself in. At one time, I would turn my eyes up the river, to the banks; at another, down to the island which divided the waters. Here the waters suddenly failed, as though cut off in the sky.

After a quarter of an hour of vague and perplexed admiration, I went on to the falls. The reader will find in the *Essai sur les révolutions*[1] and in *Atala*[2] the two descriptions which I have written of the scene. To-day, high-roads run to the cataract; there are inns on the American side and on the English side, and mills and factories overhang the chasm.

I was unable to utter the thoughts that stirred me at the sight of so sublime a disorder. In the desert of my early life, I was obliged to invent persons to adorn it; I drew from my own substance beings whom I did not find elsewhere and whom I carried within myself. In the same way, I have placed memories of Atala and René on the edge of the cataract of Niagara, as the expression of its sadness. What meaning has a cascade which falls eternally in the unfeeling sight of heaven and earth, if human nature be not there, with its destinies and its misfortunes? To be steeped in this solitude of water and mountains and not to know with whom to speak of that great spectacle! To have the waves, the rocks, the woods, the torrents to one's self alone! Give the soul a companion, and the smiling verdure of the hill-slopes, the cool breath of the water, will all turn into charm : the journey by day, the sweetest repose at the end of the day's march, the gliding over the billows, the sleeping upon the moss, will call forth from the heart its deepest tenderness. I have seated Velléda upon the shores of Armorica, Cymodocea beneath the porticoes of Athens, Blanca in the halls of

---

[1] *Essai sur les révolutions :* Book I. Part ii. chap. 23.—B.
[2] *Atala :* Epilogue.—B.

the Alhambra. Alexander created towns wheresoever he hastened: I have left dreams behind me wherever I have dragged my life.

I have seen the cascades of the Alps with their chamois and those of the Pyrenees with their izards; I did not go sufficiently high up the Nile to meet its cataracts, which are reduced to rapids; I will not speak of the azure zones of Terni or of Tivoli, graceful fragments of ruins or subjects for the poet's song:

Et præceps Anio ac Tiburni lucus.[1]

Niagara eclipses everything. I gazed upon the cataract the existence of which was revealed to the old world, not by puny travellers like myself, but by missionaries who, seeking solitude for the love of God, flung themselves upon their knees at the sight of some marvel of nature and received martyrdom while completing their hymn of admiration. Our priests greeted the fine sites of America and consecrated them with their blood; our soldiers clapped their hands at the ruins of Thebes and presented arms to Andalusia: the whole genius of France lies in the double army of our camps and of our altars.

I was holding my horse's bridle twisted round my arm; a rattlesnake came and rustled in the bushes. The startled horse reared and backed towards the falls. I was unable to release my arm from the reins; the horse, still more terrified, was dragging me after it. Already its fore-feet were off the ground; cowering over the edge of the abyss, it maintained its position only by the strength of its loins. It was all up with me, when the animal, itself astonished at its fresh peril, gave a sudden turn and vaulted inwards. Had my soul left my body amidst the Canadian woods, would it have carried to the Supreme Tribunal the sacrifices, the good works, the virtues of the Pères Jogues[2] and Lallemant,[3] or empty days and wretched idle fancies?

This was not the only danger I encountered at Niagara. A ladder of creepers was used by the savages to climb down to the lower basin; it was at that time broken. Wishing to see the falls from below, I ventured, in the face of my guide's

---

[1] HOR., *Od.* I. 7.—T.
[2] Isaac Jogues (1607-1646), a Jesuit priest placed at the head of the Canadian Mission in 1636. He suffered martyrdom at the hands of the Mohawks ten years later.—B.
[3] Jérôme Lallemant (1593-1673), also a Jesuit father, preached the Gospel to the savages of Canada for nearly forty years. He died at Quebec as Superior-General of the Canadian Mission.—B.

representations, down the side of an almost perpendicular rock. In spite of the roar of the water which seethed below me, I kept my head and climbed down to within forty feet of the bottom. When I had reached so far, the bare and vertical rock gave me nothing to lay hold of; I was left hanging by one hand to the last root, feeling my fingers open beneath the weight of my body: few men have spent two such minutes, as I counted them. My tired hand let go; I fell.   By an unparalleled stroke of good fortune, I found myself upon the pointed back of a rock upon which I ought to have been smashed into a thousand pieces, and yet I felt no great hurt; I was at half a foot from the abyss and had not rolled into it; but when the cold and the damp began to penetrate me, I saw that I had not come off so cheaply : my left arm was broken above the elbow.   The guide, who was watching me from above and saw my signals of distress, ran off to fetch some savages.   They hoisted me with ropes along an otter's path, and carried me to their village.   I had only a simple fracture : two splints, a bandage and a sling were enough to effect my cure.

I stayed twelve days with my surgeons, the Niagara Indians. I saw tribes pass which had come down from Detroit or from the districts lying south and east of Lake Erie.   I inquired into their usages; in return for small presents, I was given representations of their former customs, for the customs themselves no longer exist.   Nevertheless, at the commencement of the War of American Independence, the savages still ate the prisoners, or rather the killed: an English captain, helping himself to soup with a ladle from an Indian stew-pot, drew out a hand.

The practices attendant upon birth and death have lost least, because these do not pass lightly like the life which divides them; they are not things of fashion that come and go.   The Indians still bestow upon the new-born, in order to do him honour, the name of the oldest person under his roof: his grandmother, for instance; for the names are always taken in the maternal line. From that time forward, the child fills the place of the woman whose name it has taken; in speaking to it, they give it the degree of relationship which the name revives; thus an uncle might address his nephew by the title of "grandmother." This apparently ludicrous custom is nevertheless touching. It restores the old dead to life; it reproduces the weakness of the last in the weakness of the earliest years; it brings closer the two extremities of life, the commencement and the end of the family; it confers a kind of immortality upon the ancestors and implies that they are present in the midst of their posterity.

In what regards the dead, it is easy to find motives for the savage's attachment to sacred relics. Civilized nations are able to preserve the memory of their country by means of the mnemonics of literature and the arts: they have cities, palaces, towers, columns, obelisks; they have the track of the plough in fields once cultivated; their names are carved in marble and brass, their actions recorded in the chronicles.

The desert peoples have none of these advantages: their names are not written upon the trees; their huts, built in a few hours, disappear in a few moments; the butt of their ploughing only grazes the ground, and is not able even to raise a furrow. Their traditional songs perish with the last memory which retains them, and die away with the last voice which repeats them. The tribes of the New World, therefore, have but one monument: the tomb. Take away from savages the bones of their fathers, and you take away their history, their laws, and their very gods; you rob those men, in the future generations, of the proofs both of their existence and of their annihilation.

I wished to hear my hosts' songs. A little Indian girl of fourteen, called Mila and very pretty (the Indian women are pretty only at that age) sang something very pleasant. Was it not perchance the canzonet quoted by Montaigne? "Adder stay, stay good adder, that my sister may by the patterne of thy partie-coloured coat drawe the fashion and worke of a rich lace, for me to give unto my love; so may thy beautie, thy nimblenesse or disposition be ever preferred before all other serpents."[1]

The author of the *Essaies* saw Iroquois at Rouen, who, according to him, were "not verie ill; but what," he adds, "of that? They weare no kinde of breeches nor hosen!"[2]

If ever I publish the Στρωματεῖς or patchwork of my youth, to talk like St. Clement of Alexandria,[3] you shall there see Mila.[4]

---

[1] Florio's MONTAIGNE, I. 30: *Of the Caniballes.*—T.

[2] *Ibid.*—T.

[3] St. Clement of Alexandria (*d.* 217) does not figure in the Roman Calendar. The work in question, the Στρωματεῖς, is a medley or patchwork of philosophical maxims and Christian thoughts set down at random, without order or connection, as the title implies.—T.

[4] She appears in the *Natchez*, which was published in 1826, four years after the above was written.—B.

The Canadians are no longer the same as when they were described by Cartier, Champlain,[1] La Hontan,[2] Lescarbot,[3] Lafitau,[4] Charlevoix,[5] and the *Lettres édifiantes;* the sixteenth century and the commencement of the seventeenth were still the time of a boundless imagination and ingenuous customs: the marvel of the first reflected a virgin nature, and the candour of the second reproduced the simplicity of the savage. Champlain tells us at the end of his first journey to Canada, in 1603, that "near Chaleur Bay, verging to the south, there is an island where dwells a frightful monster which the savages call Gougou."

Canada had its giant as well as the Cape of Storms. Homer is the true father of all these inventions; it is always the Cyclopes, Scylla and Charybdis, ogres or *gougous*.

The savage population of North America, not including the Mexicans and Esquimaux, does not to-day amount to four hundred thousand souls on either side of the Rocky Mountains; there are travellers who put it so low as one hundred and fifty thousand. The degradation of Indian manners has kept pace with the depopulation of the tribes. Their religious traditions have become confused; the instruction spread by the Canadian Jesuits has mixed foreign ideas with the inborn ideas of the natives: through their rude fables, one sees the Christian beliefs disfigured; the majority of the savages wear crosses by way of ornaments, and the Protestant traders sell them what the Catholic missionaries give them. Let us say at once, to the honour of our country and to the glory of our religion, that the Indians had become greatly attached to us; that they never cease to regret us; and that a "black robe," or missionary, is still an object of veneration in the forests of America. The savage continues to love us under the tree where we were

[1] Samuel Champlain (*circa* 1570-1635) explored a part of Canada, in 1608 founded the city of Quebec, and in 1620 became governor of the province. He was attacked by the English in 1627, and obliged to capitulate; in 1629 Canada was restored to France and Champlain resumed his command, which he retained until his death.—T.

[2] Armand Louis de Delondarce, Baron de La Hontan (*circa* 1667-1715) served in Canada in 1703 and was subsequently the King of France's lieutenant in Newfoundland; he was accused of peculation and fled to Portugal and thence to Denmark. In 1705 he published his *Voyages dans l'Amérique septentrionale.*—T.

[3] Marc Lescarbot (*circa* 1590–*circa* 1630) served in Florida under Admiral Coligny. He annotated an edition of Champlain's Voyages.—T.

[4] Père Joseph François Lafitau (1670-1740), a Jesuit priest of the Canadian Mission, author of the *Mœurs des sauvages américains comparées aux mœurs des premiers temps* (1723), &c.—T.

[5] Père Pierre François Xavier de Charlevoix (1682-1761), another Jesuit, author of the *Histoire de la Nouvelle-France* (1744).—T.

his first guests, on the soil which we have trod, where we have left tombs in his care.

When the Indian was naked or clad in skins, he had something great and noble about him; at present, rags of European clothing, without covering his nakedness, bear witness to his destitution : he is a beggar at the door of a counting-house, he is no longer the savage in his forest.

Lastly, a kind of hybrid people has been formed, born of colonial fathers and Indian mothers. ' These men, called "Burnt-woods," because of the colour of their skin, act as brokers between the authors of their dual origin. They speak the language of their fathers and of their mothers, and have the vices of both races. These bastards of civilized and of savage nature sell themselves to the Americans and the English by turns, to hand over to them the monopoly of the fur-trade ; they keep alive the rivalry between the English companies, the Hudson's Bay Company and the North-West Fur Company, and the American companies, the Columbian American Fur Company, the Missouri Fur Company and others : they themselves go hunting for account of the traders and with hunters paid by the companies.

The great war of American Independence is the only one which people know of. They are ignorant of the fact that blood has been shed on behalf of the paltry interests of a handful of merchants. The Hudson's Bay Company in 1811 sold to Lord Selkirk[1] a tract of land on the bank of the Red River. The North-West or Canadian Company took umbrage at this transaction. The two companies, allied to various Indian tribes and seconded by the "Burnt-woods," came to blows. This domestic conflict, so horrible in its details, took place on the frozen wastes of Hudson's Bay. Lord Selkirk's colony was destroyed in the month of June 1815,[2] at the exact period of the Battle of Waterloo. Upon those two theatres, one so brilliant, the other so obscure, the misfortunes of the human species were the same.

Seek no longer in America the skilfully constructed political constitutions of which Charlevoix has written the history : the monarchy of the Hurons, the republic of the Iroquois. A somewhat similar destruction has been accomplished and is

[1] Thomas Douglas, fifth Earl of Selkirk (1771-1820). This tract of land covered forty-five million acres, and comprised large portions of what are now Manitoba and Minnesota.—T.

[2] The date of the defeat of the Hudson's Bay Company by the North-West Company and their half-breed allies was 10 June 1815.—T.

still being accomplished in Europe under our very eyes; a Prussian poet, at a banquet of the Teutonic Order, held about the year 1400, sang in old Prussian the heroic deeds of the ancient warriors of his country: no one present understood him, and he received one hundred empty walnuts by way of recompense.   To-day, the language of Lower Brittany, the Basque and Gaelic languages, are dying out from cottage to cottage, keeping pace with the deaths of the goatherds and husbandmen.

In the English County of Cornwall, the language of the natives became extinct about the year 1676.   A fisherman said to some travellers:

"I know hardly more than four or five persons who speak Cornish, and they are old folk like myself, between sixty and eighty years of age; none of the young people know a word of it."

Whole tribes of the Orinoco have ceased to exist; of their dialect there remain but a dozen words articulated in the tree-tops by parrots that have regained their freedom, like Agrippina's thrush, which warbled Greek words upon the balustrades of the Roman palaces.   This, sooner or later, will be the fate of our modern jargons, the remains of Latin and Greek.   Some raven escaped from the cage of the last Franco-Gallic curate will say, from the top of a ruined steeple, to peoples that shall be foreign to our successors:

"Accept these last strains of a voice once known to you; you will put an end to all this talk."

It is well worth while to be Bossuet, so that, in the ultimate event, your masterpiece may survive, in the recollection of a bird, your language and your memory among men!

When speaking of Canada and Louisiana, when considering on the old maps the extent of the former French colonies in America, I asked myself how the government of my country could have suffered the loss of those colonies, which would be an inexhaustible source of prosperity for us at this day.

From Arcadia[1] and Canada to Louisiana, from the mouth of the St. Lawrence to the mouth of the Mississippi, the territory of "New France" surrounded what formed the confederation of the first thirteen United States: the eleven others,[2] together

---

[1] The French name for New Brunswick and Nova Scotia.—T.

[2] The original thirteen United States, in the order of their ratification of the National Constitution, were Delaware, Pennsylvania, New Jersey, Georgia, Connecticut, Massachusetts, Maryland, South Carolina, New Hampshire, Virginia, New York, North Carolina, and Rhode Island.   The eleven others, completing

with the District of Columbia, the North-Western Territory, the Territories of Michigan, Missouri, Oregon, and Arkansas either belonged to us or would now belong to us, as they belong to the United States by the cessions of the English and Spaniards, our successors in Canada and Louisiana.[1] The country enclosed by the Atlantic on the north-east, the Arctic Ocean on the north, the Pacific Ocean and the Russian possessions on the north-west, and the Gulf of Mexico on the south, in other words more than two-thirds of North America, would now be recognizing the laws of France.

I fear that the Restoration will ruin itself through holding ideas contrary to those which I have here expressed: the mania for adhering to the past, a mania which I never cease impugning, would be in no sense fatal if it subverted only myself, by robbing me of the Sovereign's favour; but it may yet subvert the Throne. Political stagnation is impossible; it is absolutely necessary to keep pace with human intelligence. Let us respect the majesty of time; let us reverentially contemplate past centuries, rendered sacred by the memory and the footsteps of our fathers: but let us not try to go back to them, for they no longer possess a vestige of our real nature, and if we endeavoured to seize hold of them, they would fade away. The Chapter of Our Lady of Aix-la-Chapelle caused the tomb of Charlemagne[2] to be opened, we are told, about the year 1450. The Emperor was found seated in a gilt chair, holding in his skeleton hands the Book of the Gospels written in letters of gold; before him were laid his sceptre and his golden buckler; by his side hung his sword "Joyeuse," sheathed in a golden scabbard. He was clad in the imperial robes. On his head, which was held erect by a golden chain, was a winding-sheet covering what had been his face and surmounted by a crown. They touched the phantom: it crumbled into dust.

We once possessed vast countries beyond the seas: they

the twenty-four existing at the time at which Chateaubriand was writing, were Vermont (detached from New York, 1791), Tennessee (detached from North Carolina, 1796), Kentucky (detached from Virginia, 1796), Ohio (created, 1802), Louisiana (purchased from France in 1803 and raised into a State in 1812), Indiana (created, 1816), Mississippi (separated from Georgia, 1817), Illinois (created, 1818), Alabama (detached from Georgia, 1819), Maine (detached from Massachusetts, 1820), and Missouri (detached from Louisiana, 1821).—T.

[1] The western portion of Louisiana was ceded to Spain in 1763, but restored to the French in 1800. In 1803 Bonaparte, despairing of being able to hold it against the English, sold it to the United States for 80,000,000 francs.—T.

[2] Charles I., King of France and Emperor of the West (742–814), known as Charlemagne, had been dead for more than six centuries when this experiment was made.—T.

offered a refuge for our surplus population, markets for our commerce, stations for our navy. We are now excluded from the new world in which the human race is beginning life afresh: in Africa, Asia, Oceania, in the South Sea Islands, on the continent of North and South America, the English, Portuguese, and Spanish languages serve to interpret the thoughts of many millions of men ; and we, disinherited of the conquests of our valour and our genius, scarce hear the tongue of Colbert and Louis XIV. spoken in some petty market-town of Louisiana or Canada, under a foreign government : it lingers there only as a witness to the reverses of our fortune and the errors of our policy.

And who is the king whose dominion now succeeds the dominion of the King of France in the forests of Canada ? He who yesterday caused this note to be sent to me :

> "ROYAL LODGE, WINDSOR,
> "4 *June* 1822.
>
> "MONSIEUR LE VICOMTE,
> "I am commanded by the King to invite Your Excellency to dine and sleep here on Thursday the 6th instant.
> "Your Excellency's most humble and obedient servant,
> "FRANCIS CONYNGHAM."[1]

It was fated that I should be plagued by princes. I lay down my pen ; I recross the Atlantic ; I mend my arm broken at Niagara ; I take off my bearskin ; I resume my gold-laced coat ; I leave the wigwam of an Iroquois to repair to the Royal Lodge of His Britannic Majesty, King of the United Kingdom of Great Britain and Ireland and Lord of the Undies ; I leave my hosts with the exposed ears and my little girl-savage with her bead : wishing Lady Conyngham[2] the charm of Mila, together with the age which as yet belongs only to the earliest spring-time, to the days which precede the month of May and which our Gallic poets called the *avrillée*, the April shower.

The tribe of the little girl with the bead departed ; my guide, the Dutchman, refused to accompany me beyond the cataract ; I paid him and joined a party of traders who were leaving to go

---

[1] Lord Francis Nathaniel Conyngham (1797-1876), second son of the first Marquess Conyngham, and first groom of the Bedchamber and Master of the Robes to George IV. He succeeded to the Marquisate in 1832.—T.

[2] Elizabeth Marchioness Conyngham (1769-1861), *née* Dennison, married in 1794 to the third Lord Conyngham, Lord Steward of the Household to George IV., and created successively Viscount Conyngham, Earl of Conyngham, and Marquess Conyngham by that monarch. She was George IV.'s mistress, and presented a complete contrast to Mila in other respects than age alone.—T.

down the Ohio; before setting out, I took a glance at the Canadian lakes. There is nothing so mournful as the aspect of these lakes. The liquid plains of the Atlantic and the Mediterranean open highways to the nations, and their shores are, or were, inhabited by civilized, numerous, and powerful peoples; the lakes of Canada display only the nakedness of their waters, which, in its turn, is joined to a bare soil: they are deserts dividing other deserts. Shores devoid of inhabitants look upon seas devoid of ships; you alight from the unfrequented waves upon unfrequented coasts.

Lake Erie is over one hundred leagues in circumference. The nations of the water-side were exterminated by the Iroquois two centuries ago. It is an appalling thing to see the Indians venturing in their birch-bark wherries upon this lake famed for its tempests, in which myriads of serpents swarmed in former days. These Indians hang their manitous upon the prow of their canoes and dart into the midst of the eddies among the heaving waves. The waves, level with the aperture of the canoes, seem ready to swallow them up. The hunters' dogs, with their front-paws resting on the side, utter loud barks, while their masters, preserving a profound silence, beat the waves in cadence with their paddles. The canoes proceed in Indian file: in the prow of the first stands a chief who repeats the diphthong *oah: o* in a long, dull note, *ah* in a short, sharp tone. In the last canoe is another chief, who also stands up, and works an oar by way of rudder. The other braves squat upon their heels at the bottom of the well. Across the mist and the winds one perceives nothing save the plumes adorning the Indians' heads, the outstretched necks of the baying dogs, and the shoulders of the two sachems, the pilot and the augur: as it were the gods of these lakes.

The rivers of Canada play no part in the history of the world of antiquity: how different from the destiny of the Ganges, the Euphrates, the Nile, the Danube, and the Rhine! What changes have not these beheld upon their banks! How much sweat and blood has been poured forth by conquerors to cross, in their current, waters over which, at their source, a goatherd passes with a single step!

Leaving the lakes of Canada, we came to Pittsburg at the confluence of the Kentucky and Ohio rivers; here the landscape unfolds an extraordinary stateliness. Nevertheless, this magnificent country is called Kentucky after its river, whose name means "river of blood." It owes this name to its beauty:

for more than two centuries the nations on the side of the Cherokees and of the Iroquois nations fought for the possession of its hunting-fields.

Will the European generations be more virtuous and more free upon those banks than were the exterminated American generations? Shall slaves not till the soil beneath the lash of their masters, in these deserts of man's primeval independence? Shall prisons and gallows not fill the places of the open hut and the tall tulip-tree where the bird builds its nest? Shall the richness of the soil not cause new wars to burst forth? Shall Kentucky cease to be the "Land of Blood," and shall the monuments of the arts beautify the banks of the Ohio to better purpose than the monuments of nature?

After passing the Wabash, the Cypress, the Cumberland, the Cherokee, or Tennessee, the Yellowbank, one comes to a tongue of land often submerged beneath the mighty waters: here is formed the confluence of the Ohio and the Mississippi in latitude 36° 51'. The two rivers oppose an equal resistance to one another and relax the force of their currents; for some miles they sleep side by side without mingling in the same bed, like two great peoples at first of different origins and then combining to form but one race; like two illustrious combatants sharing the same couch after a battle; like a husband and wife born of hostile blood, who at first have but little inclination to mingle their destinies in the nuptial bed.

And I, too, even as the mighty urns of the rivers, have poured forth my life's small current, now on this, now on that side of the mountain; capricious in my straying, but never malignant; preferring the poor glens to the rich plains, stopping at the flowers rather than at the palaces. For that matter, I was so charmed with my rambles that I gave scarce a further thought to the Pole. A party of traders, who had come from among the Creeks, in Florida, gave me leave to accompany them.

We set out for the countries known at that time by the general name of the Floridas, to-day divided into the States of Alabama, Georgia, South Carolina, and Tennessee. We followed, more or less closely, paths now connected by the high-road which runs from Natchez to Nashville, through Jackson and Florence, and which enters Virginia by way of Knoxville and Salem: a country very little frequented at that time, although Bartram[1] had explored its lakes and sites. The planters of

---

[1] William Bartram (1739–1823), an American traveller and naturalist, author of *Travels through North and South Carolina, East and West Florida, the Cherokee country, &c.*—T.

Georgia and Florida proper went to the various tribes of the Creeks to buy horses and half-wild cattle, which multiplied indefinitely in the savannahs pierced by the wells at whose edges I placed Atala and Chactas. They even extended their journey as far as Ohio.

We ran before a stiff breeze. The Ohio, swollen by a hundred rivers, passed now through the lakes which opened out before us, now through the woods. Islands stood out in the middle of the lakes. We made sail for one of the largest of these : we came alongside at eight in the morning.

I crossed a meadow strewn with ragwort with its yellow flowers, hollyhocks with their pink plumes, and obelarias with purple egrets. An Indian ruin struck my eyes. The contrast between this ruin and the youth of nature, this monument of men in a desert, caused a great emotion. What people dwelt upon this island ? Its name, its race, the time of its passing ? Did it live at the time when the world in whose midst it lay hidden was as yet unknown to the three other quarters of the globe ? The silence of this people was perhaps contemporaneous with the fame of some great nations that have in their turn lapsed into silence.[1]

Sandy anfractuosities, ruins or *tumuli* issued from amid poppies with red flowers hanging at the end of bent, pale-green stalks. The stem and the flower have an aroma which clings to the fingers when one touches the plant. The perfume which outlives the flower is an image of the memory of a life spent in solitude.

I observed the nymphæa : it was preparing to hide its white lily beneath the surface at the close of day; the "tree of sadness "[2] was awaiting the night before unfolding its own : the wife retires to bed at the hour when the courtesan rises.

The pyramidal œnothera, which is seven or eight feet high, with pale leaves dentated with dark green, has other habits and another destiny: its yellow flower begins to half-open in the evening, during the space of time which Venus occupies in descending below the horizon ; it continues to expand by the light of the stars ; the dawn discovers it in all its brilliancy ; midway through the morning it fades ; it falls at noonday. It lives for but a few hours ; but it despatches those hours beneath a placid sky, between the breaths of Venus and Aurora: what matters, then, the shortness of life ?

---

[1] The ruins of Mitla and Palenque in Mexico prove to-day that the New World rivals the Old in antiquity.—*Author's Note* (Paris, 1834).

[2] *Arbor tristis*, the nyctanthes or night-jasmine.—T.

A streamlet trickled through a garland of dionæas; a multitude of day-flies buzzed all around. There were also humming-birds and butterflies which, decked in their brightest gauds, rivalled the motley flowers in splendour.

In the midst of these walks and studies, I was often struck by their futility. What! Did the Revolution, which already weighed down upon me and drove me into the woods, inspire me with no graver thoughts than these? What! Was the time of my country's confusion that which I chose to occupy myself with descriptions of plants, and butterflies, and flowers? The individuality of mankind serves as a measure of the littleness of great events. How many men are indifferent to those events! To how many others do they remain unknown! The aggregate population of the globe is estimated at from eleven to twelve hundred millions; a man dies every second: thus in each minute of our existence, of our smiles, of our joys, sixty men expire, sixty families moan and weep. Life is a permanent pestilence. The chain of mourning and funerals that winds us about is never broken, grows ever longer: we ourselves form one of its links. And then tell us to magnify the importance of the catastrophes of which seven-eighths of the world will never hear speak! To pant for a fame which will spread its wings at but a few leagues from our tomb! To plunge into the ocean of a felicity of which each minute slips away between sixty graves incessantly renewed!

> Nam nox Nulla diem, neque noctem aurora sequuta est
> Quæ non audierit mixtos vagitibus ægris
> Ploratus, mortis comites et funeris atri.

The savages of Florida tell of an island in the middle of a lake where live the most beautiful women in the world. The Muskhogulges have repeatedly attempted its conquest; but this Eden flees before the canoes, a natural image of the chimeras which retreat before our desires. The country also contained a fountain of youth: who would wish to rise from the dead?

But little was wanting to make these fables assume a semblance of reality in my eyes. At a moment when we least expected it, we saw a flotilla of canoes come out of a bay, some with oars, others with sails. They landed at our island. They were two families of Creeks, of which one consisted of Seminoles, the other of Muskhogulges, including some Cherokees and Burnt-woods. I was struck with the grace of these savages, who in no respect resemble those of Canada.

The Seminoles and Muskhogulges are fairly tall, and, by an

unusual contrast, their mothers, wives, and daughters are the smallest race of women known in America. The Indian women who landed near us, born of mixed Cherokee and Castilian blood, were tall in stature. Two of them were like the creoles of San Domingo and Mauritius, but yellow and delicate as the women of the Ganges. These two Floridan women, cousins on the father's side, served as my models, one for Atala, the other for Céluta: they excelled the portraits I drew of them only by that variable and fugitive truth of nature, that physiognomy of race and climate which I was not able to express. There was something indefinable in that oval visage, in that shaded complexion, which one seemed to see through a light, orange-tinted smoke, in that hair so black and soft, those eyes so long, half-hidden beneath the veil of two satiny eyelids that opened indolently; in short, in the two-fold seduction of the Indian and the Spanish woman.

The meeting with our hosts occasioned a certain alteration in our movements: our trading agents began to inquire about horses; it was decided that we should go to fix ourselves in the neighbourhood of the studs. The plain in which our camp stood was covered with bulls, cows, horses, bisons, buffaloes, cranes, turkeys, pelicans: these birds mottled the green background of our savannah with white, black, and pink stains.

Our traders and hunters were stirred by many passions: not passions of race, education, or prejudice, but natural passions, full and absolute, making straight for their object, having for witnesses a tree fallen in the depths of an unknown forest, a nameless stream. The relations between the Spaniards and the Creek women formed the ground-work of the adventures; the "Burnt-woods" played the principal part in those romances. One story was famous: that of a trader in strong waters seduced and ruined by a "painted woman" or courtesan. This story, put into Seminole verse with the title of *Tabamica*, was sung in passing through the woods.[1] Carried off in their turn by the colonists, the Indian women soon died forsaken at Pensacola:[2] their misfortunes went to swell the *Romanceros* and to be numbered among the ballads of Ximenes.

The earth is a charming mother; we issue from her womb: in childhood, she holds us to her breasts swollen with milk and

---

[1] I have quoted it in my Travels—*Author's Note* (Geneva, 1832). The story of *Tabamica* is told in the *Voyage en Amérique*, where it is called the Song of the Pale-face.—B.

[2] The Spanish capital of Florida.—T.

honey; in youth and old age, she lavishes upon us her refreshing waters, her harvests and her fruits; she offers us, wherever we may go, a shade, a bath, a table and a bed; she opens her entrails again to receive us after death, and throws a coverlet of herbs and flowers over our remains, while she secretly transforms us into her own substance, to reproduce us under some graceful shape.   That is what I said to myself on waking, when my first look fell upon the sky, the canopy of my bed.

The hunters had set out for the work of the day; I remained behind with the women and children.   I never left the side of my two sylvan goddesses: one was proud, the other sad.   I did not understand a word of what they said to me, and they did not understand me; but I went to fetch water for their cup, shoots for their fire, mosses for their bed.   They wore the petticoat and the wide, slashed sleeves of the Spanish women, the body and cloak of the Indian women.   Their bare legs were cross-gartered with a lace-work of birch.   They plaited their hair with posies or filaments of rushes; they mailed themselves in chains and necklaces of glass beads.   From their ears hung purple berries; they had a fine talking paroquet: the bird of Armida; they fastened it on their shoulder like an emerald, or carried it hooded on their hand, as the great ladies of the tenth century carried their hawks.   To harden their breasts and arms, they rubbed themselves with the apoya, or American gallingale.   In Bengal the nautch-girls chew the betel-nut, and in the Levant the almes suck the mastic of Chio: the Floridan maidens pounded, between their teeth of a bluey whiteness, tears of liquid-amber and roots of *libanis*, which blended the fragrance of angelica, cedrat, and vanilla.   They lived in an atmosphere of perfumes emanating from themselves, like orange-trees and flowers living in the pure exhalations from their leaves and chalices.   I amused myself by placing a little ornament upon their heads: they submitted, gently dismayed; witches themselves, they thought I was working a charm upon them.   One of them, the "proud" one, often prayed; she seemed to me half a Christian.   The other sang in a voice of velvet, uttering at the end of each phrase a note that troubled one.   Sometimes they spoke hastily to each other: I thought I could recognize the accents of jealousy, but the "sad" one wept, and silence was restored.

Weak as I was, I sought examples of weakness, in order to encourage myself.   Had not Camoëns in the Indies loved a black Barbary slave, and might not I in America do homage to two young jonquil sultanas? Had Camoëns not addressed *endechas*, or stanzas, to his *Barbaru escrava?* [1]

A fishing-party was arranged. The sun was nearing its setting. In the foreground appeared sassafras, tulip-trees, catalpas, and oaks, from whose boughs hung skeins of white moss. Behind this foreground rose the most charming of trees, the papaw, which might have been taken for a chased silver style, surmounted by a Corinthian urn. In the background reigned balsam-trees, magnolias, and liquid-ambers.

The sun dropped behind that curtain: a ray piercing through the crown of a thicket sparkled like a carbuncle set in the sombre foliage; the light diverging between the trunks and branches projected heightening columns and mobile arabesques upon the sward. Below were lilacs, azaleas, annulated creepers with gigantic sheaves; above, the clouds, some fixed, like promontories or old towers, others fleeting, like rosy vapours or carded silk. By means of successive transformations, one saw the mouths of furnaces opening up in those clouds, heaps of embers piling themselves up, streams of lava flowing: all was dazzling, radiant, gilded, opulent, saturated with light.

After the Morean insurrection in 1770, some Greek families took refuge in Florida; they could still believe themselves in that Ionian climate which seems to have relented, together with men's passions: at Smyrna, in the evening, nature sleeps like a courtesan wearied with love.

On our right were ruins belonging to the great fortifications that were found on the Ohio, on our left an old savage camp. The island on which we were, pictured in the water and reproduced by a mirage, poised its double perspective before us. In the east, the moon rested upon distant hills; in the west, the vault of the sky was melted into a sea of diamonds and sapphires, in which the sun, half-immersed, appeared to be dissolving. The animals of creation were keeping watch; the earth, in adoration, seemed to offer incense to the sky, and the amber exhaled from its bosom fell back upon it in the form of dew, as prayers fall back upon those who pray.

Abandoned by my companions, I lay resting by the edge of a clump of trees: its darkness, glazed with light, formed the penumbra in which I sat. Fire-flies gleamed among the crape-covered shrubs and became obscured when they passed through

---

[1] I omit a quotation from Camoëns.—T.

the irradiations of the moon. I heard the sounds made by the rise and fall of the lake, the leap of the gold-fish, and the rare cry of the diver. My eyes were fixed upon the water; I gradually lapsed into the state of drowsiness known to men who travel the world's highways: I lost all clearness of recollection; I felt myself living and vegetating with nature in a kind of pantheism. I leant back against the trunk of a magnolia-tree and fell asleep; my slumbers floated upon a vague surface of hope.

When I emerged from this Lethe, I found myself between two women: the odalisks had returned; they did not wish to arouse me; they had sat down silently by my side; whether they had feigned sleep or had really slumbered, their heads had fallen on my shoulders.

A breeze blew through the grove and deluged us in a shower of rose-leaves from the magnolia. Then the younger of the Seminoles began to sing: let whomsoever is not sure of his life beware of ever thus exposing himself! No one knows the strength of the passion that glides with melody into a man's breast. A rude and jealous voice replied: a " Burnt-wood " was calling the two cousins; they started and rose: the dawn was beginning to break.

In the absence of Aspasia alone, I have since repeated this scene on the shores of Greece; ascending to the columns of the Parthenon with the dawn, I saw the Cithæron, Mount Hymettus, the Acropolis of Corinth, the tombs, the ruins, bathed in a dew of golden, transparent, shimmering light, reflected by the seas and wafted like a perfume by the zephyrs from Salamis and Delos.

We finished on the bank our voyage without words. At noon, we broke up the camp to inspect the horses which the Creeks wished to sell and the traders to buy. Women and children, all were summoned as witnesses, according to the custom in solemn bargains. Stallions of every age and colour, foals and mares, with bulls, cows and heifers, began to scamper and gallop around us. Amid this confusion, I became separated from the Creeks. A thick group of men and horses gathered on the skirt of a wood. Suddenly, in the distance, I perceived my two fair Floridans; vigorous hands seated them upon the cruppers of two barbs ridden bare-backed by a " Burnt-wood " and a Seminole. O Cid, why had not I thy swift Babieça that I might overtake them! The mares galloped off, the immense squadron followed them. The horses rushed, jumped, bounded, neighed, amid the horns of the bulls and buffaloes, their hoofs clashed in mid-air, their tails and manes flew blood-stained. A whirlwind of voracious insects swarmed about this wild cavalry. My Floridans disappeared from sight like Ceres' daughter, snatched by the god of the nether world.

Thus does everything prove abortive in my life, thus is nought left me save pictures of what has passed so quickly; I shall descend to the Elysian Fields with more shades than mortal man has ever taken with him. The fault lies with my organization : I am never able to take advantage of any piece of good fortune ; I can never take an interest in anything whatever that interests others. Putting religion aside, I have no beliefs. Shepherd or king, what should I have done with my sceptre or my crook ? I should have wearied equally of glory or genius, work or leisure, prosperity or misfortune. Everything tires me : laboriously I tow my weariness after my days, and, wherever I go, I yawn away my life.

Ronsard[1] shows us Mary Stuart[2] ready to set out for Scotland after the death of Francis II.[3] Was I like Mary Stuart wandering through Fontainebleau, when I wandered about my savannah after my widowerhood? One thing is certain, that my mind, if not my person, was wrapped in "a long crape, subtil and flowing," as Ronsard also says, that old poet of the new school.

The devil having flown away with the Muskhogulge damsels, I was told by the guide that a "Burnt-wood," who was in love with one of the two women, was jealous of me and had resolved with a Seminole, the brother of the other cousin, to carry Atala and Céluta off from me. The guides spoke of them bluntly as "painted girls," which shocked my vanity. I felt the more humiliated in that the "Burnt-wood," my favoured rival, was a lean, ugly, dark-skinned mosquito, possessing all the characteristics of the insects which, according to the entomologists of the Grand Lama, are animals whose flesh is inside their bones. Solitude appeared empty to me after my misadventure. I gave the cold shoulder to my sylph, who generously hastened to console her faithless lover, like Julie when she forgave Saint-Preux his Parisian Floridans.[4] I

---

[1] I omit a quotation from Ronsard.—T.

[2] Mary Stuart (1542-1587), Queen of Scots, was married in 1558 to the Dauphin of France, who in 1559 became king, with the title of Francis II. She was left a widow eighteen months after marriage, in the seventeenth year of her age.—T.

[3] Francis II., King of France (1544-1560).—T.

[4] *Cf.* ROUSSEAU, *La Nouvelle Héloïse.*—T.

lost no time in quitting the desert in which I have since re-suscitated the drowsy companions of my night. I know not whether I gave back to them the life they gave me : at least I made a virgin of one, a virtuous spouse of the other, by way of expiation.

We again crossed the Blue Mountains, and approached the European clearings in the neighbourhood of Chillicothe. I had gathered no light upon the principal object of my enterprise; but I was escorted by a world of poetry :

> Comme une jeune abeille aux roses engagée
> Ma muse revenait de son butin chargée.[1]

On the bank of a stream I saw an American house : at one end a farm-house, at the other a mill. I went in, asked for food and shelter, and was well received.

My hostess led me by a ladder to a room above the shaft of the hydraulic apparatus. My little casement-window, festooned with ivy and cobæas with iris bells, opened above the stream which flowed, narrow and solitary, between two thick borders of willows, elms, sassafras, tamarinds, and Carolina poplars. The moss-grown mill-wheel turned beneath their shade and let fall long ribands of water. Perch and trout leapt in the foam of the eddy ; water-wagtails flew from bank to bank, and various kinds of kingfishers fluttered their blue wings above the current.

How happy should I have been there with the " sad " one, had she been faithful to me, seated dreaming at her feet, my head laid upon her knees, listening to the noise of the weir, the rotations of the wheel, the rolling of the mill-stone, the sifting of the bolter, the even beating of the clapper, breathing the freshness of the water and the scent from the husks of the pearl-barley.

Night came. I went down to the sitting-room of the farm-house. It was lighted only by maize-straw and husks of beans blazing in the hearth. The fire-arms of the master of the house, lying horizontally in the gun-rack, gleamed in the reflections from the fireplace. I sat down upon a stool in the chimney-corner, near a squirrel, which jumped from the back of a large dog to the shelf of a spinning-wheel and back again. A kitten installed itself upon my knee to watch this sport. The miller's wife put a large stew-pot on the fire, the flames of which

---

[1] " Like a young bee which 'mong the roses toils,
My muse returned to me all laden with rich spoils."—T.

played round the pot's black bottom like a radiant golden
crown. While I watched the sweet potatoes boiling for my
supper, I amused myself by reading by the firelight, with
lowered head, an English newspaper which had fallen on the
floor between my legs. Printed in large letters I read the
words:

FLIGHT OF THE KING.

It was the story of the flight of Louis XVI., and the arrest
of the unfortunate monarch at Varennes.[1] The paper also described the progress of the emigration and the gathering of the
officers of the army around the flag of the French Princes.

A sudden conversion took place within my mind. Rinaldo
beheld his weakness in the mirror of honour in Armida's
gardens; I was not Tasso's hero, but the same looking-
glass showed me my image in the midst of an American
orchard. The clash of arms, the world's tumult resounded
in my ears under the thatch of a mill hidden in unknown
woods. I abruptly interrupted my travels, and said to myself:
"Go back to France."

Thus it happened that my sense of duty upset my early
plans, and occasioned the first of the revolutions that have
marked my career. The Bourbons no more needed that a
cadet of Brittany should return from across the seas to offer
them his obscure devotion than they have needed his services
since he has emerged from his obscurity. Had I lit my pipe
with the newspaper which changed the course of my life, and
continued my journey, no one would have remarked my
absence; my life was at that time as unknown and weighed
as little as the smoke from my calumet. A simple contest
between myself and my conscience flung me upon the world's
stage. I could have acted as I pleased, since I alone was a
witness of the struggle; but, of all witnesses, that is the one
before whose eyes I should most fear to blush.

Why is it that the solitudes of Erie and Ontario present
themselves to my thoughts to-day with a charm which the
brilliant spectacle of the Bosphorus is not able to possess in
my memory? It is because, at the time of my journey in the
United States, I was full of illusions: the troubles of France
commenced at the same time as the commencement of my existence; nothing was complete in myself or in the land of my
birth. Those days are dear to me because they recall to me

[1] Louis XVI. was arrested at Varennes on the 22nd of June 1791.—T.

the innocence of sentiments inspired by the family and the pleasures of youth.

Fifteen years later, after my journey in the Levant, the Republic, swollen with ruins and tears, had discharged itself like a torrent from the deluge into despotism. I no longer deluded myself with chimeras; my recollections, thenceforth taking their source in society and passions, lacked candour. Deceived in both my pilgrimages to the West and to the East, I had failed to discover the passage to the Pole, I had failed to snatch glory on the banks of Niagara, where I had gone in search of it, and I had left it seated on the ruins of Athens.

After setting out to be a traveller in America and returning to be a soldier in Europe, I did not go the whole length of either of those careers: an evil genius snatched the staff and the sword from my hand, and put the pen there in its stead. Fifteen more years have elapsed since, finding myself at Sparta, and contemplating the sky during the night, I recalled the countries that had already witnessed my peaceful or troubled sleep: on the commons of England, in the plains of Italy, upon the high-seas, in the Canadian forests, I had already saluted the same stars which I saw shine upon the land of Helen and Menelaus. But what would it avail me to complain to the stars, the fixed witnesses of my vagrant destinies? One day their gaze will cease to tire itself by pursuing me; meantime, indifferent to my fate, I will not ask those stars to move it with a gentler influence nor to restore to me that portion of life which the traveller leaves behind in the places at which he touches.

Were I to revisit the United States to-day, I should no longer recognize them: there where I left forests, I should find tilled fields; there where I traced a path for myself across the thickets, I should travel on the high-roads; at Natchez, instead of Céluta's hut, stands a town of some five thousand inhabitants; Chactas might to-day be sent to Congress. I have lately received a pamphlet printed among the Cherokees and addressed to myself, in the interests of those savages, as "the defender of the liberty of the press."

In the land of the Muskhogulges, the Seminoles, the Chickasaws, we find a city of Athens, another of Marathon, another of Carthage, another of Memphis, another of Sparta, another of Florence; there is a County of Columbia and a County of Marengo: the glory of every country has placed a name in the same wastes where I met Father Aubry and the obscure Atala.

Kentucky exhibits a Versailles; a territory called Bourbon has a Paris for its capital.

All the exiles, all the fugitives from oppression who have taken refuge in America have carried there the memory of their country.

> Falsi Simoentis ad undam
> Libabat cineri Andromache.[1]

The United States offer in their bosom, under the protection of liberty, an image and a memory of the greater part of the famous spots of antiquity and of modern Europe: the Emperor Hadrian caused copies of the monuments of his empire to be placed in his garden in the Roman Campagna.

Thirty-three high-roads run out of Washington, as formerly the Roman roads started from the Capitol; spreading asunder, they end at the circumference of the United States and trace a circulation of 25,747 miles. Posting-stations are established on a large number of these roads. One now takes the coach for the Ohio or Niagara as in my time one took a guide or an Indian interpreter. The means of transport are two-fold: lakes and rivers abound, and are connected by canals; you can travel alongside of the high-roads in rowing or sailing-boats, barges or steamers. Fuel is inexhaustible, since immense forests cover coal-mines level with the surface.

The population of the United States has increased in every decade from 1790 to 1820 at the rate of 35 per cent. It is calculated that in 1830 the population will amount to 12,875,000 souls. Continuing to double every twenty-five years, it should amount in 1855 to 25,750,000 souls, and twenty-five years later, in 1880, it should exceed fifty millions.[2]

This human sap causes the wilderness to thrive on every side. The Canadian lakes, on which lately no sail was to be seen, now resemble docks in which frigates, corvettes, cutters and barks pass Indian pirogues and canoes, in the same way in which the big ships and galleys mix with the pinks, sloops and caiques in the waters of Constantinople. The Mississippi, the Missouri, the Ohio no longer pursue a solitary course: three-masters ascend their currents; over two hundred steamboats enliven their banks. This immense inland navigation, which alone would ensure the prosperity of the United States,

---

[1] VIR., Æn., I. 302-303.—B.
[2] These predictions have been verified with wonderful accuracy. According to the census of 1 June 1880, the population of the United States on that day amounted to 50,445,336 inhabitants.—B.

does not lessen their distant expeditions. Their vessels sail all the seas, engage in all forms of enterprise, carry the Stars and Stripes from the horizon of the setting sun to the shores where the sun rises, shores that have never known aught but slavery.

To complete this surprising scene, one must picture to one's self cities like Boston, New York, Philadelphia, Baltimore, Charleston, Savannah, New Orleans, lighted at night, filled with horses and carriages, adorned with coffee-houses, museums, libraries, ball-rooms, theatres, displaying all the enjoyments of luxury.

At the same time, the United States must not be searched for that which distinguishes man above the other beings of creation, for that which constitutes his certificate of immortality and the ornament of his days: literature is unknown in the new republic, although called for by a multitude of institutions. The American has replaced intellectual by positive operations. Do not impute to him as an inferiority his mediocrity in the arts, for it is not in that direction that he has turned his attention. Cast through various causes upon a desert soil, he made agriculture and commerce the first objects of his cares: before thinking, one must live; before planting trees, one must fell them, in order to till the ground.

The primitive colonists, it is true, their minds steeped in religious controversy, carried the passion for disputation into the very heart of the forests; but it was necessary for them first to shoulder their axes and march to the conquest of the desert: their sole pulpit, in the intervals between their labours, was the elm they were engaged in squaring. The Americans have not passed through the ages of other nations: they left their childhood and their youth in Europe; the artless words of the cradle were unknown to them; they enjoyed the delights of home only through the medium of their regrets for a native land which they had never seen, and of which they mourned the eternal absence and the charm they had heard of from others.

The new continent has no classical literature, nor romantic literature, nor Indian literature: for the classical, the Americans have no models; for the romantic, no middle-ages; for the Indian, the Americans despise the savages and loathe the sight of the woods as of a prison to which they were once condemned.

And thus it comes that literature as a thing apart, literature properly so-called, does not exist in America; what one finds is applied literature, answering to the different needs of society: the literature of workmen, merchants, sailors, farmers. Americans succeed in mechanics and science, because science has its material side.   Franklin [1] and Fulton [2] took possession of lightning and steam for the benefit of mankind.   It fell to America to endow the world with the discovery, thanks to which no continent can henceforward escape the mariner's search.

Poetry and imagination, the portion of a very small number of idlers, are regarded in the United States as puerilities appertaining to the first and to the last age of life.   The Americans have had no childhood and have as yet had no old age.

Hence it follows that men engaged upon serious studies have necessarily been obliged to take part in the affairs of their country in order to become acquainted with them, and in the same way they inevitably found themselves actors in their revolution.   But one melancholy fact must be observed, which is the prompt degeneration of talent, from the first men, who figured in the American troubles, down to the men of these latter days ; and yet those men all touch.   The old presidents of the Republic have a religious, simple, lofty, calm character, of which we find no trace in the blood-stained tumults of our own Republic and Empire.   The solitude with which the Americans were surrounded reacted upon their nature; they achieved their liberty in silence.

General Washington's farewell address [3] to the people of the United States might have been uttered by the gravest characters of antiquity:

" How far in the discharge of my official duties," says the General, " I have been guided by the principles which have been delineated, the public records and other evidence of my conduct must witness to you, and to the world.   To myself, the assurance of my own conscience is, that I have at least believed myself to be guided by them. . . .

" Though, in reviewing the incidents of my Administration, I am unconscious of intentional error—I am nevertheless too sensible of my defects not to think it probable that I

[1] Benjamin Franklin (1706-1790), discoverer of the identity of lightning and electricity.—T.

[2] Robert Fulton (1765-1815), one of the first to apply steam to the propulsion of vessels ; he built a steamboat to navigate the Hudson River in 1807; it made five miles an hour.—T.

[3] Issued 17 September 1796, before his retirement from his second presidency.—T.

may have committed many errors. Whatever they may be, I fervently beseech the Almighty to avert or mitigate the evils to which they may tend. I shall also carry with me the hope that my country will never cease to view them with indulgence; and that, after forty-five years of my life dedicated to its service, with an upright zeal, the faults of incompetent abilities will be consigned to oblivion, as myself must soon be to the mansions of rest."

Jefferson[1] in his house at Monticello, wrote, after the death of one of his two children:

"The loss which I have experienced is a really great one. Others may lose of that which they possess in abundance, but I, of my whole portion, have now to deplore the loss of one-half. The declining years of my life are now held up by the slender thread of one human life. Perhaps I am destined to see the last tie of a father's affection broken!"

Philosophy, which is rarely touching, is here touching in the highest degree. And this is not the idle grief of a man who had played no part in life. Jefferson died on the 4th of July 1826, in the eighty-fourth year of his age, and the fifty-fourth year of the independence of his country. His remains lie covered with a stone, having for sole epitaph the words:

THOMAS JEFFERSON,

AUTHOR OF THE DECLARATION OF INDEPENDENCE.

Pericles and Demosthenes pronounced the funeral oration of the young Greeks who had fallen for a people that disappeared soon after themselves: in 1817, Brackenridge[2] celebrated the death of the young Americans whose blood gave birth to a nation.

We have a national gallery of portraits of distinguished Americans, in four volumes octavo, and what is more singular, a biography containing the lives of over one hundred of the

---

[1] Thomas Jefferson (1743-1816), third President of the United States, 1801-1805, and again, 1805-1809. Jefferson died at Monticello, Virginia, on the anniversary of the Declaration of Independence, 4 July 1826. John Adams, the second President of the United States, died at Quincy, Massachusetts, on the same day.—T.

[2] Henry M. Brackenridge (1786-1871), author of, among other works, the *History of the late War between the United States and Great Britain*. Baltimore, 1817.—T.

principal Indian chiefs. Logan,[1] the Virginian chief, uttered these words before Lord Dunmore:[2]

"Colonel Cresap,[3] the last spring, in cold blood and unprovoked, murdered all the relations of Logan. There runs not a drop of my blood in the veins of any living creature that called on me for revenge. I have sought it; I have killed many. . . . Who is there to mourn for Logan? Not one."

Without loving nature, the Americans have applied themselves to the study of natural history. Townsend[4] set out from Philadelphia and traversed on foot the regions separating the Atlantic from the Pacific Ocean, jotting down numerous observations in his journal. Thomas Say,[5] who travelled in Florida and in the Rocky Mountains, has published a work on American entomology. Wilson,[6] a weaver who became an author, has left some rather finished pictures.

To turn to literature proper, although it does not amount to much, there are, nevertheless, a few writers to be mentioned among the novelists and poets. Brown,[7] the son of a Quaker, is the author of *Wieland*, which is the source and model of the novels of the new school. Unlike his fellow-countrymen:

"I prefer," said Brown, "roaming in the forests to thrashing corn."

Wieland, the hero of the novel, is a Puritan whom Heaven has commanded to kill his wife:

"'I have brought thee hither,' says he to her, 'to fulfil a divine command. I am appointed thy destroyer, and destroy thee I must.'

---

[1] Tah-Gah-Jute (*circa* 1725-1780), a famous Cayuga chief, named John Logan, after James Logan, secretary of Pennsylvania. The famous speech was not spoken in person, but sent by an interpreter in October 1774. Logan was eventually shot by an Indian through a misunderstanding.—T.

[2] John Murray, fourth Earl of Dunmore (1732-1809), Governor of Virginia at the outbreak of the American Revolution.—T.

[3] Captain Michael Cresap (1742-1775). His memory was attacked by Thomas Jefferson, and vindicated by his son-in-law, J. J. Jacob.—T.

[4] John K. Townsend (1809-1861), author of *Narrative of a Journey across the Rocky Mountains and a Visit to the Sandwich Islands, Chili, &c.*, 1833-37 (1839).—T.

[5] Thomas Say (1787-1834), author of an *American Entomology* (1824) and an *American Conchiliology* (1830).—B.

[6] Alexander Wilson (1766-1813), a Scotsman by birth, emigrated at an early age to America. He was by turns a weaver, a schoolmaster, and a pedlar. He applied himself to the study of birds, and eventually published his *American Ornithology* in seven volumes, containing the finished illustrations referred to by Chateaubriand.—T.

[7] Charles Brockden Brown (1771-1810), author of several novels, of which *Wieland* was the most popular.—B.

"Saying this, I seized her wrists. She shrieked aloud, and endeavoured to free herself from my grasp. . . .

"'Wieland. . . . Am I not thy wife? And wouldst thou kill me? Thou wilt not; oh! . . . Spare me—spare—help, help—'

"Till her breath was stopped she shrieked for help—for mercy."

Wieland strangles his wife, and experiences unspeakable delights by the side of her dead corpse. The horror of our modern inventions is here surpassed. Brown had trained his mind by reading *Caleb Williams*,[1] and in *Wieland* he copied a scene from *Othello*.

At the present day, the American novelists Cooper [2] and Washington Irving [3] are obliged to take refuge in Europe to find chronicles and a public. The language of the great English writers has been "creolized," "provincialized," "barbarized," without gaining anything in energy in the midst of a virgin nature; it has become necessary to draw up catalogues of American expressions.

As to the American poets, their language has charm, but they rarely rise above the common-place. Still, the *Ode to the Evening Breeze*, the *Sunrise on the Mount*, the *Torrent*, and some other poems, deserve a passing glance. Halleck [4] has sung the death of Bozzaris, and George Hill [5] has wandered among the Ruins of Athens:

> Alas! for her, the beautiful, but lone,
> Dethroned queen![6] . . .

And again:

> There sits the queen of temples [7]—grey and lone.
> She, like the last of an imperial line,
> Has seen her sister structures, one by one,
> To time their gods and worshippers resign.[8]

It pleases me, a traveller on the shores of Hellas and

---

[1] *Caleb Williams*, by William Godwin (1756–1836), father of Mary Wollstonecraft, Shelley's second wife, appeared in 1794, one year before the publication of *Wieland*.—T.

[2] James Fenimore Cooper (1780–1851), probably the most popular of American novelists.—T.

[3] Washington Irving (1783–1859). He was American Minister in Madrid for a short period (1842).—T.

[4] Fitz-Greene Halleck (1795–1867), author of *Marco Bozzaris*. The curious will find a criticism of his work in Poe's *Literati of New York*.—T.

[5] George Hill (*b.* 1796), author of the *Ruins of Athens*, and a few shorter poems.—T.   [6] *Ruins of Athens*, II.—T.

[7] The Parthenon.—T.   [8] *Ruins of Athens*, XVII.—T.

Atlantis, to hear the independent voice of a land unknown to antiquity lamenting the lost liberty of the old world.

But will America preserve her form of government? Will the States not become divided? Has not a representative of Virginia already maintained the theory of ancient liberty with slaves, the result of paganism, against a representative of Massachusetts, defending the cause of modern liberty without slaves, as Christianity made it? Are not the Northern and Southern States opposed in mind and interests? Will not the Western States, so far removed from the Atlantic, wish to have a separate government? On the one hand, is the federal bond sufficiently powerful to maintain the union, and to compel each State to draw closer to it? On the other hand, if the presidential power be increased, will not despotism come with the guards and privileges of the dictator?

The isolation of the United States has permitted them to spring into being and to increase: it is doubtful whether they would have been able to exist and grow in Europe. Federal Switzerland subsists in our midst; but why? Because she is small, poor, cantoned in the bosom of the mountains, a nursery of soldiers for kings, a goal for travellers.

Separated from the old world, the population of the United States still inhabits the solitude: its deserts have been its liberty; but already the conditions of its existence are altering.

The existence of the democracies of Mexico, Columbia, Peru, Chili, Buenos Ayres, always troubled as they are, constitute a danger. When the United States had nothing near them except the colonies of a Transatlantic kingdom, no serious war was probable; now, are there not rivalries to be dreaded? Let men on both sides have recourse to arms, let the military spirit seize upon the children of Washington, and a great captain may rise to the throne : glory loves crowns.

I have said that the Northern, Southern, and Western States were divided in interests; that is common knowledge : if these States break up the union, will they be reduced by force of arms? In that case, what a leaven of hatred will be spread through the social body! Will the dissenting States maintain their independence? In that case, what discords will not break out among those emancipated States! Those republics across the sea, once uncoupled, would no longer form aught save feeble units without weight in the social balance, where they would be successively subjugated by one of their number (I leave on one side the serious question of alliances and foreign intervention). Kentucky, peopled as it is with a race of men bred in the open air, harder and more soldier-like, would seem destined to become the conquering State. In this State devouring the others, the power of one would soon rise upon the ruins of the power of all.

I have spoken of the danger of war ; I must point out the dangers of a long peace. Since their emancipation, the United States have, with the exception of a few months, enjoyed the most profound tranquillity; while Europe was shaken with a hundred battles, the United States tilled their fields in safety. Hence we find an overflowing population and riches, with all the drawbacks of a superabundance of riches and population. If hostilities came unexpectedly upon an unwarlike people, would it be able to offer resistance ? Would its fortunes and habits consent to sacrifices ? How could it give up the bland usages, the comfort, the indolent well-being of life ? China and India, asleep in their muslin draperies, have constantly endured the foreign yoke. That which is best suited to the complexion of a free society is a state of peace moderated by war, and a state of war tempered with peace. The Americans have already worn the olive-crown too long continuously: the tree that provides it is not a native of their shores.

The commercial spirit is beginning to take possession of them; self-interest is becoming their national vice. Already the speculations of the banks of the different States clash with one another, and bankruptcies threaten the fortunes of the community. So long as liberty produces gold, an industrial republic does wonders; but when the gold is acquired or exhausted, it loses its love of independence, which is not based upon a moral sentiment, but arises from the thirst for gain and the passion for trade.

Moreover, it is difficult to create a mother-country among States which have nothing in common in religion or interests, which, issuing from various sources and at various times, live on a different soil and under a different sun. What connection is there between a Frenchman of Louisiana, a Spaniard of Florida, a German of New York, an Englishman of New England, Virginia, Carolina, Georgia, who are all reckoned as Americans ? One is thoughtless and a duellist; the next a Catholic, lazy and haughty; the other a Lutheran, a husband-man, with no slaves; another, an Anglican and a planter, with negroes; yet another, a Puritan and a merchant: how many centuries will be needed to make these elements homogeneous ?

A chrysogenous [1] aristocracy is ready to appear with the

---

[1] Chateaubriand coins the word *chrysogène* to express the idea of being born in wealth : I have ventured to retain it.—T.

love of distinctions and the passion for titles. Men think that
a general level prevails in the United States: that is a complete mistake. There are sets in their society which despise
one another and refuse to mix; there are houses in which the
arrogance of the master exceeds that of a German prince with
sixteen quarterings. These plebeian nobles aspire to form a
caste in the face of the progress in enlightenment which made
them equal and free. Some of them speak of nothing but their
ancestors, proud barons, bastards apparently and companions
of William the Bastard. They display the knightly blazons
of the Old World, enriched with the serpents, lizards, and
parrots of the New. A Gascon younger son, landing on the
republican shores with nothing but his nobility and his umbrella,
becomes a person of consideration on the steam-boats, if he
will only take care to call himself "marquis."

The enormous inequality of fortunes threatens still more
seriously to kill the spirit of equality. There are Americans
with incomes of one or two millions a year; and already the
Yankees of high society are no longer able to live as Franklin
did: the true "gentleman," disgusted with his new country,
goes to Europe in search of the old; one meets him at the
inns, making "tours" in Italy like the English, tours marked
by extravagance or spleen. These ramblers from Carolina or
Virginia buy ruined abbeys in France, and lay out English
gardens with American trees at Melun. Naples sends its
singers and perfumers to New York, Paris its fashions and
dancers, London its grooms and prize-fighters: exotic delights which do not add to the gaiety of the Union. There they
amuse themselves by jumping into the Falls of Niagara, amid
the applause of fifty thousand planters, semi-savages whose
merriment is with difficulty aroused by the sight of death.

And what is so extraordinary is that, at the very time when
the inequality of fortunes is extending and an aristocracy is
springing into being, the great levelling movement outside
obliges the industrial or landed proprietors to hide their
luxury, to dissimulate their wealth, for fear of being knocked
on the head by their neighbours. These refuse to recognize
the executive power; they dismiss the local authorities whom
they have chosen at will, and elect others in their stead. This
in no way disturbs order; practical democracy is observed,
while the laws laid down by the same democracy in theory are
laughed at. The family spirit scarcely exists; so soon as the
child is fit to work, he has to fly with his own wings, like the
newly-fledged bird. Out of these generations emancipated in

a premature orphanage, and out of the emigrants arriving from Europe, are formed nomadic companies which clear the land, dig canals, and carry their trade in every direction without becoming attached to the soil; they run up houses in the desert in which the transient owner will live scarce a few days.

A cold and hard egotism reigns in the towns; piastres and dollars, bank-notes and silver, the rise and fall of stocks, these form the sole subject of conversation: one imagines one's self on 'Change or in the counting-house of a large shop. The newspapers, huge in dimensions, are filled with business articles or scurrilous gossip. Could the Americans be unconsciously submitting to the law of a climate in which vegetable nature seems to have benefited at the expense of living nature, a law combated by some distinguished minds, and yet not put entirely out of court by its refutation? It might be worth while to inquire whether the American has not been too soon used up in philosophic liberty, as the Russian has been in civilized despotism.

To sum up, the United States give the idea of a colony, not of a parent country; they have no past, their manners owe their existence to the laws. These citizens of the New World took rank among the nations at the moment when political ideas were entering upon an upward phase: this explains why they change with such extraordinary rapidity. A permanent form of society seems to become impracticable in their case, thanks, on the one hand, to the extreme weariness of individuals; on the other, to the impossibility of remaining in one spot, the necessity for movement, by which they are dominated: for one is never very firmly fixed where the household gods are wandering gods. Placed on the ocean road, at the head of progressive opinions as new as his country, the American seems to have received from Columbus a mission to discover fresh worlds rather than to create them.

On returning to Philadelphia from the desert, as I have already said, having hurriedly written on the road "what I have just related," like the old man in La Fontaine, I did not find the remittances I expected: this was the commencement of the pecuniary difficulties in which I have been plunged ever since. Fortune and I conceived a mutual dislike at first sight. According to Herodotus, certain Indian ants used to heap together piles of gold; according to Athenæus, the sun gave Hercules a golden ship in which to accost the island of

Erythia, the home of the Hesperides: ant though I be, I have not the honour to belong to the great Indian family; and navigator though I be, I have never crossed the sea, save in a wooden bark. It was a vessel of this kind which brought me back to Europe from America. The captain gave me my passage on credit. On the 10th of December 1791, I embarked with several of my fellow-countrymen who were returning to France, like myself, for various reasons. The ship's destination was the Havre.

A westerly gale caught us at the mouth of the Delaware and drove us right across the Atlantic in seventeen days. Often, scudding under bare poles, we were scarcely able to bring to. The sun did not appear a single time. The vessel, steering by a dead reckoning, flew before the waves. I crossed the ocean among shadows; never had it looked to me so sad. I myself, sadder still, was returning deceived, after my first step taken in life:

"Palaces are not built upon the sea," says the Persian poet Feryd-Eddyn.[1]

I felt a vague heaviness of heart, as at the approach of a great misfortune. Turning my eyes over the waves, I asked them to tell me my destiny, or else I used to write, more inconvenienced by their motion than troubled by their threats.

So far from calming, the tempest increased the nearer we came to Europe; but it blew steadily: the uniformity of its raging produced a sort of furious lull in the wan sky and leaden sea. The captain, having no means of taking the altitude, was uneasy; he climbed into the shrouds and scanned each point of the horizon through a telescope. A look-out was placed on the bowsprit, another in the main-top-mast crosstrees. The sea became choppy, and the colour of the water changed, signs that we were approaching land: what land? The Breton sailors have a proverb, "Who sees Belle-Isle sees his isle; who sees Groie sees his joy; who sees Ouessant's shore sees his gore."

I had spent two nights in walking the deck, to the hissing of the waves in the dark, the moaning of the wind in the rigging, and the constant dashing of the sea which swept the decks: the waves rioted all around us. Tired with the shocks and jerks of the vessel, I went below early on the third night. The weather was terrible; my hammock creaked and rocked with the blows of the sea, which, breaking over the vessel,

[1] Feryd-Eddyn-Atthar (circa 1226–circa 1280), author of the *Pend-Nâmeh*, or Book of Counsels.—T.

threatened to dislocate her very planks. Soon I heard men running from one end of the deck to the other, and coils of rope falling: I experienced the motion which one feels when a vessel is put about. The hatch of the steerage ladder was thrown open; a frightened voice called for the captain: that voice, in the middle of the night and the tempest, sounded tremendous. I listened; I thought I heard sailors discussing the lie of a coast. I tumbled out of my hammock; a sea drove in the quarter-deck, flooded the captain's room, knocked over and rolled pell-mell tables, mattresses, chests, furniture, and arms; I made my way on deck half-drowned.

When I put my head out of the steerage, a splendid sight met my eyes. The ship had tried to put about; but, failing in this attempt she had become embayed under the stress of the wind. By the light of the moon, her horns broken by the clouds, from beneath which she emerged only to be hidden by them again, we discovered on either side of the ship, through a yellow fog, a coast bristling with rocks. The sea threw up waves like mountains in the channel in which we found our-selves engulfed: now they scattered into foam and spray; again they presented merely an oily and vitreous surface, mottled with black, coppery, or greenish stains, according to the colour of the bottom over which they roared. During two or three minutes, the moaning of the abyss and that of the wind would be confused; the next moment, one distinguished the ripple of the currents, the hissing on the reefs, the voice of the distant surge. From the hold of the ship issued sounds which made the hearts of the stoutest sailors beat faster. The stem of the vessel cut through the thick mass of waves with a hideous crash, and, at the helm, torrents of water flowed away eddying as from the mouth of a sluice. Amid all this uproar, nothing was so alarming as a certain dull, murmuring sound, like that of a vase filling.

Lighted by a ship's lantern and held down by weights, harbour-books, charts, and log-books lay spread out upon a hen-coop. A gust of wind had put out the binnacle-lamp. Every one was at variance about the land. We had entered the Channel without noticing it; the vessel, staggering under each wave, was drifting between the islands of Guernsey and Alderney. Our shipwreck appeared inevitable, and the pas-sengers put up their valuables to save them.

The crew included some French seamen; one of them, in the absence of a chaplain, raised the hymn to "Our Lady of Succour," the first thing I had learnt as a child; I repeated it in sight of the coast of Brittany, almost under my mother's eyes. The American Protestant sailors joined in chorus in the song of their French Catholic mates : danger teaches men their weakness and unites their prayers. All, passengers and sailors, were on deck, one clinging to the rigging, another to the sides, another to the capstan, others to the bills of the anchors, in order not to be swept away by the sea or thrown overboard by the heaving of the ship. The captain shouted, "An axe! an axe!" to cut away the masts; and the rudder, of which the tiller had been forsaken, swung from side to side with a harsh sound.

One experiment remained to be tried : the lead marked only four fathoms on a sand-bank which crossed the channel; it was just possible that the swell might enable us to clear this bank and carry us into deep water; but who would dare to seize the helm and charge himself with the common safety? One false turn of the tiller, and we were lost.

One of those men who spring from events and who are the spontaneous children of danger was found : a New York sailor took the post deserted by the steersman. I seem still to see him in his shirt and canvas trousers, his bare feet, his tangled streaming hair, holding the tiller in his powerful grasp, while, with turned head, he looked over the stern at the sea which was to save or sink us. See that great wave coming, embracing the whole width of the channel, rolling high without breaking, as it were a sea invading the billows of another sea : large white birds go before with a calm flight, like the birds of death. The ship touched and struck; there was a complete silence; every face turned pale. The swell came : at the moment when it touched us, the sailor put down the helm; the vessel, just ready to fall on her side, turned her stern, and the swell, which seemed about to swallow us, lifted her. The lead was heaved; it registered twenty-seven fathoms. A cheer rose to the sky, and we added a shout of "Long live the King!" God did not hear it for Louis XVI.; it benefited none save ourselves.

Although clear of the two islands, we were not out of danger; we were unable to run up above the coast of Granville. At last the ebbing tide carried us out, and we doubled Cape La Hougue. I experienced no agitation during the semi-shipwreck and felt no delight at being saved. Better to give up possession of one's life while young than to be evicted from it by time.

The next day we entered the Havre. The whole population

had come out to see us. Our top-masts were broken, our boats carried away, our quarter-deck cut down, and we shipped water at every pitch of the vessel. I landed on the jetty. On the 2nd of January 1792, I once more trod my native soil, which was soon again to slip from under my feet. I brought with me no Esquimaux from the Polar regions, but two savages of an unknown species: Chactas and Atala.

END OF VOL. I.

Printed by BALLANTYNE, HANSON & Co.
Edinburgh & London

.

CPSIA information can be obtained at www.ICGtesting.com
Printed in the USA
BVOW06s1814040813

327820BV00004B/15/P

9 781175 467089